# The Old Soldiers Show

*Stories from the 1913 Gettysburg Reunion*

Lee Vetter

Stackpole
Books
*Essex, Connecticut*

STACKPOLE BOOKS
An imprint of Globe Pequot Publishing Group Inc.
64 South Main Street
Essex, CT 06426
www.globepequot.com



British Library Cataloguing in Publication Information available

**Library of Congress Cataloging-in-Publication Data available**
9780811778596 (cloth)
9780811778350 (paperback)
9780811778367 (electronic)

*This book is dedicated to my dad, who never made it to Gettysburg.*

# Contents

# Author's Note

This book began as a script for a documentary, something I started during the 2020 COVID-19 lockdown to keep myself from going stir-crazy. My grand plan was to write a script and produce a full-length documentary once the world reopened. However, there was one small problem: Making documentaries is expensive, and I don't have access to a Hollywood-sized budget. A friend suggested turning the script into a book to build interest for a future documentary. So here we are. Let's see what happens next . . .

I wrote both the script and this book with a specific audience in mind: people who hate history.

Let's be honest. High school history class ruined history for many people. Too many teachers focus on dry facts, forcing students to memorize dates, locations, and treaties that feel completely irrelevant to real life. I remember learning about the Louisiana Purchase in middle school. We spent forever studying the trade agreements with the French—or at least it felt that way. In reality, it was probably just a few days, but as a kid, it was pure torture. I memorized enough facts to pass the test and then immediately forgot everything. The only lasting impression? How much time we wasted on it.

The problem isn't history itself—it's how it's taught. Too many facts, not enough fun. I learned more about the French and Indian War from watching *The Last of the Mohicans* (1992) than I ever did in school. And I bet I'm not the only one.

After being taught history the wrong way for twelve years, it's no surprise that so many people hate it.

However, people love stories. We can't get enough of them. Who doesn't like a good ghost story while sitting around the campfire? Do you know what people don't like hearing around the campfire? Mind-numbing statistics.

But everyone loves a good story.

Here's an example: A few years ago, my wife and I adopted a little, red-haired dachshund named Scooter. While researching the breed, I stumbled across a fantastic story online.

A man living in the Florida Everglades had a beloved dachshund. One day, the dog went missing. The man searched everywhere but found no trace of it. Fearing the worst, he headed to the swamp at the back of his property, where the alligators lived. Sure enough, he spotted one lounging nearby, looking suspiciously satisfied. Heartbroken, he assumed the worst but kept searching.

Days passed with no sign of his pup. Then, on the third morning, he opened his door and there was his dachshund, sitting on the step, looking perfectly fine, except for being covered in a foul-smelling slime. Suspicious, the man went back to the swamp. There, he found that same alligator, dead, with a dachshund-sized hole chewed through its belly—from the *inside* out.

Dachshunds are small, but they are mighty.

I love that story. Now, here's the thing. You don't need to know the man's name, address, or profession to enjoy that story. You don't even need to know the dog's name, either. The only relevant detail is that a man owned a dachshund and lived near a swamp. The details might add some authenticity, but they're not needed to enjoy the story.

And that's the approach I'm taking with this book.

Everyone loves a good story.

Some people can't get enough of their midday soap operas, while others are hooked on epic adventures like *Star Wars* or *Star Trek.* Superheroes dominate movies, comics, and TV—some even live up to the hype. And remember when *Lost* took over the world? People dropped everything to watch and then spent the next week dissecting every plot twist with their coworkers. More recently, *Game of Thrones* had the same effect—love or hate the ending, you can't deny the story kept people on the edges of their seats.

So why not bring that same storytelling magic to history?

That's exactly what I hope to achieve with *The Old Soldiers Show.* Instead of getting lost in dates and statistics, I want to highlight the human side, the moments that made it an event like no other. I'm a filmmaker, not a historian, so my aim is to tell a compelling story rather than nitpick every historical nuance. I've spent years researching to get the details right, and if you spot a mistake, know it's purely mine. Any simplifications are meant to keep the story moving and not bog it down.

The Gettysburg Reunion was a massive event, and this isn't an exhaustive, in-depth examination of every speech, meeting, and detail. Otherwise, this book would be four times longer and half as interesting. Instead, I'll focus on what happened when the former enemies met each other again on the battlefield.

When you finish this book, I don't expect you to remember every name, regiment, or historical detail, though you may remember that crazy bastard, Dan Sickles. But I do hope some of the stories from the Gettysburg Reunion resonate with you.

So let's get started.

# Introduction

July 3, 1913. The sun hung heavy in the sky that day, a cruel, blistering orb pouring its relentless heat over the fields of Gettysburg. The air was thick, like a wet woolen shroud, wrapping around every living thing and choking the breath from their lungs.

They stood along the weathered fence on the Emmitsburg Road—150 men, old warriors draped in the tattered remnants of a lost cause. Some stood tall, backs straight with stubborn pride, but they were the few. The rest bore the weight of time, with sunken faces, hollow eyes, and bodies broken long ago by war. Sleeves hung empty where arms had once been, and wooden crutches groaned under the weight of those who had left pieces of themselves on these fields half a century before. They wore their Confederate gray like a second skin, faded and threadbare, yet clinging to them like memories that refused to die.

Across the field, beyond the stone wall, another army waited—an equal number of Union veterans, watching in silence. Some wore civilian clothes; a few leaned on canes, while others shaded themselves under umbrellas. They had no reason to march, no ghosts to pursue. All they needed to do was wait.

Then, at precisely 3:00 p.m., the signal was given.

The old Confederates moved. Slowly at first, like specters rising from the past, their feet dragged through the tall grass. The younger, stronger among them bore the weight of their frailer comrades, half-carrying, half-marching toward the low stone wall that had once been their undoing. A murmur passed through the crowd of onlookers. Some shook their heads at the pitiful sight. There was certainly nothing to fear from these old men.

But then a sound cut through the thick air.

At first, just one voice, raw and cracked with age. Then another. And another.

A cry, high and wild. The Rebel Yell.

It swept through their ranks like fire in dry grass, rising in a crescendo that sent shivers racing up spines. Time unraveled. The shuffle of feeble feet became a determined march. Bent backs straightened. Trembling hands curled into fists. Something fierce and untamed flickered to life in their eyes.

Across the field, the Union men stiffened. The sound—dear God, the sound—it was the same. The same chilling cry that haunted their nightmares. The weight of fifty years evaporated, and suddenly they were young men again, standing shoulder to shoulder in the chaos of battle.

As the Confederates surged forward, the Union men found their voices. "Vicksburg!" one shouted. It was a challenge hurled into the storm.

A Confederate shot back, breathless but defiant: "Chancellorsville!"

"Gettysburg!"

And then they collided.

Canes, meant for support, became clubs. Crutches were thrust like bayonets. Hands grasped, shoved, and fought for purchase. Punches were thrown. Entwined, the old men fell to the ground, smothering each other's faces into the dirt. The low stone wall, that cursed boundary, became a battleground once more.

"You didn't cross this wall fifty years ago, you son of a bitch," a Union man declared as he fought against the tide, "and you're not crossing it today!"

Old hatreds flared. Ancient wounds, long scarred over, split open anew. The war—their war—was not over. Not yet.

The peace of the Grand Reunion was shattered. The past refused to stay buried.

Except . . .

That's not how it happened.

Not even close.

# 1

# The Civil War

All right, settle in close and listen well. This is not just history; it's a story of men who bled, fought, and fell beneath the weight of something far greater than themselves. A tale of tides that rose and receded, of a war that swallowed a nation whole . . . and spat out something unrecognizable on the other side.

It began in April 1861.

A shot. A single, defiant shot was fired into the dawn over Fort Sumter, just off the coast of South Carolina. A shot that cracked through the stillness and split a nation in two.

Initially, they believed it would be over in a matter of weeks. They said one big fight, and the Rebels will scatter like leaves in the wind.

But war doesn't listen to idle speculation. War has a hunger of its own.

When the first battle happened, not far from Washington, DC, it wasn't the ragtag Confederate army that broke and ran. Instead, the proud and confident men of the North turned and fled, their banners trampled in the dust, their rifles abandoned along the road. And in that moment, both sides knew—this would not be a war of weeks or months.

This war would drag on for years.

Two years passed. Two years of blood and thunder, of men thrown against each other in the fields, forests, and mountains. Two years of gunsmoke and shattered bodies.

And then, in the summer of 1863, the storm swept northward to a quiet town in Pennsylvania. A place that had never wanted war but, on July 1, found itself drowning in it.

Gettysburg.

The numbers were staggering—ninety-four thousand men from the North, seventy-two thousand from the South. They came like thunderclouds rolling over the hills, drawn into battle by fate.

For three days, the earth trembled beneath them. Muskets roared. Cannons split the sky. Bayonets turned the wheatfields red. And when the smoke cleared, when the cries of the dying had faded into silence, fifty-one thousand men were gone—dead, wounded, or missing.

It was the bloodiest battle of the war. And it was the high-water mark of the Confederacy.

Think of the tide at the beach. It rushes forward, surging over the sand, hungry to claim new ground. That was the Southern army at Gettysburg—crashing like a wave, flooding into Northern territory.

But some tides never reach the shore.

Because at Gettysburg, they met something they could not break. Something they could not push aside. The Union army under the command of General George Meade stood like a wall of iron, and when the Confederates crashed against it, it did not move.

After three bloody days, the tide turned.

The Southern army receded, dragged back into the depths from which it came. Never again would it rise so high. Never again would it come so far north.

But the war was far from over. It raged on for another two years. Two more years of fire and ruin, of men dying in the mud. But the Confederate army never truly recovered from the Battle of Gettysburg. The Confederates under the command of Robert E. Lee were forced onto their collective back foot, retreating into their own territory, fighting not to win but to survive.

And in the end, survival was not enough.

The tide had turned and slithered into the sea.

General Ulysses S. Grant took command of the Union army, and together they crashed into the South like an unstoppable wave, washing away the Confederacy piece by piece, until at last, on an April morning in 1865, in a quiet courthouse in Appomattox, Virginia, Robert E. Lee laid down his sword.

The war was over.

And yet, what did that truly mean?

The numbers tell their own story: 620,000 men—dead. Enough to fill entire cities, wiped from the earth.

And those who lived? They went home, if they had a home to go to.

But tell me—How does a man return from war? How does he walk back into his old life, knowing what he has done and what he has seen?

The truth is some never do.

Because war does not end on a battlefield; it lingers. In the land. In the blood. In the bones of those who fought it.

And if you listen, on certain nights—when the wind is just right, when the air is heavy, when the fire burns low—you might still hear it. The echo of marching feet. The thunder of distant guns. And the whisper of a tide that never rose again.

But time moved on, as it always does. The war faded into memory, the battlefields grew quiet, and the soldiers who once tore into each other went home—or at least what was left of them, anyway.

And then, fifty years later, something strange happened.

They came back.

Not as young men with rifles in hand, not as warriors eager for glory, but as old men—very old men. Men in their seventies, their eighties, even their nineties. Time had ground them down, but it had not erased them. And so, from all corners of the country, they returned to Gettysburg to the fields where they had fought and bled so long ago.

The plan was to host forty thousand veterans. But war doesn't follow plans, and neither did these men.

Fifty-five thousand of them showed up.

And suddenly there weren't enough tents. There wasn't enough food. There wasn't enough room. Veterans were turned away, some forced to wander back home, and their reunion was stolen from them before it could even begin.

The organizers had picked the first week of July for this gathering—the exact dates of the battle and the hottest week of the year. The sun beat down without mercy. The temperatures soared into the nineties every day, and the air was thick enough to choke on. Men who had once braved bullets and bayonets now collapsed beneath the weight of heat and age. Hundreds ended up in the hospital.

But the organizers had planned for this situation.

Doctors and nurses from the Red Cross stood ready, sweat dripping from their brows as they tended to the fallen. And in the shadows of the tents, lined up in grim silence, were five hundred empty coffins. A temporary morgue had been set up, waiting—just in case.

And then, on July 3, under that blazing, unrelenting sun, the impossible happened.

They reenacted Pickett's Charge.

But this was no staged performance. Nor were these young actors in crisp blue and gray uniforms choreographed for an audience. No, this was a real-life battleground, and these were the men who had been there—the same souls who had once charged across that killing field for real.

And there they went, stepping forward one last time—hobbling, shuffling, leaning on canes, held up by the hands of their comrades. Across the field they marched, not as soldiers or enemies but as something else entirely. The sight of it—hundreds of old warriors, moving through the heat and the haze, retracing the footsteps of their youth—must have been something to behold.

There is nothing else like it in the annals of history. No other event at which two armies—once bitter enemies—returned to the battlefield, not to fight but to make peace.

It was an American thing, through and through.

But close your eyes for a moment and picture it.

Fifty-five thousand old men, who had once sworn to kill each other, wandering the same blood-soaked ground under the July sun.

What could go wrong?

Hundreds, if not thousands, of books have been written about the Civil War by those much smarter than I am. I'm not a historian or a college professor. So, what can I add to the equation? Almost nothing. But let me present my drop-dead simple understanding of the Civil War. I hope this will provide some insight into our upcoming cast of characters, especially those from the South.

Let me start by saying that I grew up in New Jersey, and the only thing I was taught in school about the Civil War was that it was fought over slavery.

Done.

End of story.

In my mind, it played out like this: The noble, righteous people of the North (especially those from New Jersey, naturally) saw the great injustice of slavery and decided enough was enough. The South, by contrast, was ruled by a wicked empire, an iron-fisted regime of plantation overlords who kept millions in chains. The stakes? Nothing less than the soul of a nation.

And so, the two sides clashed in battle after battle, an epic struggle of good versus evil. If the North won, freedom would reign, the slaves would be liberated, and justice would triumph. Cue the soaring orchestral music—YAY! But if the South won? Oh, then the world would plunge into darkness, the cries of the oppressed would go unanswered, and slavery would still exist to this very day. Cue the ominous villain theme—BOO!

It was practically *Star Wars* before *Star Wars* was a thing.

Jefferson Davis? The brooding, manipulative Emperor Palpatine. Robert E. Lee? The noble and yet tragically misguided Darth Vader. Abraham Lincoln? The steadfast, destiny-bound Luke Skywalker. Ulysses S. Grant? The rough-and-tumble Han Solo, whiskey bottle in one hand, battle plans in the other.

I mean, doesn't that sound like a marvelous story?

When framed in such simple, black-and-white terms, it's easy to vilify the South, to see them as the mustache-twirling villains of the grand American saga. And as a kid from New Jersey—firmly on the "good guy" side—I basked in that moral superiority. After all, my state fought to free the slaves. That made me, by default, one of the heroes.

It wasn't until I was in my late twenties that I heard anything different, and it was my future father-in-law, Mike Bell, who challenged me on it. He asked a simple question: "If the Civil War started in 1861, but the Emancipation Act, which freed the slaves, wasn't signed until 1863, then what were the first two years of the war about?"

I had no idea. My high school history class had not prepared me with an answer.

I wanted an easy answer, but Mike didn't give me one. Instead, he encouraged me to think for myself and seek out my own answers. To actually pick up a book and form my own opinions. I wasn't thrilled with the idea, but I did it anyway.

I read about the Dred Scott case, which stated that slaves were not US citizens and therefore not eligible for government protection. I also learned about the Three-Fifths Compromise, which specified that for taxation and representation purposes, slaves were only counted as three-fifths of a person. Then there was the question of the expansion of slavery into the western territories and how it would affect the economics of Manifest Destiny.

These things all backed up my original premise: The war was about slavery. Plain and simple.

I was disappointed. Was Mike sending me on a wild-goose chase? Was this his punishment for keeping his daughter out too late that one night?

I didn't think he was that malicious.

I read some articles by more Southern-leaning folk, who proposed that the war was about states' rights and their ability to self-rule. My off-the-cuff rebuttal to such statements was "Yeah, the states' right to own slaves." This was not a satisfactory answer, so I continued my research.

Then I discovered that it wasn't always referred to as the American Civil War. Some called it "The War Between the States," which I thought was a pretty balanced perspective. Other names reflected their inherent bias, such as "The War of Southern Independence" or "The War for the Union." The name varied depending on your location. If you lived in the North, you might have referred to it as "The War of the Rebellion," while if you lived in the South, you might have called it "The War of Northern Aggression."

That name resonated with me.

Many other names are associated with the Civil War, but, interestingly enough, no contemporary ever referred to it as "The War to Free the Slaves." (Although this term was used *after* the war.)

Pair that with what Abraham Lincoln said on March 4, 1861, in his First Inaugural Address: "I have no purpose, directly or indirectly, to interfere with the institution of slavery in the States where it exists. I believe I have no lawful right to do so, and I have no inclination to do so."

Congress passed the Corwin Amendment, the originally proposed Thirteenth Amendment, to reinforce this idea. This was a last-ditch effort to allow the Southern states to keep their slaves if they remained in the Union. The Corwin Amendment never became law, but it does illustrate the extent to which the federal government was willing to go to maintain control over the South.

So, if the Civil War wasn't about slavery, what was it about?

In a letter dated August 22, 1862, Lincoln spelled it out: "My paramount object in this struggle is to save the Union, and is not either to save or to destroy slavery. If I could save the Union without freeing any slave I would do it, and if I could save it by freeing all the slaves I would do it; and if I could save it by freeing some and leaving others alone I would also do that."

According to Lincoln, the primary cause of the Civil War was to save the Union. He believed it was unconstitutional for a state to secede from the Union and was willing to do whatever it took to keep them together.

Ending slavery became an important issue for the North *during* the war, but it wasn't the reason why the North *went* to war. A reporter for the *Boston Evening Transcript* summed it up like this in 1913: "The abolition of slavery was not the object of the war, but it was, of course, its only logical conclusion."[1]

The freeing of the slaves was, in many ways, a powerful *byproduct* of the Civil War—an outcome that reshaped the nation but wasn't exactly the war's opening act. Ever the strategist, Lincoln kept emancipation tucked in his back pocket, waiting for a crucial Northern victory before unveiling it. And when he finally signed the Emancipation Proclamation, it sent shockwaves throughout the world.

But here's the catch—it was largely symbolic. The proclamation applied only to the rebellious Southern states—places that, inconveniently for Lincoln, were no longer under his control. Meanwhile, the slaves in the North? They had to wait.

The war officially ended in April 1865, but freedom didn't come overnight. It wasn't until June 19 that federal troops rolled into Galveston, Texas, with orders to enforce emancipation, bringing freedom to those still in bondage. Today, we celebrate this moment as Juneteenth, and it's now a federal holiday.

But even then, the chains hadn't been broken everywhere.

The Thirteenth Amendment—the real legal hammer that abolished slavery across the entire United States—wasn't ratified until December 1865, a full nine months after the Civil War ended.

And just when I thought I could take comfort in my home state's moral high ground, history had one last sucker punch waiting for me. Turns out, New Jersey—yes, the same New Jersey that taught me we were champions of freedom—held onto its final slaves until January 1866—the last state in the Union to do so.

Oof. So much for that moral superiority I grew up believing in.

As I continued my research, one thing that surprised me was how people in the nineteenth century viewed the government. They saw themselves as a loose collection of states mildly supervised by the federal government. In other words, the states came first, and the federal government came second. This all changed after the Civil War, when a strong central government emerged, diminishing the power of the individual states. This might be a complex concept for twenty-first-century Americans to imagine, but, fortunately, we have a modern-day example to help us better understand it.

In 1993, the nations of Europe came together and formed the European Union (EU)—a sort of economic club where everyone pooled their resources, made trade easier, and (in theory) prospered together. And for nearly three decades, it seemed to work well enough.

But then, in 2016, Great Britain decided it had had enough. The very reason it had joined—the promise of economic benefits—was now the reason it wanted out. "Brexit" was born, a messy, controversial breakup that left many of its European neighbors fuming. But no matter how bitter they were, no armies marched, and no battles were fought. Britain simply packed its bags and walked away.

Now, imagine for a moment that it hadn't been so simple. Imagine the rest of Europe wasn't willing to let Britain go so easily. Imagine the EU responded with force, sending troops across the English Channel, demanding Britain stay put.

In that scenario, who would the British people have fought for? Spain? France? Or would they have defended their homeland?

And if they did fight for Great Britain, would that make them traitors to the EU? Or, if they fought for Spain or France, would that make them traitors to Britain?

Now, take that thought and rewind the clock to early America.

In the eighteenth century, a group of autonomous states came together primarily for economic and strategic reasons. The idea was simple: United, they were stronger. But by the mid-nineteenth century, that bond began to crack. Some states wanted out, primarily over economic concerns—yes, including slavery.

And here's where history takes a hard turn. Unlike Brexit, when the Southern states tried to leave, the federal government didn't let them walk away. Abraham Lincoln could have allowed them to secede peacefully, much like the EU allowed Britain to secede. Instead, he chose a different route—one paved with gunpowder and blood.

And so the Civil War began.

The issues of slavery affected each state differently. In the declarations of secession written by South Carolina, Georgia, Mississippi, and Texas, there can be no doubt that the issue of slavery was the primary reason they withdrew. Meanwhile, Kentucky, Missouri, Maryland, Delaware, and my home state of New Jersey stayed in the Union but kept their slaves! North Carolina and Virginia were both pro-Union states that ended up leaving the Union, not because of slavery but because of Lincoln's aggressive nature in suppressing the rebellion with military force. The term "The War of Northern Aggression" came from this viewpoint.

Virginia put the issue to a vote, and the state convention overwhelmingly decided to remain with the Union. This decision satisfied Lincoln, but he took a step too far and ordered the Virginia militia to help take back the Southern states *by force*. This aggressive nature shocked the Virginia delegates, who took a second vote two weeks after the first one. This time, they voted for secession.

After the Battle of Gettysburg, the Southern states that suffered the highest casualties were North Carolina with 6,160; Virginia with 4,470; and Georgia a distant third with 2,700.[2] What I find interesting is that the two states with the heaviest losses left the Union for reasons other than slavery.

Meanwhile, Robert E. Lee was offered the command of the entire Union army by none other than Abraham Lincoln. Lee was one of the finest officers in the army and the apparent choice for the role. He was born and raised in Virginia, and for him that was home. Lee said he would accept the command only if Virginia stayed in the Union. Now, imagine if Lincoln had played his cards differently; Virginia would have remained in the Union with Robert E. Lee at the head of the Union army! The Civil

War would have played out very differently. However, Lincoln rattled his saber too loudly, losing Virginia and Lee to the South.

Many people have accused the Confederates of being traitors to their country, but in their minds, at that time, they were fighting for *their* country. Virginia was their country. Remember, this was an era when most people lived and died within twenty miles of where they were born. In a fictional war between the EU and Great Britain, most Britons would fight for Britain. So it was in America, where the Virginians fought for Virginia.

Let's make this real.

Imagine this: One day, a foreign army marches into your neighborhood. They're not just passing through; they're there to take control. Houses are set ablaze, crops torched, families left with nothing but the clothes on their backs. Now ask yourself—Who would you fight for? Would you stand alongside the invaders as they burn everything you love to the ground? Or would you fight with your family, friends, and neighbors, doing everything you can to keep them out?

This wasn't just a hypothetical question for thousands of Southerners during the Civil War. It was reality.

Things got uglier as the war dragged on, especially when General William Tecumseh Sherman unleashed his infamous March to the Sea. He didn't just battle enemy soldiers—he made war against everything in his path. Towns were burned, fields reduced to ash, homes stripped bare. He wasn't marching against an army that could fight back. He was tearing through civilian life, leaving men, women, and children with nothing.

For those caught in the path of destruction, it didn't matter what side they'd started on. Survival became the only cause worth fighting for.

In the Ken Burns documentary on the Civil War, historian Shelby Foote sums it up nicely. He relates a story in which a federal soldier is talking to a Confederate and asks, "Why are you fighting us?" and the Confederate replies, "Because you're down here!"

Regardless of the issues of slavery and policies in Washington and Richmond, the average Southern soldier was fighting for his home.

With this in mind, does that make a Confederate soldier a traitor?

At the end of the Civil War, when General Ulysses S. Grant was in hot pursuit of Lee's army, Lincoln advised Grant to "let them surrender and go home." When Lee and his army finally yielded at the Appomattox Courthouse, they were not tried as traitors, put in chains, and hauled off to prison but instead paroled, given food, and sent home.

Lincoln knew the best way to unify the country was not through further violence against the beaten soldiers. This would have hardened their hearts and stiffened resistance. By being generous, the Confederates had nothing to lose and everything to gain by laying down their arms. In doing so, Lincoln made it easy for the Confederates to surrender.

Unfortunately, only a few days after Lee surrendered, Lincoln was assassinated. When Andrew Johnson assumed the presidency, he demanded that General Lee and his Confederates be arrested and tried for treason. However, the Southerners received support from an unlikely ally. General Ulysses S. Grant openly opposed the new president and threatened to resign his commission if Lee was arrested. As a result, President Johnson backed down. He needed Grant's support more than he needed Lee in chains.

Let's take a closer look at this situation.

General Ulysses S. Grant wasn't some distant politician or armchair warrior. He was in the thick of it, face-to-face against the Confederate army, watching his men fall to Southern bullets. He fought and bled with them, ultimately outmaneuvering them until the war was won. If anyone had the right to call them traitors, it was Grant.

But he didn't.

He did the opposite. Grant didn't demand their heads when the war ended—he defied the new president of the United States to protect them. He saw the Confederates not as enemies to be punished but as Americans who needed to be brought home. To him, the war was over. They weren't traitors—they were countrymen.

Lincoln saw it the same way. And if neither Grant nor Lincoln—the very men who fought and won the war—labeled the Confederates traitors, then what right do we have to do so today?

We weren't there. We didn't see what they saw. We can't hold nineteenth-century soldiers to twenty-first-century standards and pretend we understand their world. The best we can do is try to see it through their eyes.

And that's why not a single Confederate was ever charged with treason.

Now, I'm not here to give you a deep dive into all the reasons behind the Civil War—that's better left to smarter historians with their fancy books and clever words. Honestly, this is the only time I'll talk about how it all started. But here's the deal: The war happened and that's that. Everyone had their reasons for being there, no doubt about it. But what I'm really curious about is why they came back.

One last thing about this book: I'm not here to throw moldy old facts and figures at you—stuff you'll forget in two sentences. Instead, I want to summon the dead and breathe life into lungs that have been dust for more than a century. I want to peer into the dim mirror of the past and call forth the ghosts of yesterday. To wake them, put flesh on their brittle bones, and show you they were once real people, just like us, even if their presence lingers only for a heartbeat before fading back into the shadows of history.

2

# The Beginning of an Idea

THE STORY OF GETTYSBURG ISN'T JUST A SINGLE MOMENT IN HISTORY—it's a three-act drama, each part essential to understanding the full impact of the Civil War. Like any great story, it has a beginning, a middle, and an end. While most people remember the first two, the third act is often overlooked, even though it is the most relevant to us today.

The first part of the story is the battle itself, which took place over three brutal days from July 1 to 3, 1863. Gettysburg became the deadliest clash of the war, leaving more than fifty thousand wounded and seven thousand dead in its wake. It was the Confederacy's "high-water mark," their last real shot at breaking the Union on Northern soil. But beyond strategy and statistics, Gettysburg was a human catastrophe. The fields were littered with the fallen, and the town was left to deal with the unimaginable aftermath.

Then came the second part: the mourning. President Abraham Lincoln arrived in November of that same year to dedicate the Soldiers' National Cemetery. His Gettysburg Address transformed a graveyard into hallowed ground, redefining the war's purpose in just 272 words. It was a moment of reflection, a time to honor the dead, and an opportunity to grapple with what the nation was fighting for. But mourning wasn't just about words. The process stretched on for years as the country struggled to heal its wounds.

And then, after half a century, the third and final act came, the least remembered but perhaps the most remarkable. In 1913, the battle's survivors—men who had once tried to kill each other—returned to

Gettysburg for the fiftieth anniversary of the battle. They came as old men, not enemies, to retrace their steps, reconnect with comrades, and walk the battlefield one last time. Their goal wasn't reconciliation, but something unexpected happened somewhere between the monuments and the memories. The Grand Reunion became a powerful symbol of healing and unity.

Gettysburg's story didn't end with cannons or speeches. It ended with handshakes across a stone wall that had once divided a nation. In many ways, it was the final chapter of the Civil War. And though history often forgets this part, it may just be the most important lesson of all.

Picture a bent, old soldier standing at the edge of the battlefield, the wind stirring the tall grass like ghosts from the past. Fifty years had passed, and yet the land still echoed with cries and the smell of gunpowder. He clutched a worn map, its edges frayed from decades of handling, but in the end, it was not ink or paper that guided him—it was memory. The shape of a distant hill, the curve of a stone wall along the field, the feeling in his gut.

This was the place.

Or close enough.

As he wandered, he caught sight of another man moving slowly across the ground, stopping now and then, as if listening for something long buried beneath the earth. The stranger wore the same haunted expression, the exact weight of years in his eyes. Their gazes met and instinct took over: a nod, a cautious step closer.

"Where are you from?" the first asked.

"New York," came the reply.

"North Carolina," the other answered.

There was a pause as the two old soldiers studied each other. They asked each other more questions. They exchanged military details, including division, regiment, and company names. They traded pieces of the past like puzzle fragments, fitting them together until realization struck.

"I was posted right over here," the man from New York said, pointing to a rise in the land.

"And I was just over there." The Southerner gestured at a cluster of trees.

For a moment, silence. Then a chuckle.

"Hell, we might've been trying to kill each other."

"Wouldn't be surprised."

And then, something neither expected. They exchanged names and shook hands, firm and steady. No longer soldiers, no longer enemies. Just two men, bound by history.

"What did things look like from your side of the field?"

The man from North Carolina squinted at the land and then motioned. "Come on. Let me show you."

Together, they walked—not as adversaries rekindling past aggressions but as old men revisiting a shared experience. Their conversation wove a bridge across half a century—one step, one story, and one unexpected friendship at a time.

Though this exchange is a product of my imagination, similar experiences happened dozens, hundreds, if not thousands of times during the Gettysburg Grand Reunion. And we'll explore as many of these stories as we can.

The politicians belted out their long-winded speeches, full of lofty rhetoric about national healing, reconciliation, and the march of progress. They spoke in grand terms of unity and destiny, as if healing could be declared from a podium. But that wasn't what the reunion was really about.

The real reunion didn't unfold beneath the banners and speeches but out on the fields themselves. It happened quietly, in ones and twos, as old men in blue and gray wandered back over the ground they had once fought to the death to hold. There, away from the crowds, they found each other—sometimes with a handshake, sometimes with a shared memory, sometimes with nothing more than a nod of recognition. They hadn't set out to reconcile; most came to relive, to remember, perhaps to mourn. And yet, in those small, human encounters across a once-bloody field, reconciliation was exactly what took place.

Before we dive into the stories, let's take a quick look at how the Grand Reunion came about. I'm not going to drag you through every little detail—the nuance would make your eyes glaze over. My focus is on the reunion's events, so I'll stick to the highlights to keep things moving. Still, it's worth pausing for a moment on how it all came together, if only to set the stage properly.

The battle's first day lined up perfectly with the calendar—July 1, 1863. There's a long-standing myth that the Confederate army marched into

Gettysburg looking for shoes, but the truth is much less dramatic—they were following the road system. That's where a popular Civil War saying came from: "All roads lead to Gettysburg."

Here's the ironic part: While the Southern army approached the town from the north, the Northern army came from the south. They quite literally bumped into each other. Neither side had planned to fight at Gettysburg, but once they crossed paths . . . they couldn't pass up the opportunity to shoot at each other. And just like that, the battle was on.

Henry S. Huidekoper was just twenty-three years old during the Battle of Gettysburg and a member of the 150th Pennsylvania Volunteer Infantry. The 150th was engaged near McPherson's Farm, just outside town. This area saw much of the fighting on the first day of the battle. Although the farmhouse is long gone, McPherson's barn still stands and is an excellent landmark while touring the battlefield.

But let's get back to Huidekoper. He was in command of the 150th regiment, and during the fighting, a Rebel bullet struck his leg and cut him to the bone. A Civil War–era bullet was called a Minié ball. It was conical in shape and made from soft lead that created devastating wounds. The soft lead would spread out on impact, splintering bones and leading to many battlefield amputations. The Minié ball didn't pierce as much as it bludgeoned the body. It was a painful wound, but Huidekoper took it like a champ.

A medic bandaged his leg in the field, but no sooner had he been treated than a second Minié ball smashed into his arm. Despite the pain, Huidekoper continued to command the 150th during a desperate portion of the battle, and his tenacity helped hold the line against the enemy. Every officer of the 150th had been either killed or wounded during the struggle, and despite his injuries, Huidekoper remained in command until he grew faint from loss of blood.

Huidekoper described the battle in his after-action report, where he wrote that "a wound compelled me to relinquish the command to Captain Widdis."[1] Such a modest statement!

After the first day's battle, the doctors determined that his shattered arm could not be saved, and it was amputated. Huidekoper survived the surgery, but his wound never fully healed, and he was forced to resign from the army.

As a result of his actions during the Battle of Gettysburg, Henry S. Huidekoper received the Congressional Medal of Honor. His citation read, "While engaged in repelling an attack of the enemy, received a severe wound of the right arm, but instead of retiring, remained at the front in command of the regiment."[2]

After the war, Huidekoper was drawn back to Gettysburg, often walking through the quiet fields that had once been drenched in blood. Although the armies were gone, the scars remained. Bullet-riddled trees dotted the landscape and stood as silent witnesses to the carnage of battle. I wonder what went through his mind as he revisited the site where his arm was sawn off. To my knowledge, he never wrote about it, but it's evident from his frequent visits that the battlefield held a particular significance for him.

Huidekoper attended many Civil War reunions, gathering with the old boys to relive the days when they had stood shoulder to shoulder in battle. He cherished those meetings because only another soldier could truly understand the horrors they had endured. The camaraderie forged in fire was something his family could never fully grasp.

But as the years passed, those reunions changed. He would arrive searching for a familiar face, only to find that friend's chair empty, their name read solemnly among the dead. With each gathering, the ranks grew thinner. More empty chairs marked each gathering, more names read in memoriam, and a growing sense that time was running short for all of them.

Huidekoper lived long enough to witness this steady disappearance of comrades, and the weight of it pressed on him. While there was still time, he sought something greater than another fading reunion.

Because of this, Henry Huidekoper is generally credited with the idea for a combined fiftieth reunion of the Battle of Gettysburg. In 1908, he met with Edwin Stuart, the governor of Pennsylvania at the time, and suggested a joint reunion, to honor not just those who had fought and died but also those who had fought and *survived*.

In a way, this reunion embodied the same spirit as the Last Man's Banquet—a final gathering of comrades before the march of time claimed them all. Whether he realized it or not, Huidekoper's vision was more than just a commemoration; it was an acknowledgment that one day the

(*Top left*) Henry S. Huidekoper in 1864, reproduced from his *A Short Story of the First Day's Fight at Gettysburg* (1906); (*top right*) from John P. Nicholson's *Pennsylvania at Gettysburg* (1914); (*bottom*) McPherson's Farm in 2025, near where Huidekoper lost his arm, photographed by the author.

battlefield would no longer echo with the voices of those who had fought there. If the veterans could not stop time, they could at least decide how they would be remembered—together as brothers rather than as enemies.

Governor Stuart caught the vision and presented the idea to the Pennsylvania General Assembly, establishing the Fiftieth Anniversary of the Battle of Gettysburg Commission. The Commission members, all of whom were Civil War veterans, were responsible for planning the reunion.

Before we continue, let's stop and reconsider that last statement. Every single member of the Commission was a veteran of the Civil War. This means that the 1913 Gettysburg Reunion was by veterans for veterans. Notice they didn't consult the HR department before selecting who should be on the committee. I have read criticism from twenty-first-century Americans who feel the reunion wasn't inclusive enough, and maybe there is some merit to that discussion. However, the reunion was organized *by* the veterans *for* the veterans, and ultimately they decided what they wanted to include. Please keep this point in mind if you believe they should have handled things differently. Perhaps they should have, but the reunion went precisely as the veterans planned and criticizing it will not change the past.

The First General Conference of Pennsylvania's Fiftieth Anniversary of the Battle of Gettysburg Commission took place in October 1910 and met in Gettysburg to discuss the logistics for the reunion. The Second Conference met in Washington, DC; the Third at the Union League of Philadelphia; and the Fourth and Final General Conference met again at Gettysburg in May 1913, just six weeks before the reunion, to inspect the camp and make final preparations. These conferences contained sixty-five participants and featured the "Who's Who" of the Civil War, from Elisha Hunt Rhodes to Daniel Sickles to Joshua Lawrence Chamberlain. The conference discussed whether the blue and gray uniforms should be worn during the reunion, whether the Union and Confederate flags should appear, or if only the American flag should be flown.

As you can imagine, both sides had a lot to say on the matter.

Colonel Charles Borrows from New Jersey motioned that no uniforms should be worn and the only flag allowed should be the Stars and Stripes. General Felix H. Robertson from Texas opposed the idea.

*We tried our best to get out of the Union, but you kept us in the house. . . . Take me just as I am. I want to bring it there and show you and wave in your faces again the very Texas Brigade battle flag that we shook in your faces there on July 3rd, 1863. If you were able to drive it back then, its faded colors can do you no harm now.*[3]

General J. Thompson Brown had a different view: "Virginia does not agree with the views expressed by Texas. We would not dictate to our hosts. . . . I am going as a citizen. The moths have eaten my old gray uniform, and I am glad of it. . . . We want to show the world that we can bury the past."

By this time, Pennsylvania governor Stuart's term had ended, and he was succeeded by John K. Tener, who settled the debate: "We shall not quibble, we do not care what uniforms are worn." All flags were welcome. However, the Confederate flag would not be used in any official capacity during the celebration, and only the American flag would be flown above the camp.

This settled the matter, and Colonel Charles Borrows withdrew his motion.

Regardless of this decision, a rumor spread on both sides of the Mason-Dixon Line claiming that the Confederate uniform would not be welcomed back at Gettysburg. This caused quite a stir in the veteran community, prompting several Union veterans to denounce the rumor. Dr. Samuel E. Eastman from Grand Army of the Republic (GAR) Post 6 in Elmira, New York, declared that such opposition was "ridiculous." He expressed that it was his "earnest hope to meet there in cordial fellowship the old boys in gray in their familiar uniforms."[4] Dr. Eastman believed that anyone opposed to the gray uniform probably did not fight in the Civil War, and this view did not accurately reflect the general sentiment of the Northern veterans.

Retired colonel Jerome A. Watrous from Whitewater, Wisconsin, replied to Dr. Eastman:

*I was delighted to know that your large post had promptly cuffed the ears of the little fellows who are prating against the old veterans of the*

> *South appearing at the Gettysburg Reunion in their uniforms. Good Lord, save us! Speaking for myself, I would vote to have them come in their old uniforms or new uniforms in gray and bring along their voices and now and then indulge in the old-time Rebel yell. I want to see the uniform and hear the yell when it will not scare the life out of me as they used to do when I saw them coming over the field. . . . Let us convey to the old fellows of the South, who had the hardest end of the stick, that with us the war is over, and that we look upon them as American soldiers, and shall be delighted to meet them on the field of Gettysburg.*[5]

These quotes appeared in newspapers nationwide and did much to assure the Southern veterans of the welcome they would receive at Gettysburg.

However, in June 1913, a new rumor spread only a few weeks before the start of the reunion. Despite Governor Tener's assurance that the Confederate flag would be welcome, this latest rumor stated, "The word has gone out to the veterans of the Confederate Army not to bring their tattered battle flags to Gettysburg, that it shall not be unfurled or floated to the breeze." This news shocked the Southerners, causing some to stay home. It angered Alexander Hunter so much that he wrote a letter to the editor of *The Baltimore Sun*. Hunter concluded with "Well, each Confederate veteran must decide the question for himself. As for myself I feel that all the soul, all the sentiment . . . of the reunion has been shattered by that 'no battle flag' order. No Gettysburg for me."[6]

It's a real shame that a mere rumor caused this veteran to miss such a marvelous event. Days before the reunion, *The Philadelphia Inquirer* reiterated, "The War Department has issued no order prohibiting the display of the Confederate flag in the big camp, and the men of the South may be expected with gray uniforms, campaign hats, battleflags and all."[7]

A little later in this book, we'll discuss how the veterans felt about the Confederate flag and whether it belonged at the Grand Reunion.

During the planning, the reunion was referred to by many different names, including:

The Celebration of the Semi-Centenary of the Civil War

| | |
|---|---|
| The Gettysburg Celebration | The Grand Reunion |
| The Reunion Celebration at Gettysburg | The Gettysburg Reunion |
| The Gettysburg Reunion | The Blue and Gray Reunion |
| The Great Peace Reunion | The Gettysburg Peace Reunion |
| The Golden Jubilee | The Great Peace Jubilee |
| | The Great Reunion |

And the all-encompassing Grand Reunion of the Blue and Gray on the Fiftieth Anniversary of the Battle of Gettysburg. That's quite the mouthful, but for our purposes, from here on, we'll refer to it as the Grand Reunion.

Since the Civil War ended in 1865, numerous reunions have been held for veterans, but none as impressive as the Grand Reunion of 1913. It took three years of planning and more than a million dollars to make the event happen, with the goal of having former enemies put aside their animosity and honor those who fought and died at Gettysburg.

If you were a Civil War veteran and lived in the North, you likely belonged to a fraternal organization called the Grand Army of the Republic, or GAR for short. Hundreds of posts popped up around the country. They served as a social network for veterans, helping many receive government pensions. A similar organization called the United Confederate Veterans (UCV) was created in the South. These organizations died out with the passing of their members. Still, they served as precursors to the modern-day American Legion or the Veterans of Foreign Wars posts in towns across America.

In the early twentieth century, the commander of the Grand Army of the Republic wrote a letter to the commander of the United Confederate Veterans about the upcoming Gettysburg Reunion: "Let us assemble there, and meet and greet each other hand to hand and heart to heart in the spirit of true friendship and brotherhood, born out of love for the Flag and devotion to our common Country."[8]

The UCV commander enthusiastically accepted the invitation in hopes "that this event may mark the final and complete reconciliation . . . and the permanent establishment of harmonious and fraternal relations between the North and South."[9]

After the bloody Civil War, the United States entered a painful and chaotic period known as Reconstruction. During this time, the federal government faced the enormous task of reintegrating the Southern states and redefining freedom for millions of former slaves. The era was further marred by widespread political corruption, as opportunistic "carpetbaggers" from the North and self-serving "scalawags" in the South exploited the upheaval for personal gain. By the time the nation reached the fiftieth anniversary of Gettysburg, it was clear that America desperately needed reconciliation.

As the reunion approached, politicians made flowery speeches about brotherly love and unity, but many believed that true reconciliation would exist only within the politicians' empty rhetoric. Words were one thing, but actions were another. How would the veterans, the actual people doing the killing in the 1860s, react when meeting their enemies on the battlefield again? Could all be forgiven and forgotten, or had time caused the old wounds to fester and blister with bitterness? Only time would tell.

The Grand Reunion had something uniquely powerful going for it—something crucial to remember when considering its significance. This wasn't a gathering of Civil War–era generals, high-ranking officers, or politicians. Men like General Robert E. Lee, General Ulysses S. Grant, and General George Meade had long since passed into the history books.

Instead, this reunion belonged to the privates and enlisted men—the foot soldiers who made up the vast majority of both armies. These were not the men who debated causes or drafted strategies. They didn't sit in halls of power or draw up declarations. They were the ones who followed orders, marched twenty miles a day on foot, and bled on the front lines.

Because of this, the cause of the Civil War—the politics and ideologies that led to it—wasn't the central focus. For them, it wasn't about preserving the Union or defending states' rights. It was about surviving the chaos and returning home. The memories of the battles, not the politics, stayed with them.

They didn't meet each other at the reunion as enemies or symbols of a divided nation. They met as old soldiers. And instead of facing off with bayonets, they greeted one another with handshakes—men who had once stood on opposite sides of the battlefield, now stood in peace.

The governor of Virginia, William Hodges Mann, put it like this: "We are not here to discuss the Genesis of the war, but men who have tried each other in the storm and smoke of battle are here to discuss this great fight. . . . We came here, I say, not to discuss what caused the war from 1861 to 1865, but to talk over the events of the battle here as man to man and as comrade to comrade, to shake hands as brothers and to recognize in each the splendid courage displayed upon this remarkable field of battle."[10]

The average age of the veterans in 1913 was seventy-two[11] years old, meaning they were a mere twenty years old at the start of the Civil War in 1861. Three million men fought in the war; according to the War Department, 2.3 million were between the ages of ten and eighteen.[12] At such a young age, they did not have much say in the cause of the war, but they certainly did fight in it!

Let's consider why the veterans returned to Gettysburg. They had all sorts of reasons to go. The *New York Tribune*[13] shared an interesting story about Jacob J. Blake, an old Confederate living with his family in Milford, Connecticut. (The *Tribune* listed his age as seventy-nine, but it's interesting to note that another paper claimed he was eighty-nine.) During the war, Jacob Blake fought in McIntosh's Artillery Battalion under Southern general A. P. Hill. At Gettysburg, Blake was engaged with the enemy on all three days of the battle and was eventually wounded.

As an old man, Blake was looking forward to going to the reunion and spent months planning his trip, but his physician advised against it; his health was poor, and the trip could kill him. Blake was disappointed and agreed to stay home.

But then he read in the newspaper that Sergeant James Russell from the Massachusetts Infantry was making the trip, and Blake immediately changed his mind. He was going to the Grand Reunion, regardless of the risk.

According to the *Tribune*, Blake and Russell were pickets in opposite armies during the Battle of Gettysburg. They shot at each other for three days, but at night, when things quieted down, they met in the middle. They swapped food and tobacco. During this time, one man in blue and one man in gray became friends.

Jacob Blake said he would die happy if only he could see his old friend James Russell one last time.

On May 16, 1913, the Anniversary Commission and state representatives met at Gettysburg for the fourth and final time to review the camp and finalize the program. It was decided that there would be two official welcome addresses: one by a representative of GAR and another by the UCV. Each would welcome the other to the battlefield. The program would open with a prayer from the GAR chaplain and close with a benediction from the UCV's chaplain.

Each participating state had a representative in attendance, and the representative from Maine was Major General Joshua Lawrence Chamberlain. If you've ever read *The Killer Angels* or seen the 1993 *Gettysburg* movie, then you'll be familiar with Chamberlain, as portrayed by actor Jeff Daniels in the film.

In battle, it's always good to hold the high ground. At Gettysburg, there is a small mountain called Big Round Top and a rocky spur beside it called Little Round Top. This area, located approximately two miles south of Gettysburg, is one of the most popular places to visit on the battlefield. Little Round Top rises 650 feet above sea level and has a commanding view of the area, making it an advantageous location for either army. Both sides wanted to place artillery on the summit, and on July 2, 1863, they raced to see who could get there first. The Twentieth Maine Volunteer Infantry, under the command of Joshua Lawrence Chamberlain, reached the top only ten minutes before the Alabama Brigade did. The men from Maine were stretched thin along the crest of Little Round Top and fired down at the Confederates.

Meanwhile, the men from Alabama had a tough time climbing up the mountain while under fire. The Confederates charged up the hill multiple times, only to be repulsed by the Twentieth Maine time and again. After ninety minutes of battle, the Twentieth Maine was running low on ammunition, so Chamberlain made a bold decision. He ordered his men to fix bayonets and charge down the hill into the enemy. This move surprised the Confederates. Some were wounded, many were captured, and the rest retreated, leaving Little Round Top firmly in the hands of the Union.

For his actions on July 2, Joshua Lawrence Chamberlain was awarded the Medal of Honor. The citation reads, "Daring heroism and great tenacity in holding his position on the Little Round Top against repeated assaults and carrying the advance position on the Great Round Top."[14]

But there's more to Chamberlain's story than what happened at Gettysburg. During the Civil War, he was wounded six times. At Petersburg in 1864, he raised his sword to command his men and was shot by a Minié ball. The bullet passed through his right hip, crushing bone, puncturing his bladder, and severing his urethra.

OUCH!

The surgeons did what they could, but the battlefield medicine of the 1860s was practically barbaric. The wound never fully healed and constantly leaked, leaving Chamberlain susceptible to chronic bladder infections that caused him "unspeakable agony." And all of this was before antibiotics were invented. He lived with this weeping wound for almost fifty years. The pain often left him bedridden, but he managed it as best he could and didn't let it keep him down. After the war, he served as the Republican governor of Maine and spent twelve years as the president of his alma mater, Bowdoin College. He was also very active in the Grand Army of the Republic, and, despite his chronic pain, he participated in reunions and visited Gettysburg many times.

His last trip to Gettysburg was on May 16 and 17, 1913, to participate in the Fourth General Conference, which focused on final preparations for the Grand Reunion. While there, the Commission answered the one question everyone wanted to know: How many veterans would be attending the reunion? Chamberlain, as the Maine delegate, claimed that 600 veterans from his state would be in attendance. Each of the other state representatives offered a number, and when tallied up, it came to 43,998 veterans planning the trip to Gettysburg. At that point, the Great Camp was prepped to host 40,000 veterans, meaning they needed to find tents, cots, and food for an additional 4,000 people.

That was their number as of mid-May. By June 1, the anticipated attendance had risen to 49,405; by June 15, it had increased to 54,928. They needed more provisions, and they needed them fast!

While at Gettysburg during the May conference, the Commission surveyed the construction of the Great Camp and took a group photo in front of the Pennsylvania Monument, in which Chamberlain can be seen. Because of that image, many assume Chamberlain attended the Grand Reunion. However, this journey was painful for Chamberlain; the constant

The fourth and final conference of the Pennsylvania Commission met at Gettysburg on May 17, 1913, to inspect the Great Camp. Joshua Lawrence Chamberlain is fourteenth in the second row, third from the left. Reproduced from Pennsylvania, *Fiftieth Anniversary of the Battle of Gettysburg: Report of the Pennsylvania Commission*, ed. and comp. Lewis Eugene Beitler (Harrisburg, PA: Wm. Stanley Ray, State Printer, 1913); hereafter cited as the *Fiftieth Anniversary Report*.

jostling on the train ride from Maine to Pennsylvania inflamed his old wounds, and he didn't think he could physically tolerate another trip just six weeks later. So as the Grand Reunion kicked off on July 1, Joshua Lawrence Chamberlain was resting at his home in Portland, Maine.

However, Chamberlain still wanted to support his old comrades, so when the Maine veterans left on the train for Gettysburg, he was at the station to see them off.[15] It's a real shame that he helped plan the reunion but could not attend himself.

His health continued to deteriorate, and he died on February 24, 1914. Joshua Lawrence Chamberlain is often considered one of the last soldiers to die from Civil War–related injuries.

One indispensable source for discussing the Grand Reunion is the "Fiftieth Anniversary of the Battle of Gettysburg Report of the Pennsylvania Commission." It is considered the Holy Bible of the Grand Reunion and is chock-full of facts, figures, photos, and transcripts of the speeches given during the event. It is the go-to source for the Grand Reunion, and I will draw heavily from it.

The reunion was scheduled to take place from July 1 to 4, 1913, precisely fifty years after the Battle of Gettysburg. From the outset, it was decided that all honorably discharged veterans of the Civil War would be invited, not just those who fought at Gettysburg. This also included veterans from the US Navy and the US Colored Troops, although few chose to go. With invites going out across the nation, the state of Pennsylvania prepared a "Great Camp" on the battlefield and estimated that they would need to host forty thousand veterans.[16]

In 1913, the United States consisted of only forty-eight states. Arizona and New Mexico had joined the Union only the previous year, while Alaska and Hawaii were nearly fifty years away from achieving statehood. With forty-eight states came a forty-eight-star flag, its design set in a neat grid of six rows by eight columns—a layout noticeably different from the one we recognize today.

In many cases, the states provided transportation for the veterans, and forty-six out of forty-eight states sent representatives to attend the event. Nevada and Wyoming were the only states that didn't send veterans to Gettysburg.

The exact number of attendees at the reunion varies by source. Still, the official report from the Pennsylvania Commission claimed that there were 53,407 veterans in attendance—44,713 from the Union and 8,694 from the Confederacy. The Confederate veterans were vastly outnumbered at the reunion, probably because they were commemorating a Southern defeat in Northern territory. Also, the Union veterans were financially better off than many of their Confederate counterparts. The Pennsylvania veterans numbered 22,203, with New York State coming in second with 8,500 veterans. Both states offered free transportation to and from the reunion, which is why they had far more veterans show up than anywhere else in the country. Other states weren't as financially capable and thus had lower attendance. For instance, Colorado claimed that the "State [was] not in shape financially to appropriate any money for transportation."[17] Any veteran who wanted to attend had to pay their way. As a result, only twelve veterans from the Rocky Mountain state made the trip.

According to *The Washington Herald*, "There are many more veterans in the South, but their failure to attend the great reunion should not be misconstrued. Many were ready to go, but the financial resources were inadequate."[18] This is unfortunate, but it makes sense, as it took significantly more money to send a veteran from Texas than it did to send one from Philadelphia.

Illinois paid only for veterans who participated in the Battle of Gettysburg. These men traveled in style on luxurious railway cars called Pullman cars, which had electric lights, cooling fans, and enough space for each passenger to have a bed to sleep in. They were also given ten dollars each for spending money. Other Civil War veterans from Illinois who did not participate in the Battle of Gettysburg were still welcome to attend, but they had to go on their own dime.

In nearly every Southern state, the veterans had to pay for their transportation. Virginia provided some money for travel expenses, and the Daughters of the Confederacy provided brand-new gray uniforms for anyone who wanted one. In attendance were 3,329 Virginia veterans, and thanks to the brand-new Confederate uniforms, they are very easy to spot in the photos from the event.

Washington State spent $15,000 transporting one hundred veterans to and from Gettysburg. However, when it came time to depart, 160 veterans showed up at the train station, and there wasn't enough money to pay for everyone's ticket. At the last minute, a wealthy veteran stepped forward and provided an additional $6,000 to ensure no one was left behind.[19]

It's important to note that the states provided money only for veterans and nothing for their families. If wives, children, and grandchildren wanted to go to Gettysburg, they had to pay their own way. Consequently, the Pennsylvania Commission only allowed veterans to stay at the Great Camp, so their family members had to find food and lodging elsewhere. In 1913, Gettysburg had an approximate population of four thousand people. During the reunion, the town itself hosted another ten thousand people. Some of these were veterans who didn't want to sleep in a tent or wanted to stay with their families.

The Great Camp stood just southwest of Gettysburg, sprawling along the Emmitsburg Road like a pop-up city built of brown tents. It was a logistical marvel—a temporary home prepared for the tens of thousands of aging veterans who would soon descend on it, returning not as soldiers to the battlefield but as old men chasing memories.

The scale of the project was staggering. For two months, laborers transformed open farmland into a functioning military encampment, thankfully without the chaos of war. New wells were drilled, and water was pumped into towering tanks, cooled by ice-packed coils and delivered by gravity to thirty-two scattered fountains. On a hot July day, nothing would be more welcome.

Initially, five thousand tents were raised across 280 acres, a sea of canvas flapping in the summer breeze. Each tent, initially intended to hold twelve men, was reduced to accommodate eight, providing the veterans with space to stretch, breathe, and rest their weary bones. Inside, every man was given a cot, a blanket, and a mess kit. Buckets of water, hand basins, and candle lanterns were distributed to each tent.

The camp pulsed with energy and innovation. The Army Signal Corps laid over two hundred miles of cable, wiring the grid-like company streets with one hundred telephones so the old soldiers could call home and let their families know they'd arrived safely. Five hundred electric lights illuminated the grounds, allowing the veterans to navigate their way back to their tents at any hour of the day.

The streets of the camp were organized in numbered camps, ranging from 1 to 49, with each tent clearly labeled. For example, veterans from Vineland, New Jersey, were located on Street 39, Tent 17. This system provided an orderly arrangement for men who were accustomed to regimented military life.

A temporary railroad spur split the camp in half. A platform was built to allow the trains to stop in the middle of the Great Camp so the aged veterans wouldn't have to walk as far to their tents.

At the southern edge of the camp stood the aptly named Great Tent. Part circus tent, part cathedral, it towered above the rest of the encampment and could hold between twelve thousand and fifteen thousand people. It was the heart of the camp, where official ceremonies, speeches, and commemorations would take place. Between events, it could be sectioned off to host smaller regimental reunions. A wooden stage and lectern were built for speakers, but there was a catch—the Grand Reunion took place just before the invention of the loudspeaker. So, while the tent could hold thousands, it didn't guarantee everyone could hear what was being said.

Feeding such a multitude was no small feat. The camp featured 173 field kitchens and 400 army ranges, manned by 2,000 cooks working day and night to prepare meals. Equally important were the 90 latrines, which could accommodate nearly 3,500 men at any given time. This was vital, as the organizers planned to make quality food with a good deal of roughage.

The camp had all the makings of a 1913 military bivouac, except this time the soldiers were no longer young recruits, but rather gray-haired veterans with canes and stories to tell. Considering their age and condition, health services were critical. The Red Cross set up a hospital and fourteen aid stations throughout the grounds. Every detail had been considered. Even five hundred coffins were shipped in—just in case.

From a modern perspective, one detail stands out: These men camped in the sweltering July heat on the very ground where they had once fought and fallen, without a single shower available. Each tent had a water basin, but towels and soap were not supplied. One can only imagine the body odor after a week under the sun; the collective bouquet of thousands of unwashed men must have lingered like ghosts over the battlefield.

And yet they came. Despite the heat, the dust, the aches in their joints, and the years between them, they came. The Great Camp was not just a location; it was a temporary city built for remembrance and commemoration.

According to the Pennsylvania Commission Report, 53,407 veterans attended the Grand Reunion. However, that doesn't tell the whole story. Thousands of support personnel also resided within the Great Camp:

- Civil War veterans—53,407
- US Army officers—124
- US Army enlisted—1,324
- Journalists—155
- Cooking staff and laborers—2,170
- Boy Scouts—385[20]
- Medical staff—81[21]
- Total = 57,646

With the Grand Reunion only a few days away, the town of Gettysburg began to transform. Every block was covered in red, white, and blue, and practically every house displayed at least one flag. The Confederate flag also appeared, and the blue and gray were displayed on many buildings. Large pictures of both Union and Confederate generals were everywhere. The hotels filled up as the crowds arrived, while "every side yard is fitted up with alluringly pretty booths and refreshment stands."[22] Entrepreneurial townsfolk sold everything from ice cream to keepsake pins, ribbons, and relics dug up from the battlefield. The town was bursting with excitement, and music filled the air. Many veterans brought their fifes, drums, and bugles, and the wartime songs rang throughout the streets. *The Pittsburgh Press* described it like this: "Imagine the biggest street carnival you ever saw, then multiply it by a thousand."[23]

The Boy Scouts of America was still a new organization in 1913. It had been founded only three years earlier, and its original purpose was to teach boys about patriotism, courage, self-reliance, and Christian values. In March 1913, several Boy Scout troops from the Washington, DC, area assisted with Woodrow Wilson's presidential inaugural parade. They served as guides and helpers to the parade attendees. This caught the attention of Colonel Lewis Beitler, secretary of the Pennsylvania Commission,

View from the observation tower in Ziegler's Grove, highlighting some of the five thousand tents that made up the Great Camp. A train runs through the center, dividing the camp into two sections. Courtesy of the Library of Congress.

who wanted to enlist the Boy Scouts to assist at the Grand Reunion. Twenty-four troops from Washington, DC, New Jersey, Maryland, and Pennsylvania participated in the reunion, totaling 385 scouts.

It's also interesting to note that not all of the Boy Scouts were White. According to *The New York Age* newspaper, "Harold Allen and Oliver Poindexter, members of Troop 109, Afro-American Boy Scouts, have been picked out to attend the Gettysburg celebration."[24] We know that at least two of the Boy Scouts in attendance were Black, but it's possible that there were more.

The Boy Scouts arrived at the camp one week before the reunion started and were put to work unloading supplies, pitching tents, and distributing blankets. This extra time on site helped them become familiar with the camp's layout. Once the camp opened, their primary goal was to assist the veterans with their luggage and guide them to their tents. They also provided emergency medical care as needed.

To keep the reunion running smoothly, Major Edward James Normoyle was appointed as the quartermaster to handle the details of the Great

A cropped photograph taken from the observation tower in Ziegler's Grove, highlighting the immense size of the Great Tent. It is situated across from the Codori Farm along the Emmitsburg Road, where cars are visible. Courtesy of the Library of Congress.

Camp. The quartermaster's job was to oversee transportation logistics, sleeping arrangements, and provisions for the veterans. It was a challenging and thankless job, but they could not have picked a better man. Major Normoyle had handled relief efforts during the Great Mississippi Floods of 1912 and again during the Great Dayton Flood in early 1913. As you can see, he had considerable experience with water, and he would need that experience to handle the flood of humanity about to pour into Gettysburg. Thankfully, he was a man who knew how to get things done and keep things organized.

On June 28, Major Normoyle declared,

> *We are thoroughly prepared and have the entire situation well in hand. Every old soldier will find things in readiness for him when he comes here. He will be met at the train and shown the location of his tent. If he is not able to carry his baggage, someone will be here to do it for him. He will not even have to do a stroke of work, not even fill the water*

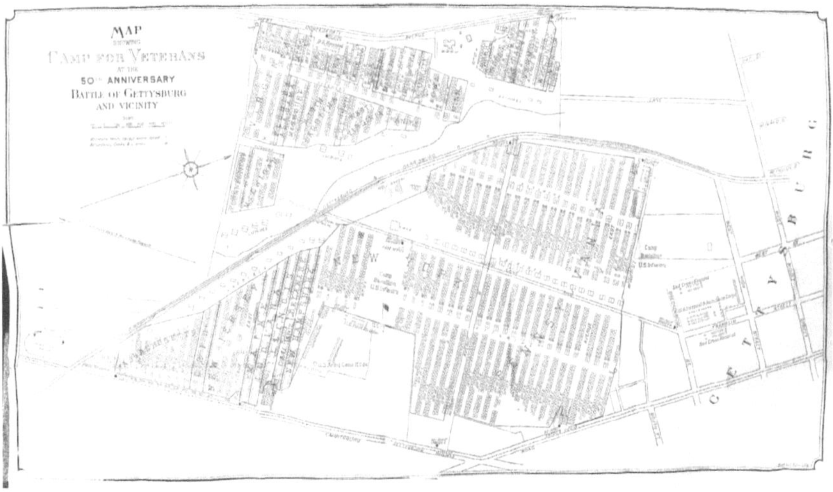

Map of the Great Camp. Reproduced from the *Fiftieth Anniversary Report.*

> *buckets in his tent. The railroads have consented to bring every train into the camp and no one will have to walk any distance. A specially built platform has been constructed so that all may unload at once and make room for others. We plan to handle the crowd without any confusion and believe we can place them in the camp as fast as the railroads can bring them here.*[25]

That was Normoyle's official statement. However, when asked how they would deal with such an influx of people into Gettysburg, he said, "We'll accommodate them if we have to pitch tents in the front yards of the houses."[26]

Famous last words . . .

Colonel James Schoonmaker formed the Fourteenth Pennsylvania Cavalry Regiment during the Civil War. He was well liked by his men and one of the youngest colonels in the army at just twenty years old. Schoonmaker received the Medal of Honor for his actions during the Battle of Winchester in 1864. His citation read, "At a critical period, gallantly led a cavalry charge against the left of the enemy's line of battle, drove the enemy out of his works, and captured many prisoners."[27]

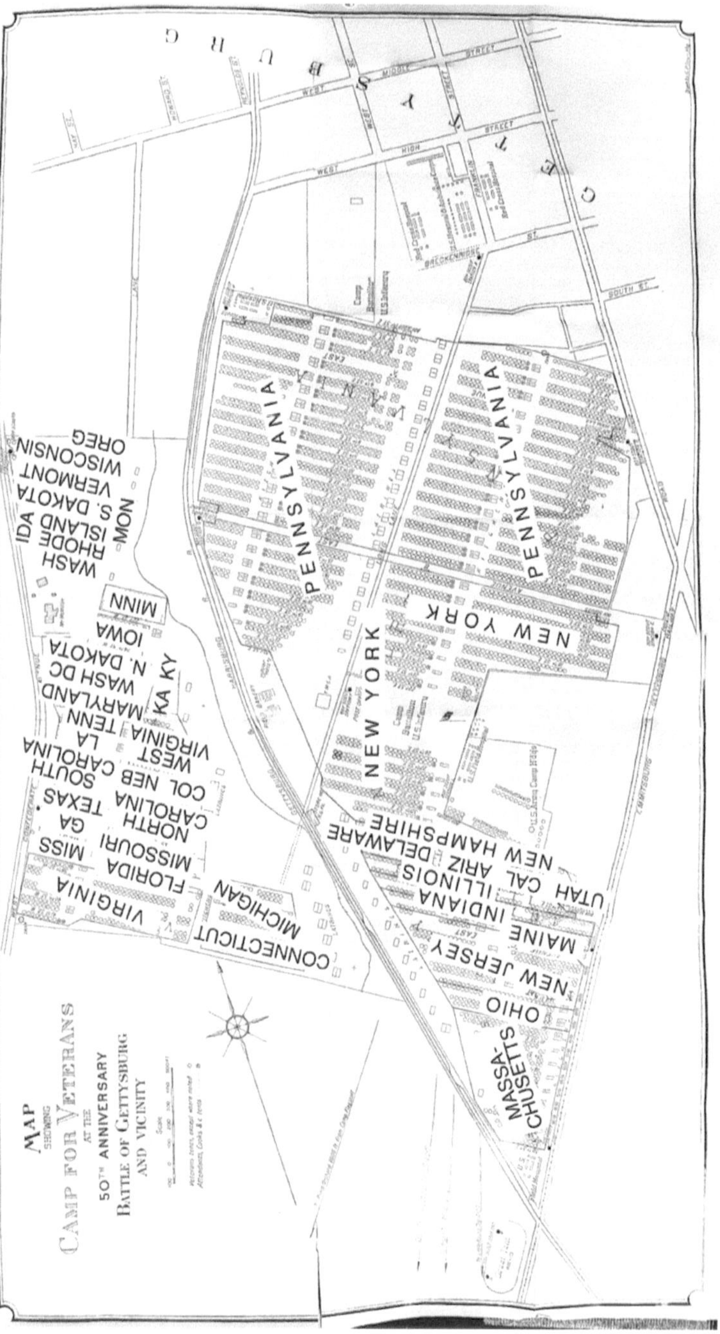


Map of the Great Camp, adapted from the *Fiftieth Anniversary Report*. State names have been enhanced by the author.

During the war, Schoonmaker was under the direct command of General Philip Sheridan, who was known for being a stern commander and a harsh disciplinarian. Schoonmaker was with Sheridan in his tent one day when a young private named Henry Schaeffer rode into camp with an urgent report. Forgetting military protocol, Schaeffer rushed into the tent and slapped down the report in front of Sheridan without even bothering to salute. Sheridan went ballistic and ordered the private hanged by his thumbs for breaking regulations.

This was an excruciating punishment. The thumbs would be tied together, and the rope would be thrown over a tree branch. The rope would then be pulled tight and tied off to the tree, leaving the victim's toes just touching the ground. They would remain in this position for several hours.

Before this punishment could be carried out, Schoonmaker intervened. He told Sheridan that the private was an exceptional soldier and requested permission to discipline him.

"All right, get him the hell out of here. You punish him!" Sheridan said.

Schoonmaker grabbed the private by the arm and threw him out of the tent, knocking him to the ground. Following him outside, he dragged the man a few feet away. Once they were out of earshot, Schoonmaker helped the private up, dusted him off, and whispered, "Next time, remember to salute."

After that, Schoonmaker and Private Schaeffer became lifelong friends.[28]

When General Lee surrendered to General Grant at Appomattox, Grant was gracious in victory and asked Lee whether he needed anything. The Confederates were starving, and General Lee requested rations for his men. Grant agreed, and soon Colonel Schoonmaker and the Fourteenth Pennsylvania Cavalry were tasked with distributing food and water to the defeated Confederates. When Schoonmaker saw the condition of the Southern army, he felt great sympathy for them and ensured they were well provided for.

In 1911, Governor Tener of Pennsylvania appointed Schoonmaker to be the chairman of the Pennsylvania Commission for the Fiftieth Anniversary Reunion of the Battle of Gettysburg. During the planning stages, Schoonmaker collaborated with veterans, governors, and two presidents to ensure the reunion's success. And it all paid off in the summer of 1913.

# 3
# June 29—Sunday

As word of the Grand Reunion spread like wildfire, veterans across the country felt the pull of history and the call to return to the hallowed fields of Gettysburg. Among them was Peter Guibert of Pittsburgh, a man who had spent his youth marching to the beat of war drums and now, at seventy years old, was determined to make one last grand journey—not by train or carriage but on foot.

Though Pennsylvania offered its veterans free passage to Gettysburg, Guibert scoffed at the idea. "I've traveled considerably since the war, in shows and circuses, always playing in the bands and have found it a great life, full of action, and sometimes nearly as bad as fighting,"[1] he declared. And so, with the same unbreakable spirit that had carried him through battle, he set off to walk the two hundred miles to the reunion.

Guibert had served as the drummer for the Seventy-Fourth Pennsylvania Infantry; his rhythmic cadence guided men through the chaos of war from the Battle of Bull Run to Lee's surrender at Appomattox. They called him "The Wizard of the Drums," and he was a true musician, a master of the fife, drum, harmonica, whistle, and guitar. Even after the war, he never set down his drumsticks, becoming a well-known performer who always wore a cap with a small American flag tucked into it.

For the fiftieth reunion, Guibert had no intention of rushing the experience. Alongside him walked his friend John Conroy, a sixty-two-year-old veteran of the Indian Wars who, while too young to have fought in the Civil War, shared the same adventurous spirit. On May 26, six weeks before the reunion began, the two men set off from Pittsburgh, their journey becoming a traveling spectacle in its own right.

And they did not travel light. Lugging a fife and drum, cymbals, a bass drum, and even a calliope—a hefty, air-powered instrument better suited for a carnival than a cross-country trek—they made their way east along the old Lincoln Highway. How they managed to carry all that weight for two hundred miles remains a mystery, but they did. Day after day, through rolling Pennsylvania hills and under the scorching summer sun, they pressed on, averaging fifteen miles per day. Wherever they stopped, they played. Their lively music bought them food, drink, and a place to sleep for the night.

Nineteen days later, on June 13, they arrived in Gettysburg, their faces bronzed by the sun, their bodies weary but unbroken. The *Adams County News* took note of their arrival, reporting, "The men show plainly the results of their exposure to the summer's sun but apparently have suffered no ill effects from their long journey."[2]

But Guibert was not yet done. For the next three weeks, he took the stage at Walter's Theater, a "one-man band" performing before eager audiences for just five cents[3] per person. His act preceded the silent film *The Battle of Gettysburg* (a spectacle we will discuss later). Night after night, his drumbeats echoed through the theater, his music breathing life into memories of an era not yet faded. And as he performed, he earned enough to cover their stay at the City Hotel, where he and Conroy lodged until the Great Camp opened on June 29.

For Guibert, the journey was never just about reaching Gettysburg; it was about honoring the past in the only way he knew—with rhythm, melody, and the unwavering spirit of a soldier who had never stopped marching to the beat of his own drum.

Thanks to the excellent reporting of *The Baltimore Sun*, we have detailed accounts of the Maryland veterans at the Grand Reunion. In this book, we will highlight four of them, following in their footsteps throughout their time in Gettysburg.

The Second Invasion of the North began not with the thunder of marching boots or the clamor of battle drums but with the slow, steady chug of a train rolling into Gettysburg on June 26. Unlike fifty years earlier, when Confederates had stormed into town as part of an invading army,

VETERANS START ON MARCH TO GETTYSBURG BATTLEFIELD

VETERANS PETER GUIBERT (IN UNIFORM) AND JOHN CONROY, OLD INDIAN FIGHTER.

Peter Guibert and John Conroy walked from Harrisburg to Gettysburg with their instruments. Photograph published in *The Pittsburgh Press*, May 26, 1913.

these Southern soldiers arrived not as foes but as guests. The train pulled into the very same station where President Lincoln had once arrived to deliver his immortal Gettysburg Address, a station built in 1858 that was bustling with activity during the battle and served as a crucial supply point for the Union army. By 1942, its days as an active station were over, and it stood as a silent witness to history, a museum of memories. But on that day in 1913, it was alive once more, welcoming men who had fought bitterly against one another but were now bound by the passage of time.

It was just another Thursday at the Gettysburg train station, and, as expected, the train arrived on time. A flurry of travelers disembarked, their chatter filling the platform. Among the familiar hustle and bustle, two men hesitated. They were older now, their backs not as straight and their steps not as quick, but their presence carried the weight of history.

*The Baltimore Sun* noted their arrival: "They were the first of men from the Southland to arrive. They were unassuming, modest, and diffident. They were unaccustomed to crowds."[4]

William E. Brawner and William Page stood side by side, as they had through so many trials before. Dressed in crisp new Confederate uniforms, provided by the state government, they had once been soldiers of the Second Maryland Infantry. They had fought on Culp's Hill during the fateful second and third days of battle. They had stood together through the long years of war, through Appomattox, and even in the quiet twilight of their lives, sharing quarters at the Old Soldiers' Home in Pikesville, Maryland.

Now they were back in Gettysburg, but the apprehension in their eyes told a deeper story. They had once arrived here as part of an invading force. Now they were guests—but what kind of reception awaited them?

They didn't have to wait long for an answer.

No sooner had their boots touched the platform than they found themselves surrounded by a crowd of Union veterans. Strong hands clapped their shoulders and hearty voices boomed in greeting. "Welcome to Gettysburg," one of the Union vets announced. "You're the first Johnnies in town, and we've been waiting and looking for you. We love you and want to know you better. Who are you?"

The sudden attention took William Page by surprise. "I'm an American," he stated. Although he wore the gray, he wanted there to be no doubt as to where his allegiance lay. Turning to his lifelong friend, he asked, "Who are you, Bill?"

Bill Brawner straightened, considered the question, and then declared, "I reckon I'm an American too, and after that I'm a Marylander." Then, with the wisdom of years, he gave an impromptu speech that would echo through the gathering:

> *But I'm thinking that first, last and all the time I'm what might be called the fellow that got an idea into his head once upon a time that he thought was right, but I found when he began to get old and see how the country was going along and ahead that he was wrong and thank God, he was big enough to say, "I'm for the union and I'm against the fellow who waves the bloody shirt." That's what I am and my first name is Bill and I want you Yanks to call me that and I'm darn glad to meet you and I hope you all will be real friendly to us, because we are two old fellas and we feel kind of lonely, seeing as how we are the only boys wearing the gray in town.*[5]

The response was immediate. The Union men erupted in cheers—not the reserved applause of old men recalling distant memories but a rousing, roof-raising cheer that shook the ground. *The Baltimore Sun* later described the sight: "a little blue cluster with the gray core." The old Confederates were no longer alone.

Their fears melted away as hands reached for theirs, shaking vigorously until their arms ached. Their faces hurt from smiling. The camaraderie was infectious. When Brawner saw the ever-growing crowd, he turned to Page with a twinkle in his eye and quipped, "See those Yanks run, and they still have the habit of running towards us. You can't break a man of some habits."

Laughter erupted, and the bonds of brotherhood were sealed. The Union veterans, determined to show their hospitality, insisted on carrying Brawner and Page's luggage to the Eagle Hotel, where they would stay until the Great Camp opened on June 29.

"They treat us well," Page said about his new Yankee friends, "and give us full credit for what we did. We love to meet and talk over the battle."

The unity on display was undeniable. Thousands of visitors in town took notice. The once-divided men, now arm in arm, marched through the streets of Gettysburg. Their uniforms provided a stark contrast, but their spirits were perfectly aligned. That night, the town made it official—the keys to Gettysburg were presented to the two Confederate veterans, symbolizing reconciliation and healing wounds once thought irreparable.

Meanwhile, another character was making his way into town.

The Blue welcoming the Gray. William Brawner and William Page with their new Union comrades. Reproduced from the *Fiftieth Anniversary Report.*

John L. Obernderfer, also a resident of the Old Soldiers' Home in Pikesville, Maryland, had planned to travel with Brawner and Page but missed the train. By the time he arrived that afternoon, Gettysburg was already bursting at the seams. Unlike his companions, he slipped quietly into town, too late for the grand reception they had enjoyed. For Obernderfer, lodging was scarce, the hotels overflowed, and no one waited with open arms or a spare key to the city. He was hot, tired, and utterly worn out.

But where desperation might have defeated another man, Obernderfer's quick wits carried him through. Perhaps it was the stifling heat, or maybe it was his natural cunning, but he devised an unconventional solution. Overcome by exhaustion, he declared himself unwell and arranged to spend the night in the hospital. When asked about his unexpected stay the next morning, he only grinned and confessed, "I only went to the hospital because I wanted a bed to sleep in last night. The hotels were filled up, and I felt played out."[6]

The Report of the Pennsylvania Commission shared a story that possibly involved Obernderfer: "The first patients to arrive at the Hospital were an aged Union veteran from Philadelphia, who entered early in the day of the 26th of June, and later on in the same day, a Confederate veteran from Hagerstown, Md. These gentlemen, quickly catching the spirit of the occasion, became friends, ate, slept, and dined together with the true campfire spirit."[7]

The next day, Oberndeřfer linked up with his pals William Brawner and William Page. They were in good spirits at the Eagle Hotel and the center of attention, surrounded by a group of old Union soldiers. "I am going to stay here until I drive every Yankee out of Gettysburg," Obernderfer declared.

Stay tuned for more adventures with Brawner, Page, and Obernderfer as they reunite with their fellow Maryland veterans.

After several years of planning, the week of the reunion finally arrived, and everything was as ready as possible. On June 28, the chefs arrived. There were six hundred first cooks, each making four dollars per day; six hundred second cooks, making three dollars per day; and twelve hundred kitchen helpers, making $1.50 per day.[8] These men were given several hundred tents to accommodate them inside the Great Camp. Among the cooks were ninety bakers who fired up the ovens and soon had fresh bread baking, a welcome smell for the incoming veterans. These ovens were large enough to crank out fifty thousand loaves of bread daily. The first meal served to the veterans would be supper from 5:30 p.m. to 7:00 p.m. on Sunday, June 29,[9] consisting of steak, fried onions, sliced tomatoes, bread, butter, and endless cups of coffee.[10] Walter H. Blake from Vineland, New Jersey, reported that "there was no fault to find with that meal."[11] Although the old veterans were camping out on the field, the Pennsylvania Commission promised quality food three times a day, not just pork and beans. The veterans received three hearty meals daily until the final breakfast on Sunday, July 6. Each veteran was issued a pint-and-a-half tin cup, a plate, a fork, a knife, a tablespoon, and a teaspoon for their use. At the end of the week, they were allowed to take their mess kit home as a souvenir.

The Great Camp opened its gates to veterans on Sunday, June 29, 1913. Since the official Grand Reunion programs were not scheduled until Tuesday afternoon, organizers expected the arriving vets would trickle in as a few early birds on Sunday, with the main influx on Monday and Tuesday.

But rather than a trickle, they were met with a flood.

Train after train pulled in, each one unloading hundreds of gray-haired veterans into the camp. The slow stream they anticipated swelled into a torrent, a ceaseless tide of humanity pouring in from dawn until midnight. And just when it seemed the deluge might ease, the next morning brought yet another wave.

In just twenty-four hours, fifty-three trains arrived—one every twenty-five minutes—carrying between two hundred and five hundred passengers.[12] By nightfall, 21,882[13] veterans had reached the camp by rail, with hundreds more arriving by automobile. The scale of the gathering was staggering, an unrelenting tide of history in motion.

The Ford Motor Company began production of the Model T in 1908. However, by 1913, automobiles were still a novelty, to the extent that the *York Dispatch* newspaper felt compelled to report that almost three hundred cars passed through York on their way to Gettysburg. W. A. Stambaugh counted 110 vehicles passing by his house between 4:00 a.m. and 8:00 p.m. Imagine if counting cars driving past your house was the highlight of your day and noteworthy enough to put in the newspaper! The *Harrisburg Telegraph* reported that as many as fifteen vehicles an hour were en route to Gettysburg![14] Nowadays, it would be newsworthy if there were *only* fifteen cars an hour driving to Gettysburg.

Despite the overwhelming flood of humanity pouring into Gettysburg, everything went somewhat smoothly, even if there were some delays in dealing with so many people. The Boy Scouts were on hand to assist the veterans with registration and to carry their luggage.[15] The scouts were familiar with the camp's layout and assisted the veterans in locating their tents. It was an exhausting job; the scouts walked countless miles each day, with few complaints. The Boy Scouts also ran errands and retrieved water for the old veterans in their tents.

"The access to the camp was fine," reported Alfred B. Beers, commander in chief of the Grand Army of the Republic (GAR). "Every railroad except one delivered the veterans in the center of the camp over tracks laid expressly for this purpose. The only railroad that did not do this ran its trains on a shuttle schedule from the main station at Gettysburg to one mile of the camp. The train service left nothing to be desired."[16]

Colonel J. M. Schoonmaker, the chairman of the Pennsylvania State Commission, said they weren't expecting so many veterans to enter the camp so quickly. They expected six thousand veterans on the first day but were flooded by almost twenty-five thousand men instead. "Although we were not looking for such a number, we were able to give every veteran something to eat before he went to bed. Tomorrow we will better handle the situation, and every man will get full rations."[17]

Even those veterans who only got a bite to eat were satisfied; most handled it without complaint. "Two meals a day is good enough," said one veteran. "It's more than we got 50 years ago."

As the veterans arrived, Surgeon General Weaver of the National Guard of Pennsylvania issued some recommendations to the veterans:

> *Get as much sleep as possible and be regular about it. Adhere in your diet to the rations furnished by the regular army, which are ample in quantity and sufficiently varied to gratify and satisfy all tastes. Don't indulge in intoxicating drinks. They disturb digestion and make you more susceptible to fatigue and disease. Don't try to meet all the old comrades at once. The camp is a big one, but you have all week of it before you. Take it easy.*[18]

I'm sure some veterans listened to these recommendations, but others were determined to see every square inch of the battlefield on the first day. While in town, one old soldier asked for directions to the Great Camp. He was told not to attempt to walk there.

"Why not? I walked all the way around Big Round Top and the Confederate Line since breakfast and I guess I can go it to camp without getting any more tired. I watched for the shady places, and I am feeling fine."[19] He could have taken numerous paths over the battlefield, but a one-way trip from the center of town, down Confederate Avenue to Big Round Top, is five miles. Depending on his route, a return trip could double that. The Great Camp was no more than a mile from the town center, a mere stroll for someone who had already walked ten miles that day.

So much for taking it easy.

On the evening of June 30, a late train arrived in Gettysburg, and twenty Virginians wearing Confederate uniforms disembarked. As they left the station, several hundred people descended on them. The crowd formed two lines and compelled the Confederates to pass through while clapping, waving handkerchiefs, and shaking hands. The crowd called out, "Welcome, Johnny Reb, we're glad to see you!" It was a very different welcome from the one they had received fifty years before.

"We are one people now," remarked an old Confederate from Richmond. He had fought through the four years of war and had surrendered at Appomattox. "These Pennsylvanians are receiving us with open arms. This will do great good all over the country."

Major Normoyle, the quartermaster for the Great Camp, didn't have time to sleep that first night the camp opened. As the sun dipped below the horizon, casting long shadows over the bustling camp, he and his men were swamped by the influx of old soldiers. Darkness settled in, but their work was far from over. Normoyle and his crew spent the night searching for more blankets, filling empty tents, and trying to assure the veterans that everything would be all right by breakfast. "They shifted trains, they ran engines, they manipulated switches with the ease of born railroad men. They became information bureaus and pack horses, but still the flood of men in blue and gray came pouring in and the tide rose around them higher and higher."[20]

The camp filled up so fast that many veterans found themselves without a tent to sleep in. Many old soldiers spent the night on makeshift chairs, gathered around campfires discussing the battle. The conversations helped them forget that their bones weren't as young as they used to be. Some slept right on the ground, staring at the stars and grumbling that the ground felt much harder than it did fifty years ago. Despite the piles of blankets provided, there didn't seem to be enough to go around, and many veterans were left shivering in the cold night air.

The veterans were supposed to receive two blankets each, but while making the rounds on the evening of July 1, some troops from the regular army discovered a Pennsylvania man hoarding them. "He was as snug as a bug in a rug,"[21] with three blankets under him, three blankets on top of him, and nine more blankets wedged beneath his cot. The regulars roused the Pennsylvanian from his slumber and questioned him about his abundance of blankets. He responded that he was keeping them for his friends. But the regulars didn't see any friends, so they quickly relieved him of all but two blankets and redistributed the rest.

While Major Normoyle and his men worked hard to support the event, others were equally determined to undermine it. On the evening of July 1, Major John H. Kerr settled in for the night in the North Carolina section of the camp. When he awoke the next morning, he found that someone had sneaked into his tent while he slept and taken his wallet, his return railroad ticket, and $50 in cash—all the money he had brought. Kerr had lost his left leg at the Third Battle of Winchester in 1864 and struggled to navigate the battlefield during the reunion. Frustrated by his misfortune, he returned home to Yanesville, North Carolina. "I came here to see the old battlefield on which I fought as a member of Company H, 57th North Carolina Regiment, but my pleasure has been destroyed. It is impossible for me to walk over the field. Having no money, I can't hire a vehicle, so I am going home."[22]

Even though troops from the regular army patrolled the camp, thousands of men were moving around the area all night long. As a result, several other veterans reported they had been robbed of their suitcases while they slept. Rumor had it that the lost luggage had suddenly disappeared, along with several civilian cooks who had left the camp. Another report spoke of a ninety-year-old veteran from Indiana who lost every cent he had when someone picked his pocket, containing seventy-five dollars. As a result, a group of Pinkerton detectives was brought into the camp to investigate and to deter any further robberies.

There were numerous reports of veterans losing their return railway tickets, and the problem became serious enough to reach the attention of the governor of Pennsylvania. Governor Tener stepped in and reassured the men that the state would pay their way home if their tickets had been lost, no matter where in the country they had come from. Considering the steep cost of a train fare from Gettysburg to California, it was an exceptionally generous promise.

A delegation of Union veterans stumbled into camp late on June 30, only to find nowhere to stay. The Great Camp had expected a big turnout, but not this quickly. Nearly twenty thousand more old soldiers than planned had shown up, and at this point, finding extra blankets and tents was about as likely as finding a quiet place to nap.

So when two hundred veterans from West Virginia arrived, they navigated the darkened camp with the determination of men who had seen worse. They reached their designated area and miraculously found their tents right where they were supposed to be. There was just one small problem: There was nothing inside the tents—no cots, blankets, or anything else.

While searching for a place to rest their weary bones, they ran into a group of Maryland veterans across the company street. Seeing their predicament, the Maryland vets wasted no time offering a solution.

"We have room for almost twice your number," said William H. Moffett from the Maryland camp. "There's plenty of tents for you, comrade."[23] As it turned out, the Maryland camp had been prepared for more arrivals from Baltimore the next day, meaning those cots were unclaimed and unused. Sorting out the logistics could wait until the morning. For now, a cot was a cot, and the men from West Virginia weren't about to turn down a little comfort.

Corporal Charles Mettee, who was in charge of the Maryland camp's Confederate section, said, "You are as welcome as the flowers in the spring."[24] So, the West Virginia Union veterans slept in the Confederate camp for the first night of the reunion.

Although the Great Camp officially opened to the veterans on June 29, the grand ceremonies beneath the Great Tent would not commence until July 1. This left the veterans ample time to reunite with old comrades, retrace the footsteps of their youth across the battlefield, and stand in quiet reverence before the monuments that bore witness to their sacrifice. Among these tributes, none loomed larger—literally or symbolically—than the Pennsylvania State Memorial, the most imposing monument on the Gettysburg Battlefield. And it was completed just in time for the fiftieth reunion.

In June 1907, Governor Edwin Stuart had entrusted nine battle-hardened Union veterans with the solemn task of selecting a site for the Pennsylvania State Memorial and ensuring that it would "commemorate the services of the soldiers of Pennsylvania in the battle."

Rising 110 feet into the sky, the monument is a colossus of nearly 4,000 tons of granite, sand, cement, steel, and bronze. Eighty-four bronze tablets encircle its foundation, each bearing the names of Pennsylvania's 34,530 sons who had fought at Gettysburg. Towering statues of key figures—President Abraham Lincoln, Governor Andrew G. Curtin, General George Meade, and five other prominent Pennsylvania generals—stand guard, their watchful gazes forever fixed on the fields where history was written in blood. Above all, the winged angel known as the "Goddess of Victory and Peace" brandishes a sword in one hand and an olive branch in the other, crafted from melted-down cannons, an eternal symbol of the war that once raged here and the fragile peace that followed.

Construction finished in April 1913, and the monument was rededicated on July 4, during the final day of the reunion. It became an instant gathering point, a beacon for veterans searching for the names of long-lost comrades. Of the thirty-five thousand names etched into its bronze tablets, an astonishing twenty-one thousand belonged to men who had returned for the fiftieth reunion. You can be sure each of them traced weathered fingers over the cool metal, seeking proof that their past had not been forgotten.

Beneath the shadow of the Pennsylvania Monument, sorrow came quietly, borne by those still searching for the names of loved ones long gone. During the reunion, a frail old woman made her way to the monument, hoping to find her husband among the bronze listings. She steadied herself before the tablet, her tired eyes scanning the regiment's roll, her trembling hands following each name as though touch might bring him back. With every line that did not bear his name, her breath grew sharper, her hope more fragile. At last, she reached the end, and still he was not there. Her strength crumbled. She sagged against the cold bronze, and a sob broke free, carrying the weight of years of longing and loss.

Nearby, two aging veterans from Harrisburg, their eyes also scanning for familiar names, caught sight of her distress. They approached with the quiet dignity of men who had seen too much sorrow in their lifetimes.

"I know he fought in the battle of Gettysburg," she said, her voice barely above a whisper. "I know he was a brave soldier; I know that every soldier who fought in this great battle has his name somewhere inscribed on this memorial, but alas! I failed to find my dear boy's name with his regiment."[25]

The two veterans stepped forward to lend a hand. Adjusting their glasses, their gnarled hands were steady despite the weight of the moment.

(*Top*) The Pennsylvania State Memorial, the largest monument on the Gettysburg Battlefield, began construction in 1910 by the Adams County Historical Society; (*bottom*) photographed shortly before the 1913 Grand Reunion (note the *Winged Angel* hasn't been installed yet). Photograph by Lewis Reed and courtesy of Jeanne Gartner.

Together, they combed through the list of names, determined to find the man who had meant everything to this grieving widow. At last, they found his name, misidentified and listed among the medical orderlies rather than with his regiment. When they pointed it out, the widow's knees buckled, and she collapsed against the monument, her body wracked with sobs.

The two veterans from Harrisburg said nothing. There was nothing to say. They stepped back, allowing the widow space to mourn. But as they turned to leave, they each reached into their coat pockets for their handkerchiefs, dabbing at their wet eyes.

Throughout the days of the reunion, the Pennsylvania veterans climbed over every inch of the monument, seeking out missing or misspelled names. By the time the Grand Reunion was over, it was clear that the memorial was incomplete. In 1914, an additional bronze tablet was added, bearing the names of 945 more soldiers—each one a name almost lost to time, now restored to its rightful place in history.

They say truth is stranger than fiction, and nowhere is that more evident than with our next star of the show. When people think of the big names at Gettysburg, they usually rattle off the usual suspects—Robert E. Lee, Joshua Chamberlain, George Meade, George Pickett, and maybe a few others if they're feeling fancy. But one name towers above them all—not necessarily for tactical genius, but rather for sheer audacity, scandal, and behavior that makes you wonder how history let this guy have a sword.

Ladies and gentlemen, meet Daniel E. Sickles. If you're a serious history buff, you might already know him. If not, buckle up, because you're in for a wild ride.

I strongly recommend James A. Hessler's book *Sickles at Gettysburg* if you want a proper deep dive into Sickles's escapades. We don't have the time or the space for a full biography, but it's essential to hear the highlights so you can fully understand why he was a madman of mythic proportions.

Quick disclaimer: I'm not a historian and don't claim to be. If I were, I'd have to tread carefully to avoid liability for defamation. I would need to use legal language to say that Sickles was an unconventional person prone to erratic behavior, known for making unorthodox decisions while engaging in high-risk activities. But since I'm approaching this more from a storyteller's perspective, I will call a spade a spade and refer to him as one crazy bastard.

Dan Sickles was originally from New York City, and his early claim to fame was helping establish Central Park. That's also where his good deeds end. When you think about the definition of a crooked politician, think no further than Dan Sickles:

> *Sickles opened law offices in New York in the early 1840s. He quickly gained a reputation for questionable ethics and business practices. He was indicted for obtaining money under false pretenses, was almost prosecuted for appropriating funds from another man, was accused of pocketing money that had been raised for a political pamphlet, stealing money from the post office, and was charged with improperly retaining a mortgage that he had pledged as collateral on a loan.*[26]

Sounds like an upstanding individual, right?

At thirty-three, he married a sixteen-year-old girl named Theresa. I'm not sure whether he married her because he wanted to "do the right thing" or because her father was holding a shotgun. Either way, they were quickly wed, and although the exact dates are a bit sketchy, their daughter, Laura, was reportedly born seven months after the wedding.

In 1856, Sickles was elected to Congress and dragged his young family to Washington, DC. Once there, he became good friends with the US attorney general Philip Barton Key, who, fun fact, was the son of Francis Scott Key, the guy who wrote "The Star-Spangled Banner." Much like his father's anthem, Philip's story would also involve a lot of drama, albeit with significantly less patriotism and a lot more bullets.

As a congressman, Sickles was often called away to New York and wasn't always home, leaving his teenage wife, Theresa, to tend the house in DC alone. Thankfully, his good friend, Philip Barton Key, stopped by *often* to check on her. During this time, Theresa's relationship with Key developed into a romantic one, and soon they were sneaking around like characters in a trashy Victorian novel. To keep their relationship hidden, the two lovers devised a secret signal to communicate whether Sickles was home.

In February 1859, Sickles received an anonymous letter spilling the tea on his wife's scandalous affair. Sickles was furious and confronted Theresa with the letter. She immediately caved and confessed to the whole thing.

Meanwhile, at that exact moment, Key was lurking outside the house, waiting for Theresa's signal to see whether she was available for a romantic interlude. But Sickles was inside and just happened to glance out the window. When he saw Key, Sickles yelled, "That villain has just passed my house! My God, this is horrible!" Sickles rushed outside to confront Key, but not before grabbing a pistol and two single-shot derringers, because when it comes to overkill, why stop at just one gun?

Key, realizing that a very angry, very armed Sickles was coming for him, did what any sensible person would do—he ran for his life. Sickles pursued and caught up with Key in Lafayette Square, directly across from the White House. Sickles called out, "Key, you scoundrel, you have dishonored my house—you must die!"

Sickles opened fire.

BANG!

But his aim was off, and he just grazed Key.

BANG!

His second shot struck Key in the groin, which is somehow fitting considering the crime. Key fell back against the wrought iron fence and slumped to the ground. Sickles slowly approached, stood over him, and fired at point-blank range.

CLICK.

But the gun misfired. Sickles stepped even closer and put the weapon barrel to Key's chest. He fired the gun a fourth time.

BANG!

The bullet lodged just below his heart. But Sickles wasn't done yet; he cocked the gun again and held it to Key's head. He pulled the trigger.

CLICK.

But it was another misfire.

At this point, bystanders, who had just witnessed a full-blown murder happen in front of the White House, finally decided to intervene. They dragged Sickles away from Key as he yelled, "Is that scoundrel dead?"[27]

Naturally, Sickles was arrested, and Key died shortly after. What followed was one of the most outrageous trials in American history—think O. J. Simpson's trial, but with more guns and fewer car chases. The scandal was so juicy that newspapers had to censor their reports. In a stroke of legal genius, Sickles became the first person ever to plead "temporary insanity" in a US court. And guess what? It worked. The jury, clearly swept up in the drama, decided that Sickles was just a "righteously aggrieved husband" and let him walk free with a "not guilty" verdict.

And that's how that crazy bastard Dan Sickles got away with murder.

But wait—it gets better.

According to legend, Sickles was up in New York City sometime after the trial at McSorley's Old Ale House. It was established in 1854 and is famous for being one of New York's oldest bars, and it's still in operation today. Sickles was a frequent visitor, and while drinking one night, someone asked him whether he had meant to kill Key. Sickles allegedly said, "Hell yes! I meant to shoot that bastard down dead!"

Did he really say that? Who knows? But let's be honest—it sounds exactly like something he would say.

And believe it or not, this was only the beginning of Sickles's long, scandal-ridden life. Buckle up, because we're just getting started.

# 4
# June 30—Monday

THEY SAY IF YOU GATHER ENOUGH OLD MEN IN ONE PLACE, SOONER OR later, they'll start acting like children. That sentiment couldn't be more genuine regarding this next story—one of my favorites from the Grand Reunion. It's a tale of mischief, nostalgia, and just a little bit of danger. Because, as it turns out, these old soldiers still had a few tricks up their sleeves—even after fifty years.

On their first night in camp, a group of Confederate veterans hatched a daring plan—one that would make their younger selves proud. These men were in the artillery and weren't content with just swapping stories by the fire. No, they wanted to hear the thunder of their old guns one last time. Under the cover of darkness, they crept along the familiar stone wall on Confederate Avenue until they found their target: two long-silent Whitworth cannons from the Alabama Battery, the same guns that had roared in battle before Pickett's Charge.

And what did they bring to the reunion, besides their uniforms and memories? Fifty-year-old sacks of black powder. Just in case.

With the giddy excitement of schoolboys up to no good, the veterans loaded the charges into the two Whitworths. They claimed to be the same men who had once fired these cannons in battle, and judging by their confidence, I believe them. I can almost hear the muffled laughter, the hushed bets on whether the powder would still ignite, and the slap of calloused hands on backs. Then, with a Rebel Yell that surely woke the dead, they struck the fuse.

At 2:00 in the morning, the silence of the Gettysburg Battlefield was shattered. The two Whitworths fired off in rapid succession, belching forth fire, thunder, and smoke. *The Baltimore Sun* later reported that "the antiquated pieces roared in great style," sending a boom across the camp and rolling more than a few sleeping veterans clean off their cots. Some sentries on duty swore they saw fire burst from the muzzles. The Great Camp was in chaos.

And the culprits? They melted into the night like ghosts and disappeared with the same stealth they had mastered decades earlier.

By sunrise, a very smug-looking group of Confederate veterans strolled back into the Virginia camp, feigning innocence but radiating satisfaction. Their prank had been a roaring success—literally. But not everyone was amused. The regular army men were livid. They claimed that the old soldiers took their lives in their hands when they fired off the rusty old guns with fifty-year-old powder; it was remarkable that the old guns didn't explode or kick. Either outcome would have meant the death of the veterans doing the firing.[1] Maybe it was luck. Perhaps it was fate. Or maybe—just maybe—those old soldiers really did know what they were doing.

Today, those same Whitworth guns, which were previously located on Confederate Avenue, now rest on Oak Hill, beside the Eternal Light Peace Memorial. During the war, they were rare and formidable, their rifled barrels offering a deadly accuracy that could send a missile whistling through the air for miles. This eerie sound often did more psychological damage than physical. And yet, of the four hundred cannons that littered Gettysburg's Battlefield, these veterans sought out the only two breech-loaded Whitworths.

Coincidence? I don't think so.

We may never know who these mischievous veterans were. The newspaper report is little more than hearsay, and the details are now lost to time. But one thing is sure—on that night in 1913, for just a few brief moments, the cannons of Gettysburg spoke once more, and a group of old soldiers relived the fire of their youth.

By the time the Massachusetts men finally arrived in camp, it was well past midnight, and their patience had worn paper-thin. Their trains had already been two hours late, but that was only the beginning of their troubles.

When they disembarked at the depot, their guide, who supposedly knew the most direct route to their tents, led them on a winding, aimless march through the darkness. Picture it: two thousand exhausted senior citizens, shuffling in circles under the night sky, muttering under their breath, desperately searching for a place to rest.

When they finally reached the Massachusetts camp, a group of cooks had worked through the night, preparing an abundance of hot food to greet the veterans. However, the men wanted nothing to do with it. Forget the meals—sleep was all they cared about. The moment they arrived, order gave way to chaos as the weary soldiers scrambled for the nearest empty cot.

And then things got worse.

Despite its best efforts, the quartermaster's department hadn't placed two blankets on each cot. The first arrivals, acting on pure survival instinct, snatched up whatever they could find, leaving the slower ones to fend for themselves. Grumbling turned to outright complaining, and soon the night air was filled with the sounds of tired, irritable old soldiers bellyaching about missing blankets and unavailable cots. In the end, five hundred men had no choice but to bed down on the hard ground inside one of the massive circus tents nearby.

But then, just when it seemed like the Massachusetts men might riot from sheer frustration, salvation arrived on four wheels. Trucks rumbled into camp, delivering two thousand extra blankets. By the time the veterans finally settled in, they had blankets to burn.

Not the smoothest welcome, perhaps—but after half a century, these men had certainly endured worse nights.

Elsewhere in the Great Camp, they ran out of blankets, and food was limited. At the Massachusetts camp, however, they had an abundance of extra blankets and a treasure trove of ready-to-go hot food that the veterans simply ignored.

The next morning, the Boy Scouts arrived at the Massachusetts camp, and the quarters were efficiently rearranged. It was quickly discovered that many of the tents, which were designed to accommodate eight men, only had three or four occupants. It took a few hours to straighten things out, but soon the camp was running smoothly.

Things were starting to get organized around the Great Camp, but not everyone was happy. Samuel Callender from Scranton, Pennsylvania, disapproved of the way the Great Camp was being run. "There was plenty of wholesome food, lots of tents, an ample supply of blankets, excellent drinking water and the most desirable sanitary arrangements for a crowd of 35,000," he said,

> *but there was a woeful lack of system in placing the old soldiers as they arrived. This was an awful hardship on account of the terrible heat. Some delegations came in and had to stand around in a shuffling, sweltering mass of humanity for hours before being assigned to quarters. And you may imagine what a hardship this was on an old man, a great many of whom were crippled. Instead of 10 headquarters for the Pennsylvania section, there was only one. We had to walk a long distance under the blistering sun to find that headquarters, only to be told to go and help ourselves. The confusion was great in the scramble for tents to get out of the sun's rays.*[2]

Captain Wilson French from Connecticut had a rough first night:

> *The Connecticut party did not arrive at the camp until 11:30 Monday night and when we got there we had some difficulty locating our tents. Then we found we had no cots or blankets. I got a cot and a blanket for the tent I was assigned to and went in search of a water bucket. When I returned I found a party of Virginians had taken possession of my tent, cot, blanket, and all.*[3]

Imagine setting up your tent for the night, then stepping out to wash up and use the bathroom, only to return and find the "enemy" occupying your space! As humorous as this situation is, it's also understandable. If you look at the map of the Great Camp, you'll find that the Virginia camp is right across the company street from the Connecticut camp. As the Great Camp filled up, the tired, old veterans were probably looking for the first empty cot they could find.

Captain French went to the camp headquarters and lodged a complaint. He was eventually assigned a new tent and settled into his cot around 5:00 a.m. One hour later, the drum corps sounded off "Reveille," and it was time to start the new day.

So many veterans arrived that they overwhelmed the camp's capacity. William Bennet of Pittsburgh, Pennsylvania, left for Gettysburg on Monday morning and was back home twenty-four hours later.[4] While at the Great Camp, he had spent hours walking, trying to find an empty cot to secure as his own. Unfortunately, there was no place to lie down, and it was many hours before he could get anything to eat. After a futile search to find accommodations, he and hundreds of other veterans got back on the train and headed home, disheartened and worn out.

Grand Army of the Republic (GAR) commander in chief Alfred B. Beers heard some of the complaints and wanted to investigate them for himself. Without revealing his identity, he walked the grounds and petitioned various veterans about their treatment and the quality of the Great Camp. He claimed that the general consensus was favorable: "It's a magnificent camp, our quarters are everything we could expect, the food is first class, and our treatment could not be excelled. So I think you may safely set it down that 99% of the veterans were perfectly satisfied." Despite the sunny words, thousands left the Great Camp after only a few hours. Beers replied, "It was to be expected that there would be some disagreeable ones in an army of more than 50,000."[5]

Several thousand eager spectators crowded the Gettysburg train station on June 30, awaiting the arrival of one of the most controversial, flamboyant, and downright stubborn figures of the Civil War—General Daniel E. Sickles. That crazy bastard had defied death, scandal, and common sense more times than anyone could count, and yet here he was, rolling into town like a conquering hero.

The Fifteenth United States Cavalry had been dispatched to escort him in a grand military gesture for the last living corps commander from the Battle of Gettysburg. If Sickles was bothered by the fact that all his fellow commanders had long since passed, he didn't show it. He had outlived them all, and without any rivals to disagree with him, he continued to tell *his* side of the story. As soon as he stepped off the train—well, more accurately, was picked up and placed in a wheelchair—he was met with a deafening cheer. The old general, reveling in the attention, was then whisked away in an automobile.

Originally, Sickles had planned to stay at the Eagle Hotel, conveniently located in the heart of town and, most important, equipped with an elevator. But Sickles changed his mind.[6] Why stay in luxury when he could plant himself right in the thick of things? He ordered his entourage to take him to the old Rogers House near the Peach Orchard on Emmitsburg Road, right on the battlefield where his controversial decisions had played out fifty years prior.

Accompanying him were several New York veterans and, most curiously, a mysterious woman who refused to give her name. Despite being almost ninety-three years old, Sickles had lost none of his legendary charm or eye for the ladies. As the photographers swarmed, the woman remained at his side, shielding her face from their prying lenses. His entourage remained tight-lipped about her identity, referring to her only as the general's (*cough-cough*) "housekeeper."

But, as with all things Sickles, the truth had a way of slipping out. Before long, it was revealed that the elusive lady was Eleanor Wilmerding. She was indeed his housekeeper on paper, but the rumors suggested she was more than "the help." Why would Eleanor hide her identity from the press if she were just a housekeeper? She wouldn't—unless something else was going on. Years after his legendary murder trial, Sickles had remarried. However, by 1913, Sickles and his second wife were separated, and it was suggested that Eleanor Wilmerding was the cause. Whatever her official title may have been, one thing was sure—Daniel E. Sickles was still living life on his terms.

Now, if I were a historian rather than just a storyteller, I'd present the facts of the following tale and move on. But there's an untold story here—one I'd love to know—and it all begins with our Maryland friends.

William Brawner and William Page were the first Confederate veterans to arrive in town. Both men lived at the Old Soldiers' Home in Pikesville, Maryland, but they weren't the only residents eager to attend the reunion. Two others, John Obernderfer and John Francis Key, also longed to make the journey. And that's where the mystery begins . . .

John Francis Key had a name that carried weight; he was the grandson of Francis Scott Key, the composer of "The Star-Spangled Banner." But sharp readers might also recall another chapter in the Key family history: the brutal murder of Philip Barton Key, gunned down in broad daylight by none other than that crazy bastard, Dan Sickles. And not only did Sickles pull the trigger, but he also walked away scot-free.

John Francis Key, the nephew of Sickles's victim, took a far different path. During the Civil War, he fought for the Confederacy alongside William Brawner and William Page in the Second Maryland Infantry. Meanwhile, Sickles—his uncle's killer—fought for the Union.

Fifty years later, fate brought both men to Gettysburg.

John Francis Key was eighty-two years old and anxious about getting to the Grand Reunion. (Perhaps to give Sickles a knuckle sandwich?) But Key couldn't afford the train ticket to Gettysburg. With tears streaming down his cheeks, Key said goodbye to Brawner and Page as they left on the trip of a lifetime. Key swore he would get to Gettysburg even if he had to walk the seventy-five miles there.

When asked about Key, William Brawner said, "Why, my boy, don't you fear about that old Marylander getting here. He's nothing but a lad, keen and quick as ever, and with a step half his age could be proud of. He'll walk here, all right, and he'll get here on time."[7]

William Page said, "Key is a right smart man and in pretty good health, and I wouldn't be surprised if he did walk here." As news of Key's misfortune spread, one of his friends purchased a train ticket for him, so he didn't have to walk after all.

On the morning of June 30, John Francis Key "arrived on the train from Baltimore wearing his gray uniform and was the happiest man in Gettysburg when he joined his Pikesville Home comrades in camp. . . . He said this evening that it was the event of his life."[8] Key then spent the rest of the day walking the battlefield, despite the heat, in remarkably good health.

However, a conflicting report claimed that "Key came into town, weak and almost dropping. He has been in failing health, but declared he was 'going to see Gettysburg on this occasion or die.'"[9] I'll leave it up to the reader to decide whether Key was in failing health or fit as a fiddle.

Almost every newspaper in the country reported John Francis Key's journey, and one reporter asked about Francis Scott Key, the author of the national anthem. "I have a dim recollection of my grandfather. . . . Grandfather Key came to visit us now and then for a day or so at a time." That was all he had to say on the matter. In my humble opinion, the reporter asked the wrong question. What I want to know is: What did Key think of his uncle's murderer? Sickles was nearby, and if Key had walked the battlefield, they must have been in close proximity to each other. Was

Key gunning for a showdown at high noon, or had he managed to forgive and forget? The newspapers are silent on the topic, but you know that one must have at least been thinking about the other.

Unfortunately, there isn't much more to tell about John Francis Key's time in Gettysburg. He had a great day touring the battlefield, but that evening Key had a tough time sleeping on the camp cots. After a restless night, he was really feeling it the next day. He was worn out, and his aching bones made him irritable. Despite having a wonderful time at the reunion, he found that camp life did not agree with his eighty-two-year-old body, and it was time to go home.[10]

If he had stayed in camp a bit longer, he might have confronted Sickles. Who knows? But it was a meeting that was never meant to be.

John Francis Key may have threatened to walk to Gettysburg, but Leopold Wolf actually made the journey.

Leopold Wolf was a very poor man who had a very tough life, and his story is quite sad. "My life hasn't been very happy," he said. "I've had a pretty hard road to travel, but it's been harder than ever during the last year. Many the time I have had no place to sleep. . . . I haven't a living relative, and it's been years since I could claim a very close friend. People aren't very kind to old men when they're poor and helpless."

As a young man in 1856, Wolf enlisted in the Third United States Cavalry but was discharged within a year. Wolf said it was "on account of disability. My mind wasn't very good, and I guess I wasn't fit for duty."[11]

A few years later, when the Civil War broke out, Wolf reenlisted with the Fourteenth New York Cavalry. His regiment did not participate in the Battle of Gettysburg, but ten days later they were sent to New York City. Congress had passed a law that conscripted men of fighting age into the Civil War. People with money could buy their way out of the draft, but the working class couldn't afford it. When the draftees' names were published, the working class rebelled and rioted through the streets of Manhattan from July 13 to 16, 1863. The riots resulted in 120 deaths and $1.5 million in property damage.[12] The Fourteenth New York Cavalry was sent to restore order to the city.

After a year in the cavalry, Leopold Wolf was once again discharged. "It was my old head trouble cropping up again." For the next few decades, Wolf was sent from one hospital to the next and eventually ended up in an insane asylum. Finally, after a two-and-a-half-year stint at the Government

Hospital for the Insane in Washington, DC, Wolf was discharged perfectly cured. "I have never had any trouble with my brain since then, but I was an old man when I got out, and life became a pretty hard struggle."

Wolf was in and out of the almshouse, and when he could earn enough money, he would stay at a boarding house, but most of the time he was homeless. He was determined to meet some of his old friends when he heard about the Grand Reunion. At the time, he was living on the streets of Harrisburg, and with no way to get to Gettysburg, Wolf decided to walk.

However, his ordeal could have been avoided if he had known that transportation was free for all Pennsylvania resident veterans. But Leopold Wolf was so poor that he couldn't afford the newspaper that would have informed him of this fact. All he knew was that a reunion would take place at Gettysburg, and he wanted to be there.

"I thought it over and decided that I would have to walk. I bought a map of the country, with the little money I had and started in early Saturday morning."

The first day wasn't so bad, but the sun was merciless, beating down on his back as he trudged along the dusty roads. Despite the heat, the kindness of strangers sustained him. Farmers and townsfolk along the way offered him water and words of encouragement. That night, he found shelter in a quiet barn, where exhaustion claimed him the moment he lay down on the hay. "I was so tired that I dropped asleep without even taking off my hat."

As the days wore on, the journey became more grueling. The roads stretched endlessly ahead, shimmering under the summer heat. His legs ached, and the dust clung to his clothes, but still he pressed on. Each morning, he was met with the generosity of strangers who had heard of his journey. A hot meal here, a shaded place to rest there—their kindness kept him moving forward.

For three days, he navigated the winding roads of Cumberland and Adams County, battling fatigue with sheer willpower. However, the last leg of the journey was the most challenging.

Wolf was described as "physically a complete wreck, but mentally he forged forward."

"I never went through worse agony in my life," he said. "About noon, I could hardly hobble twenty feet without stopping for rest, and when I finally struck the town, I thought I would never get through to the camp."

Every step was a struggle, every breath a battle. But Gettysburg was within reach, and he refused to stop now. When he finally arrived, staggering into camp, he barely had the strength to take in his surroundings. The reunion and the celebrations—none of it mattered at that moment.

"When I did get in, I just sank right down on the first unoccupied cot I could find and went to sleep."[13]

His ordeal was over for now. The road to Gettysburg had drained every ounce of his reserves, but he had made it. As he finally lay down to rest, no doubt his dreams carried him back fifty years, when the journey hadn't been so hard. But his story was far from over; in fact, it's just getting started. We'll continue Leopold Wolf's journey in another chapter.

As the morning wore on, thousands of veterans left their tents and set off across the vast battlefield. Some went to reunions with their old regiments, while others wandered around, revisiting places with deep memories.

The day was hot, with barely a breeze to stir the flags; the air felt thick and stifling. The camp lay under a shimmering haze, with smoke curling up from the camp kitchens. Off in the distance, the mountains were barely visible through the brownish mist. The veterans couldn't help but compare it to the sweltering heat they had endured fifty years earlier during the battle. They all agreed—it had been just as unbearably hot that day.

The battlefield park stretched for twenty-five square miles, and the veterans spread across it, some walking alone, others in small groups, reminiscing about the past. Many walked despite the heat, while others opted for a ride in carriages, automobiles, or any other available transportation.

If you've ever visited Gettysburg, you've probably noticed the many different ways to explore the battlefield. Sure, you can walk or drive, but why stop there? You can hop on a double-decker tour bus, cruise around on a bicycle, rent a Segway, or even ride a quirky little "scooter-coupe" (a strange mix of a motorized scooter and a motorcycle's sidecar). And if you're feeling extra adventurous, you can tour the battlefield on horseback.

But back in 1913, there was another way to see Gettysburg—one that doesn't exist today. From 1893 to 1916, visitors could ride across the battlefield in the comfort of an electric trolley car. This railway system started in town and ran along Confederate Avenue, reaching as far as Little Round Top. Since it couldn't complete a full loop, the trolley had to reverse direction and double back over parts of the same track before branching off toward the Soldiers' National Cemetery and finally returning to town. Overhead electric lines, strung along wooden poles spaced roughly every hundred feet, powered the trolleys as they glided through history.

The trolley was a popular way to tour the battlefield during the Grand Reunion—until disaster struck. On July 1, a trolley pulled onto a side track near Devil's Den to let another pass, but suddenly it derailed and collided with the oncoming trolley. Six passengers, who saw the impending crash, jumped to safety, though they sustained injuries from their falls. Thankfully, none of their injuries were fatal. Among those hurt was a Civil War veteran and one of the very few Black men visiting the battlefield. Interestingly, the passengers who remained inside during the crash walked away completely unscathed.[14]

Despite its early popularity, the trolley eventually faded into history. As personal automobiles became more common, ridership declined, and in 1916 the trolley system was permanently shut down. Looking back, it was a unique way to experience Gettysburg, and it's a shame it's no longer around.

The trolley wasn't the only way to explore Gettysburg. The monument-lined roads were packed with vehicles carrying tourists eager to witness the reunion and tour the battlefield. Tour guides, equipped with megaphones, narrated the history of the battle to captivated crowds.

However, this was before the era of licensed battlefield guides, meaning many guides prioritized entertaining over accuracy. The veterans who had fought in the battle listened with skepticism. Guides were careful when speaking in their presence, knowing these men wouldn't unquestioningly accept just any version of events.[15] And if a guide strayed too far from the truth, it wasn't uncommon for a veteran to step in and set the record straight.

In 1895, the United States War Department constructed five observation towers across the Gettysburg Battlefield, giving visitors a breathtaking aerial view of the historic landscape. Each tower stood between sixty and seventy-five feet tall and was strategically placed at Oak Ridge, Culp's Hill, Confederate Avenue, Big Round Top, and Ziegler's Grove.

These towers were bustling with visitors, and tourists eagerly climbed them for a bird's-eye view of America's most famous battlefield. The

Ziegler's Grove tower was especially popular during the Grand Reunion because it offered a sweeping view of the massive Great Camp where thousands of Civil War veterans gathered. Photographers, carrying their heavy equipment, made the trek to the top to capture stunning images of the event.

Today, only two and a half towers remain. The Big Round Top and Ziegler's Grove towers were demolished, while the Oak Ridge tower was shortened to half its original height. Though fewer in number, the remaining towers still offer an impressive view of the battlefield.

One last note about how the battlefield's layout has changed over time. Today, if you drive down Confederate Avenue, you start in town and follow a one-way loop that takes you all the way to Little Round Top. But back in 1913, the direction was reversed. Confederate Avenue ended in town rather than starting there. It's a small but interesting detail for those familiar with the battlefield's modern layout.

As the Grand Reunion wound up, thousands of stories played out each day as veterans retraced their steps from fifty years earlier, reliving moments of triumph, loss, and camaraderie. Among the many moving scenes, one particularly touching reunion took place, not on the battlefield but on the front porch of a house in town.

One of the often-overlooked chapters of the Civil War was the tireless efforts of the nurses who cared for the wounded and dying in makeshift hospitals after the battle. At the reunion, a special gathering was held in their honor at a house on the main street, which had served as an emergency hospital during those fateful days in 1863. The home's owner, Mrs. Salome Stewart, still resided there, and for the next few days her porch became a place of remembrance.

Thirty aging women, once young caregivers in the midst of chaos, now sat side by side, watching the veterans march by. They waved to the men they had once tended to, their faces lined with time but still filled with the same quiet strength that had carried them through the war.

Among the thousands who made the pilgrimage to Gettysburg was Reverend W. F. Hubbard, who had traveled all the way from California. Severely wounded during the battle, he owed his survival to the kindness and skill of one of these nurses. For fifty years, he had carried the memory

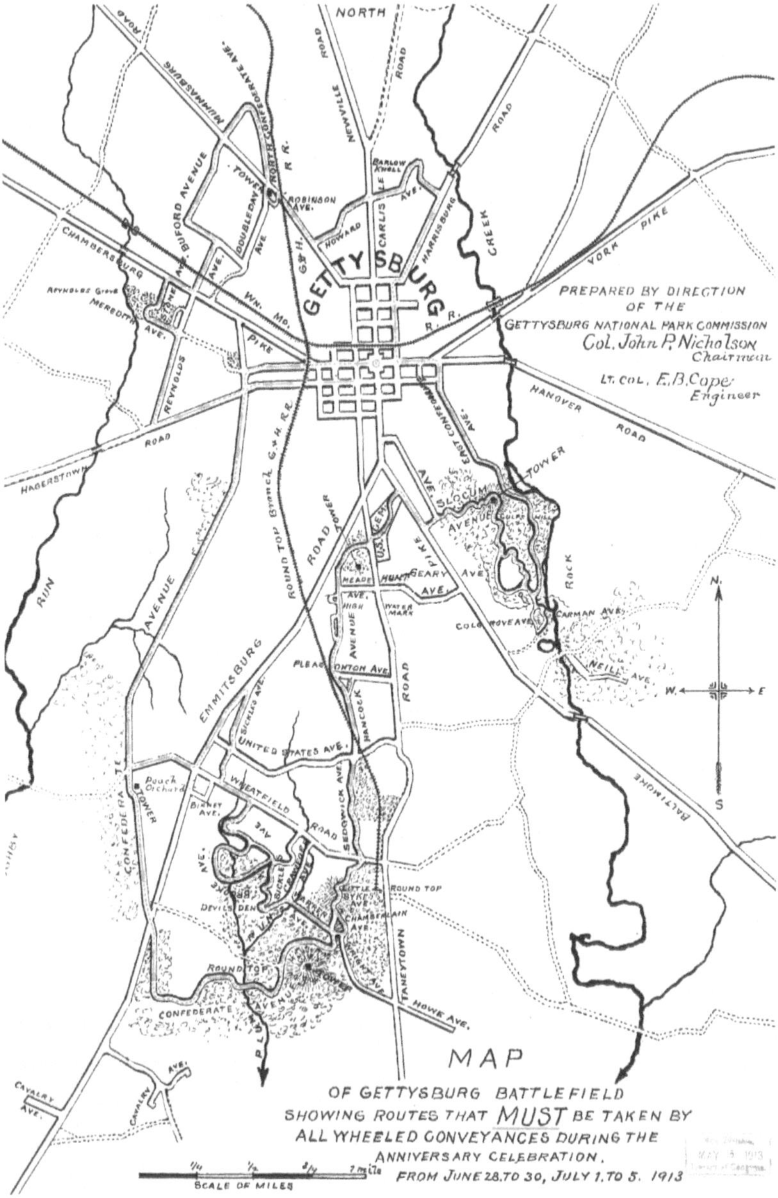


Map of Gettysburg in 1913. Note the Great Camp was southwest of town between Confederate Avenue and Emmitsburg Road, with the Round Top Branch Railroad running directly through its center. Also note the locations of the observation towers. Courtesy of the Library of Congress.

of her care, and his greatest hope was to find her and to finally thank her for the comfort she had given him in his darkest hour.

Incredibly, fate smiled on him within the first hour of his arrival. Hubbard was overjoyed to find Mrs. Margaret Young, the very nurse who had eased his suffering all those years ago. At last, he could express his gratitude, not just as a wounded soldier but as a man who had carried her kindness in his heart for decades.

In a week filled with grand speeches and historic moments, deeply personal reunions like these truly defined the spirit of Gettysburg in 1913.

The arriving veterans were described as pathetic, weak, and feeble. And many of them were. Their backs were bent, and they shuffled along on unsteady feet. Many leaned heavily on canes for support, while others relied on the sturdy young Boy Scouts to guide them to their tents. But that didn't describe all of them. Plenty were still hale and hearty, with energy and determination to spare. Not every veteran had been reduced to frailty. Some, like Walter Blake, were still strong, adventurous, and eager to make the most of their time in Gettysburg.

Walter Blake wrote an indispensable book about the Grand Reunion. In *Hand Grips*, released in December 1913, he recorded many of the events he witnessed during his attendance at the reunion. During the Civil War, Blake served in two different units: the Sixth New Hampshire Infantry Volunteers and the First New Hampshire Heavy Artillery. Shortly after the war, Blake relocated to Vineland, New Jersey. Because of this, Blake camped with the New Jersey vets rather than the men he served with during the war.

At the Grand Reunion, Blake wrote about a long zig-zag tour of the battlefield that he took with three other Union veterans. They started in the Great Camp, wandered over to the Bloody Angle, and then gazed at General Meade's equestrian statue. From there, they were drawn to the massive Pennsylvania Memorial and dozens of other monuments along the way. After spending time at each one, they headed to Little Round Top and Devil's Den. They left camp at 9:00 a.m. and returned at 3:00 p.m., claiming to have walked fifteen miles in ninety-seven-degree temperatures. After a short break and some refreshments, Blake and his companions found they weren't quite tired yet and decided to head into town and see the sights. By the time their day ended, they claimed to have walked eighteen miles.[16] Not too bad for a bunch of old guys in their seventies.

Seven survivors of Pickett's Charge arrived at camp along with the Virginia veterans. One of the first places they visited was the high-water mark of the Confederacy—the farthest point reached during Pickett's Charge. This was a significant landmark at the time, and one we'll revisit often throughout this book.

At the time of the battle, that spot was known as the "Bloody Angle." But here's where things get tricky: There's another "Bloody Angle" at Spotsylvania Court House in Virginia, where a brutal twenty-four-hour struggle of hand-to-hand combat took place. To avoid confusion between the two sites, the park service eventually dropped the "Bloody" from Gettysburg's name, leaving it simply as "the Angle."

But in 1913, the Gettysburg veterans still called it the "Bloody Angle." And that's the name we'll use here as well.

The seven survivors spent a great deal of time at the Bloody Angle, where both veterans and tourists stopped to speak with them. The old Confederates were delighted by the attention, always eager to share their memories and point out just how far they had advanced during that fateful charge. Private Richard Wilson, for instance, never missed the chance to show curious visitors the exact places where he'd been struck—once in the left knee, again in the left ankle, and the spot where his right arm had been broken.

Another unnamed Confederate said, "They say we are old . . . but I tell you I'm as tough as a mewl; yes, sir, as tough as a mewl [mule]. I've been a-looking forward to this for a long time and don't intend to miss a thing. People say we'll die from the heat, but I ain't a-going to croak; this is the greatest day of my life."[17]

To emphasize this point, Second Sergeant H. H. Moore, regardless of his ninety years, hopped over the stone wall at the Bloody Angle with the ease and grace of youth. "You see, I'm still a boy!" he shouted to some spectators. The old soldier had been close to General Lewis Armistead when he was fatally wounded during the charge.

In chapter 7, we'll spend considerably more time at the Bloody Angle and look closely at what happened there—not only during the battle but also at the reunion.

## The Angle 2025

The site known in 1913 as the "Bloody Angle," photographed during the Grand Reunion with the Great Tent in the background, courtesy of Laura Hedgecock. Today called simply "The Angle," shown again in 2025, photographed by the author.

Here's a story that has been exaggerated with each new telling.

John Hawley was no stranger to keeping an eye on rebellious Southerners. He had once been a sergeant at Fort Monroe in Norfolk, Virginia, where he served as a prison guard for none other than Confederate president Jefferson Davis.[18] But by the time of the fiftieth reunion, the eighty-five-year-old Hawley found himself under house arrest of a different kind—imposed by his own son.

Hawley was in poor health but was determined to make it to Gettysburg. His son, however, had other ideas. Convinced that the summer heat would be the death of him,[19] he outright forbade the old man from attending. To settle the matter, he dragged Hawley to the doctor, hoping for a final word of authority. The physician examined the aging veteran and agreed—it would be safer if he stayed home, since the strain of travel and the heat could prove fatal. But Hawley wasn't about to let a little thing like doctor's orders or his son's rules stand in his way.

So, on the morning of Sunday, June 29, 1913, before the household stirred, Hawley made his great escape. With the cunning of a man half his age (or maybe just the sheer stubbornness of an old soldier), he woke early, dressed, and slipped out of his bedroom window. "Like a thief in the night,"[20] he stole away to the railroad station, hopped on a train, and made his triumphant break for Gettysburg.

It wasn't until breakfast that the family realized their fugitive had escaped. Equally furious and bewildered, his son did what any good jailer would do—he called the authorities. The state police were dispatched on an urgent mission to retrieve the runaway veteran, and when they finally tracked him down in Gettysburg, they found a scene that must have left them shaking their heads.

There was John Hawley, grinning ear to ear, surrounded by his old comrades, swapping war stories, belly laughing, and generally having the time of his life. And despite the deadly heat his son had warned about, he seemed perfectly fine. The officers, perhaps with a chuckle of their own, sent word back to the family: "Don't worry, he's in good hands."

Over the years, the story of John Hawley's great escape has grown with each telling. It's been handed down with enough embellishment to become a tall tale told around the campfire. Some say that his son resorted to drastic measures by locking the old soldier in his second-floor bedroom to prevent any escape attempts. Undeterred, Old Hawley opened his window and, with the daring of a man sixty years younger, shimmied down the drainpipe like a gray-haired Houdini and hitched a ride to Gettysburg.

Of course, the official record does not mention locked doors or daredevil feats of agility, and logic suggests that a frail eighty-five-year-old probably wasn't scaling walls like an escape artist. But as with any legendary tale, the truth often lies somewhere between the facts and the flair. While the more dramatic details may not hold up under scrutiny, one thing is sure: Hawley's determination to reunite with his fellow veterans was unstoppable.

Sadly, just six months after his grand adventure, John Hawley passed away. But for one last time, he had defied the odds, outwitted his captors, and made it to Gettysburg—a final victory in a life well lived.

As more and more veterans entered the camp, impromptu mini-reunions took place all over the battlefield. Many of the old soldiers hadn't seen each other since the end of the war. In the Maryland camp, Edwin Selvage approached William Delashmutt. The two men looked into each other's eyes for a full minute. "Don't you know me?" Selvage said to Delashmutt.

"Just wait a minute," replied Delashmutt. "Let's see; you were in the First Maryland Cavalry."

"Yes," Selvage said. "And in Company D with you."

Then the two old men fell into each other's arms and wept.

They recounted the last time they had met at the Battle of Pollard's Farm in Virginia during the spring of 1864. "I saw the minie ball that struck you in the right breast," Selvage said to Delashmutt. "I recall you turned to me and said, 'They are pumping bullets at us.'" And again, the two old veterans embraced each other.

Just then, a third man joined in.

"I was there too," said Edwin Jones, a newcomer who wanted to be included, "and was fighting by your side when the bullet hit you."

"Yes, you were," Delashmutt said. "I recall it as vividly as if it took place yesterday."[21]

Although the names and circumstances changed, mini-reunions like this happened all day, every day, at the Grand Reunion.

This brings us back to an earlier question: How did the veterans feel about seeing the Confederate flag? An interesting incident on the first day of the reunion, in the Maryland camp, sheds some light on this subject. Maryland had veterans who had fought on both sides of the war, and their camps were set up right next to each other. This arrangement led to plenty of interaction between former adversaries. This also introduces the fourth and final Maryland veteran we'll follow: Charles H. Mettee.

As some Union veterans wandered into the Confederate section of the camp, they expected to see a Confederate flag—but none was there. "This isn't right until the boys in gray have their flag on Seminary Ridge. It ought to be there," remarked several New York and Pennsylvania veterans. Lucien W. Lyman of the Eighty-Third Pennsylvania Volunteers agreed, saying, "They ought to have it, let's get one up." Many other Union veterans shared this sentiment.

However, the Confederate veterans were reluctant to raise their flag. Having heard rumors about restrictions on its display, they preferred to avoid conflict. "No, the war is over. It's one country now, one flag. We fought for what we thought was right, but let's all forget it now and be brothers," one Confederate veteran said.

Despite this hesitation, the Union veterans persisted. After much encouragement, Charles H. Mettee finally produced a Confederate flag and hoisted it above the Southern section of the Maryland camp. At that moment, it was the only Confederate flag flying in the Great Camp, and as it reached its peak, both Union and Confederate veterans cheered.[22]

According to *The Baltimore Sun*, on that first day at the battlefield, twenty to thirty cameras focused on the Confederate flag as several colonels and generals eagerly posed for pictures. Mettee was surprised by all the attention. "Callers to see the old flag have kept me on the jump today,"[23] he remarked.

Once the flag was raised in the Maryland section, more Confederate flags began appearing throughout the Great Camp, flying alongside the US flag. One particularly unique flag featured the Stars and Stripes on one side and the Confederate flag sewn onto the other, with two inscriptions: "Let us have peace—Grant" and "Duty is the sublimest word in any language—Lee."[24]

Interesting, isn't it? Union veterans seem to have a surprisingly conciliatory attitude toward the Confederate flag. Rather than rejecting it as a symbol of rebellion and hatred, they viewed it as an essential representation of their former foes, deserving of a place at the reunion. Their insistence on raising the flag, despite the initial reluctance of Confederate veterans, suggests they saw it not as a threat but as a way to acknowledge and honor the shared sacrifices of both sides. For the old soldiers present, a spirit of unity transcended old divisions. For better or worse, the Confederate flag was a part of their collective history, and the actions of the Union vets suggest that they were more interested in fostering brotherhood than in erasing the past.

Many veterans were still arriving and registering at headquarters when two hundred Confederate and Union veterans from West Virginia marched through the Great Camp carrying a tattered and torn Confederate flag that was ready to fall to pieces. During the war, this particular flag had followed Stonewall Jackson and General Lee from the First Battle of Manassas to Antietam. Union veterans marched behind it as proudly as did the old Rebels in gray. As they met along the road, veterans raised their hats to honor the old flag as it passed by.

Now, I want to pause for a moment to acknowledge that the Grand Reunion was not all sunshine and rainbows. It wasn't some harmonious utopia where everyone got along perfectly and was equally accepted. The truth is, not everyone was pleased to see the Confederate flag.

The veterans from Vermont, in particular, were upset to see it paraded around. While they didn't mind the sight of gray Confederate uniforms, that flag grated on them. To them, it was an insult to the emblem of Liberty. The Confederates had spent four years trying to tear the Union apart, and the men from Vermont felt that their enemy's flag had no place at the reunion. This frustration led to a group discussion within their camp.

Cooler-headed veterans encouraged those still harboring bitterness to reconsider their stance. If the Confederate flag couldn't claim victory fifty years ago, what harm could it do now? Besides, many found the Southerners a well-meaning and friendly group. With the Vermont camp located near the Confederate camp, the two sides spent a lot of time together. They dined at the same camp kitchens and even shared the same latrines. In fact, the more time the men from Vermont spent with the Confederates, the more they liked them. After that, the matter was dropped, and no further friction over the Confederate flag was reported.[25]

So, how did the veterans feel about the Confederate flag? Well, it depends on who you ask. The vast majority supported its presence, but some still harbored resentment toward it. Fifty years had softened old animosities but hadn't erased them.

Before we continue, let's take some time to address the elephant in the room. One frequently asked question about the 1913 Grand Reunion is: Did any Black veterans attend? This is a question that many modern-day authors, professors, and historians have weighed in on, and if you read their works, the resounding answer is "No!" The reason given is that the United States Colored Troops (USCT) were purposefully excluded from the event, allegedly so as not to offend the Southern vets. The argument is that if Southern vets knew former slaves would be present, they would have refused to attend. America was ready to mend the North–South divide, but it wasn't prepared to face the history of slavery. Critics claim there's no evidence that any Black veterans attended and suggest that the event was little more than a White supremacist gathering during the Jim Crow era, and the only Black people invited were the ones cleaning the latrines.

When I first started researching the 1913 Grand Reunion, I found multiple books and articles readily available that claim there is zero evidence of Black veterans attending. However, these conclusions are based on flawed assumptions and poor research and are often repeated in the twenty-first century without a shred of supporting evidence. I call this the "Myth of the Uninvited Black Soldier."

The deeper I dug, the more evidence I uncovered, and I would like to share these findings with you.

Black veterans did indeed attend the Grand Reunion, and all it takes is some proper research to find the evidence. All honorably discharged veterans were invited to Gettysburg, regardless of race. This section presents sources proving that Black veterans were welcomed and attended the Grand Reunion. I hope that if someone spouts the Myth of the Uninvited Black Soldier, you can correct their hearsay with facts.

The *Twin City Star* was an African American newspaper circulated in Minneapolis, Minnesota, from 1910 to 1919. On July 11, 1913, it ran a brief article on page 2: "Negro Vets at Gettysburg. Comrade Henry Thomas Middleton called at the Star office Wednesday. He informed us that the Minnesota Veterans returned home in good health, also that they reported that many Negro Veterans attended the reunion, and they were seen intermingling with the Union and Confederate survivors, receiving the best of treatment. Mr. Middleton is an old employee in the Hospital of the Soldier's Home."[26]

After further research, I discovered that Henry Middleton died on October 3, 1914. His obituary states, "He served in civil war 29 months, and was honorably discharged and pensioned."[27]

Let me reiterate: Here, we have a Black veteran reporting to a Black newspaper that many Black veterans attended the Grand Reunion. That article alone is enough to dispel the myth, but I have quite a bit more evidence that I'll share throughout this book to further stomp that myth into the ground.

The state of Delaware covered the transportation fees, allowing its veterans to attend the Grand Reunion. According to the *Evening Journal*, about three hundred veterans from Delaware made the trip. "In the list are twelve men from the Confederate side, and eighteen colored veterans of [the] Union."[28] In other words, not only were the USCT invited, but some states also covered the cost of their transportation.

The *Delaware County Daily News* names two colored vets who went to Gettysburg: Walter Pyle and George Derry.[29] Meanwhile, at least one all-Black Grand Army of the Republic (GAR) post from Brooklyn, New York, attended the Grand Reunion. It was the William Lloyd Garrison[30] Post 107, and although it was reported that they sent members to Gettysburg, we don't know who attended or how many. New York was another state that provided free transportation for their veterans to and from the reunion.

Here's an excerpt from the New Jersey newspaper, the *Trenton Times*: "Bayard and Aaron Wilkes Post, G.A.R., brought to camp about 40 men each, and the colored post from the Jersey capital has about 50 members here."[31]

Pennsylvania had an all-Black GAR post called the David R. Stevens Post 520 of Harrisburg, active from 1886 to 1930.[32] At its peak, Post 520 had sixty-two members, but by 1913, the numbers had dwindled due to the attrition of time. Twelve members attended the Grand Reunion: James M. Auter, George W. Thomas, Stephen Ziegler, Cassius Mars, David Stephen, William Dixon, William White, Charles James, James Stokes,

George Gibson, Mr. Brooks, and Samuel Hall.[33] The state of Pennsylvania provided free transportation to and from Gettysburg for these men. "There aren't many of them in camp—Post 520 could hardly muster a very complete company nowadays, but the campers that are here are having the time of their lives."[34] This same article also mentions that many other Union camps at the Grand Reunion also contained Black veterans.

Let's explore the first name on that list. James M. Auter was born free in 1848. Before the war, he lived in Petersburg, Virginia, and was required to carry "a document stating that he had been born free and was a freeman."[35] If he were found without the document, he could be considered a runaway slave and arrested. In 1863, at the age of fourteen, Auter ran away from home and tried to enlist in the army. He was denied, but Auter didn't give up. He enlisted in the navy and was accepted[36] into the service. During the Civil War, the navy was more racially integrated than the army, and Auter served on board the USS *Georgia*. He was stationed off Fort Fisher in North Carolina and helped maintain the blockade against the Southern states.[37]

After the war, Auter was very active in veterans' affairs. He became the commander of GAR Post 520, regularly marched in parades on special occasions, and decorated soldiers' graves. He was a member of the Citizens' Republican Club of Philadelphia, which was a "way to do something for the one political party that had done something for his kind."[38] Auter was also an elder at the Capital Street Presbyterian Church. For a vocation, he became the messenger at the Executive Department and served under eight Pennsylvania governors.

Physically, he was described as a man who walked with a soldier's dignity, even in his later years, and always had a winning smile on his lips.[39]

At Christmas time, he delighted in a special assignment. It was tradition to distribute gifts to children at the Governor's Mansion. In 1913, two hundred children were present. While Governor John Tener and his wife looked on, "James M. Auter . . . who for years has played the part of Santa Claus to the children, passed out the candy."[40] Auter continued to dress as Santa, in "the red uniform and the white whiskers,"[41] until he died in 1932 at the age of eighty-four. It's fascinating that during the early twentieth century, a time of great racial unrest, the Pennsylvania Governor's Mansion had a Black Santa for almost thirty years.

I wish I knew more about James M. Auter; he seems like a wonderful man. I know he attended the Gettysburg Reunion, but I don't know what he did there or who he talked to. But I'm happy to have introduced you to him.

Sources indicate that Delaware sent eighteen Black veterans to the Grand Reunion, and we have confirmed fourteen from Pennsylvania. Trenton, New Jersey, sent around fifty, and an unknown number came from New York City. These were just the mentions that I could find, but that doesn't mean there weren't more. So, how many Black veterans were present? Let's find out.

Even though all honorably discharged veterans were invited to attend, very few members of the United States Colored Troops (USCT) chose to participate in the Grand Reunion. One likely reason for this decision is that the USCT did not participate in the Battle of Gettysburg. The overwhelming majority of those who attended the reunion had served in the Gettysburg campaign, and for many veterans, having fought in that specific battle was what made the event personally meaningful. This logic didn't apply only to the USCT—it extended to thousands of other veterans who chose not to attend simply because they had not fought at Gettysburg. As a result, naval veterans were also largely absent. In this regard, James M. Auter was a rare exception. Not only was he Black, but he had served in the navy and still chose to attend the reunion, making his presence especially notable.

The USCT did not fight at Gettysburg because they were six hundred miles away at Fort Wagner in South Carolina. Most notable was the Fifty-Fourth Massachusetts Infantry, famously portrayed in the 1989 film *Glory*. Veterans of the Fifty-Fourth Massachusetts held their own fiftieth-anniversary reunion in Boston a mere two weeks after the Grand Reunion.[42] It makes sense that many USCT veterans would favor the battle in which they participated rather than one they had merely heard about.

Getting back to the Grand Reunion, a reporter from the *Times Leader* newspaper wrote this account:

> *I saw a small log house at the edge of the camp that was 135 years old. A colored family now occupies it. It shows what is said to be bullet holes.*

> *On the corner of Breckinridge and Washington streets, there is a log house 100 years old, a family of colored people named Lyles, lives in it. I asked how many colored people in Gettysburg, and the answer came: "There are four or five hundred." I replied, "Seems to me I have seen more than that number," and he answered, "Yes, but there are many here visiting."*[43]

Multiple sources report that around three hundred Black veterans attended the Grand Reunion.[44] That number is an estimate, which means there could have been a few more or a few less. Although it's a small number compared to the fifty-three thousand White veterans, it's still significant. And it's certainly not zero.

In 1896, the US Supreme Court ruled on *Plessy v. Ferguson*, which instituted segregation under the guise of "separate but equal."[45] This doctrine led to separate schools for White and Black people, separate hospitals, restaurants, bathrooms, and even water fountains. The Grand Reunion took place when segregation was the norm in America, which meant that the Great Camp had a separate section for Black veterans. According to *The Philadelphia Inquirer*, Colonel Andrew James[46] arranged with the Pennsylvania Commission that all Black veterans be quartered together on one street in the Great Camp. If three hundred Black veterans attended and there were only eight men in a tent, then they must have dedicated at least thirty-eight tents to the USCT.

Except for their segregated sleeping quarters, members of the USCT were treated just like every other veteran at the reunion. They ate in the same kitchens, slept in the same style of tents as the White veterans, and even used the same latrines. (At their age, the real priority wasn't segregation—it was proximity.)

At night, they gathered at the edge of the company street, lit a campfire, tuned up a banjo, and sang some of the old plantation songs. The music always attracted a crowd; although most were Black, a few old White veterans were sprinkled among them. Between songs, they'd reminisce about the Underground Railroad and the pride they felt returning to the South in a federal uniform. After singing one of the old slave songs, one of the men said, "Comrades, the Almighty made us men, but the Republican party made us citizens."[47]

Joseph R. Winter was not a Civil War veteran, but he was at the Grand Reunion. He was born a freeman in Leesburg, Virginia, and claimed to be born in 1816 to a Black father and Shawnee Native American mother. Because of his heritage, he was given the nickname "Indian Dick." He taught himself how to read and write and later became a writer, a mechanic, a gunsmith, and an inventor. He's notable for his friendship with both Frederick Douglass and John Brown. Allegedly, he arranged a meeting between the two abolitionists before John Brown's raid on Harpers Ferry in 1859.

In 1830, he moved to Chambersburg, Pennsylvania, and was involved in the Underground Railroad. When the Confederate army entered Pennsylvania in 1863, Joseph Winter fled the area to avoid possible enslavement. After the Confederate army retreated to Virginia, Winter penned a song: "Ten Days after the Battle of Gettysburg." This song became a recruitment tool for Black men to join the Union army.

Here are some of the lyrics:

The colored people all ran away,
Likewise the composer of this song, they say—
For if I hadn't, I don't know
But I'd been in the South a'working the hoe.

It closes with:

Now, if they come back, I'll tell you what to do,
We'll give them some grape, and canister too;
Let white and black all shoulder a gun,
And then, O Lord, won't we have some fun.

After Gettysburg, Winters contributed his money and time to encourage Black men to enlist. In fact, his son, Jacob Winter, joined in December 1863 at Camp William Penn, just outside of Philadelphia. Jacob became a private in Company D of the Twenty-Second USCT Regiment and participated in the Battle of Petersburg and the Siege of Richmond.

By 1913, Winter was ninety-seven years old, and despite his age, he was quite active. According to Edward Sylvester Ellis's 1918 account of the Gettysburg Reunion, Joseph Winter was in attendance.[48] Was he there just as one of the thousands of spectators curious to see the reunion of the Blue and Gray, or was it possible that he made the journey with his son, who was a Union veteran and therefore invited to attend? Unfortunately, the documentation is scarce, and we may never know the answer. But we can place him at the Grand Reunion, and perhaps he was one of the old men sitting around the campfire telling tales about the Underground Railroad.

For years, the story has been told that Black veterans were excluded from the 1913 Gettysburg Reunion, but historical evidence proves otherwise. Official invitations were not racially exclusive, and all honorably discharged veterans were invited to attend. Some states, including Pennsylvania, New York, and Delaware, even covered travel expenses for Black attendees. Multiple accounts document their presence, including named mentions of Black veterans and an all-Black GAR post from Brooklyn. While segregation meant they were housed separately, Black veterans still participated in reunion activities, shared meals with White comrades, and gathered around campfires to reminisce about the war.

Eyewitness reports from both Black and White newspapers confirm their attendance, directly debunking the myth that they were uninvited. Their numbers were likely lower due to battlefield relevance, as the USCT did not participate in the Battle of Gettysburg. Instead, many Black veterans chose to attend reunions connected to their own battle experiences, such as the gathering of the Fifty-Fourth Massachusetts in Boston. The evidence is clear: Black veterans were present at Gettysburg in 1913, and their contributions to Civil War memory deserve recognition.

Although I don't have the numbers to prove it, I'd also claim that there were more USCT veterans at the Grand Reunion than sailors from the navy. I've read hundreds of accounts from the attendees, and only a handful involve the navy. I'd speculate that most sailors were part of a tight-knit crew who would prefer to hold a shipmates' reunion in a pub rather than travel to some far-off battlefield that they'd never laid eyes on, especially in the heat of the summer.

Here's an example: William Durst was from Philadelphia and had the distinction of being the sole survivor of the USS *Monitor*. While attending the Grand Reunion, he wore his old sailor suit so that other navy veterans could identify him from a distance. He stood out like a sore thumb and attracted a great deal of attention; unfortunately, he encountered no other

Two USCT veterans at the Grand Reunion; original caption: "Contraband of War—One of these Negroes said he belonged to a man in Norfolk and the other to one in Wayne Co., U.C., and both ran away to enlist in the Federal Army. They live now in Philadelphia." Courtesy of Edgecombe County Memorial Library (1913).

sailors. "Durst wandered about the camp like a lost gull at sea, searching for any possible seafaring companions. 'These fellows insist on talking about charges and camps and all that sort o' thing,' said Durst. 'Not one of them know a thing about sailing. I guess I'll have to go back home. An inland battlefield is no place for an old sailor man.'"[49]

Discussing the Battle of Gettysburg without mentioning General James Longstreet is almost impossible. General Robert E. Lee referred to him as his "Old War Horse" and regarded him as one of the finest corps commanders in the entire Confederate army. Longstreet was a professional soldier whose experience contributed to many Southern victories during the Civil War. As a corps commander, Longstreet was responsible for twenty thousand men and reported directly to General Lee. He and his First Corps were engaged throughout the Gettysburg campaign, but Longstreet's actions were considered quite controversial. Ask anyone who has studied the Civil War, and they'll be sure to have an opinion on what Longstreet should or should *not* have done at Gettysburg.

Helen Dortch was born in April 1863, just a few months before the Battle of Gettysburg. During her early career, she worked as a newspaper publisher, but in 1887 she returned to school at Notre Dame of Maryland University. While there, she worked as the assistant librarian and met General James Longstreet. Longstreet was writing a book called *From Manassas to Appomattox: Memoirs of the Civil War* and needed assistance with the research. While working together, sparks flew. Longstreet's first wife had passed away eight years earlier, and his children were grown and out of the house. He was lonely and "so deaf he cannot hear a word without the aid of a speaking trumpet."[50] Despite this challenge, Helen and Longstreet fell in love and married on September 8, 1897. It was a May-December romance, as she was thirty-four, while he was seventy-six.

Many scoffed at the pairing, claiming he was too old for her, but Longstreet dismissed the criticism. He said, "I am not old at all. You don't know what life is until you reach my age."[51]

When asked why she married a man forty-two years her senior, she said, "Because I love him, to be sure, for no true woman would ever marry a man whom she did not love. When he asked my hand in marriage, I granted it, knowing that I was entrusting my life and happiness to one of the noblest men God ever made."[52] The two were happily married for six years until the general's death in 1904.

Helen Dortch Longstreet was just fifty years old when she traveled to Gettysburg for the fiftieth anniversary. She was the widow of one of the most famous generals in the Civil War, and that gave her a place of honor. But she wasn't just there for the attention. She was hired as a special correspondent for *The New York Times*, and her articles would be syndicated across fifty other newspapers nationwide. Due to her last name and vocation, she was the only female allowed to stay in the Great Camp. Thanks to arrangements made by that crazy bastard, Dan Sickles, she was given not one but two tents for her use. One tent would serve as her sleeping quarters and the other as her office. She promised to call on General Sickles to thank him after she settled in. She traveled with a corps of stenographers, some lady friends, and two grandsons of General Longstreet.

However, when she arrived at the Grand Reunion, things were not as ready as she had hoped. Due to the massive influx of veterans coming to the reunion, her two tents had been given away. The camp organizers scrambled and found one tent for her use in the heart of the Great Camp. This tent served as her office, which meant she still needed a place to sleep. On her first night on-site, she walked into the town looking for sleeping quarters, but all the hotels were full. The residents of Gettysburg saw the Grand Reunion as an opportunity to make a quick buck and were renting out their spare rooms to the tourists. As a result, Helen rented an empty room without a bed and ended up sleeping on a pile of straw on the floor.[53]

We'll catch up with Helen Longstreet in the next chapter.

One of my favorite aspects of history is discovering unexpected threads. The following story has an interesting connection that spans the Civil War in the 1860s to World War II in the 1940s.

Waller T. Patton was born in Fredericksburg, Virginia, in 1835 and was just twenty-eight years old at the Battle of Gettysburg. On July 3, he served as a colonel in Kemper's Brigade, which formed the right side of the line during Pickett's Charge. While leading his men toward Cemetery Ridge, he was struck by an artillery shell fragment that tore away a portion of his jaw. He survived the battle but died a few weeks later in a makeshift hospital at Gettysburg College.

Waller's first cousin was Colonel Lewis Williams. He also fought and died during Pickett's Charge. Pickett commanded his officers to dismount and walk during the charge, but Williams felt ill and was given permission to ride his horse into battle. As they marched across an open field, the federal artillery fired on them. A shell exploded near Williams, and he was thrown from his saddle and impaled by his own sword.

Waller's brother George also fought for Virginia during the Civil War and was killed in the Third Battle of Winchester in September 1864. George left behind a widow and four children, one of whom was named George, who eventually had a son who was also named George!

In 1909, George III visited Gettysburg and wrote a letter to his future wife, Beatrice:

> *There is to me a strange fascination in looking at the scene of the awful struggles which raged over this country. A fascination and a regret. I would like to have been there too.*
>
> *This evening after supper, I walked down alone to the scene of the last and fiercest struggle on Cemetery Hill. To get in the proper frame of mind, I wandered through the cemetery and let the spirits of the dead thousands laid there in ordered rows sink into me. . . . I walked down to the scene of Pickett's great charge and seated on a rock just where Olmstead and two of my great uncles died, I watched the wonder of the day go out.*
>
> *The sunset painted a dull red the fields over which the terrible advance was made, and I could almost see them coming, growing fewer and fewer while around and beyond me stood calmly the very cannon that had so punished them. . . . I drank it in until I was quite happy. A strange pleasure, yet a very real one.*
>
> *I think that it takes an evening like that to make one understand what men will do in battle. It was a wonderful yet a very foolish battle.*[54]

George was a remarkable athlete who showcased his skills on the world stage at the 1912 Olympic Games in Stockholm, Sweden. Competing in the first-ever modern pentathlon—a grueling test of shooting, swimming, fencing, equestrianism, and cross-country running—he placed an impressive fifth overall.

By 1913, he was assigned to the Fifteenth Cavalry, the same unit that escorted that crazy bastard Sickles from the Gettysburg train station to his quarters at the Rogers House. But George's legacy wouldn't stop there.

He served in World War I and World War II, eventually earning the nickname "Old Blood and Guts." General George S. Patton became the bold and brilliant tank commander of the Third Army, leading his forces in relentless battles across Europe and Africa, all the way to the final assault on Germany. Yet, before he became a legend, he and his unit played a quiet role: helping police the Grand Reunion and ensuring that nearly eight thousand aging soldiers had warm blankets to get them through the night.

Throughout the Grand Reunion, veterans competed for bragging rights—who was the oldest, the youngest, or who had traveled the farthest to reach Gettysburg. Among them was Bennett Britten from South Plainfield, New Jersey, who had just turned one hundred in June.[55] He surprised "all who see him by his activity" and might have claimed the title of the oldest veteran at the reunion, if not for the arrival of one unforgettable character: Micajah Weiss.

Micajah Weiss was a force to be reckoned with. Hailing from Beaver Brook in Sullivan County, New York, he claimed to be 112 years old. Official pension records listed his birth year as 1805, but he insisted he was born on January 15, 1801, with proof written in the family Bible. Despite his age, Weiss was described as an "active and vivacious man who was not at all sensitive about his age." In fact, he embraced it.

In 1912, he stormed into the office of a Scranton newspaper, furious that they had printed his obituary, and threatened to give the editor a beating.

Short and bent with age, Weiss had long, white hair, a commanding voice, and sharp eyes that still held their edge. "He never used tobacco but added, 'I like a little cherry wine and have always been using it.'"[56] When asked about the secret to his longevity, he said, "Work so hard that you don't have time to grow old."[57]

By July 1913, he was 111 years, six months, and some days old—but for simplicity's sake, he rounded up to 112. And honestly, who was going to argue? He proudly announced his age to everyone at the reunion, earning plenty of attention for it.

Before the war, Weiss had worked as a lumberjack, navigating rafts of logs down the Delaware River to Philadelphia. In the spring of 1861, while on one of these trips, he heard the news—Fort Sumter had fallen, and the country was headed to war. Without hesitation, he decided to enlist. The only problem? He was already fifty-nine years old. Knowing that might be a deal-breaker, he knocked a few years off and claimed he was a spritely fifty-five.

After settling his affairs back home, Weiss officially joined the 141st Pennsylvania Infantry on August 14, 1862, serving as a private until the war's end.

Fifty years later, standing among fellow veterans at Gettysburg, he wasn't just a soldier from history—he was living proof of it.

When asked how many battles he participated in, he replied, "Most all of 'em," including Gettysburg, the Wilderness, Cold Harbor, Petersburg, and Appomattox. He later described the conditions at Petersburg: "We got there without any rations. A colored regiment. A lot of fine fellows too, they were, shared their food with us, and then we did the entrenching. I was on picket duty in the rain for days." He said that was where he contracted rheumatism, which bothered him for the rest of his life.

Weiss was regarded as a legendary hunter who used a four-barrel gun to take down bears.[58] In his younger years, he thought nothing of walking twenty miles to get a shot at a deer but had no use for the three-mile walk to the district school.[59] The *Reading Eagle* in 1913 recorded: "He told with glee how he took the saddles of 106 deer to Philadelphia in one trip, 11 of them being of bucks which he himself had killed in one day." He owned an eighty-acre farm and still had the energy to work it himself. Weiss had outlived three wives, and his fourth wife was a youthful seventy-five to his 112. Talk about robbing the cradle!

Weiss drove to the reunion in his own automobile, accompanied by his wife and stepson. Weiss drove the car, although he and his stepson took turns at the wheel. They spent the night in Allentown, Pennsylvania, where a reporter from the *Reading Eagle* interviewed him. "He still finds life sweet and worth living and has no complaints," the reporter wrote. "He works hard every day of the year and takes an interest in everything in the big world about him." He kept up with current events. He spoke of all the automobiles he saw on his way to the Gettysburg Reunion with the wide-eyed wonder of a young man. Asked whether he had been on an electric trolley, the centenarian replied, "My gracious, yes, hundreds of times, and I was on one of the first railroads built in this country. It traveled about as fast as I could walk, but I took a ride on it anyhow. And I have seen airships. They certainly are doing wonderful things these days."

At the reunion, Micajah Weiss was joined by his family, eager to see where the great battle had unfolded fifty years earlier. Acting as their guide, he led them through Little Round Top and the Peach Orchard, beaming with pride when they reached the monument to the 141st Pennsylvania Infantry.

While in Gettysburg, Weiss stayed in the Great Camp, while his family had to find lodging in town. He moved slowly through the camp, with a cane in each hand, carefully navigating the grounds. A relic from a bygone era, Weiss became something of a "guest of honor." Veterans from North and South sought him out, eager to meet and speak with the oldest man at the reunion. Despite his years, his sharp mind and eagerness to recount his wartime experiences astonished visitors.

At one point, he was photographed alongside Colonel John L. Clem, one of the youngest veterans in attendance at the reunion. Colonel Clem was only sixty-one and still an active member of the military.

Regardless of his stamina, the heat and humidity still took a toll on Weiss. When he and his wife trudged up to one of the hospital tents, an orderly sprang forward, thinking he was ill and needed help. Weiss pushed him aside with his cane. "Not yet," he said. "I only stopped in to see if a tired and hungry old man could get a bite of a sandwich and a bit of coffee to stimulate him. So he could continue on his way feeling stronger." He was fixed in a hurry. The doctor wanted him to lie down because he looked overheated, but Weiss would hear none of it. Soon he was out touring the battlefield again.

Micajah Weiss was undeniably the oldest vet at the reunion, but there is some dispute about who was the youngest. It's widely regarded that Colonel John L. Clem was the youngest, but he had some competition for

Micajah Weiss, the oldest veteran at the Grand Reunion, claimed to be 112 years old. Courtesy of Pennsylvania State Archives, RG 25.24.

the title. Clem tried to enlist in 1861 and was denied due to his age. But thanks to his persistence, he was allowed to tag along with the Twenty-Second Michigan Infantry, where he was adopted as the regimental mascot and drummer boy. He was officially allowed to enlist in 1863 at the age of eleven. Later that summer, he earned the nickname "The Drummer Boy of Chickamauga."[60]

He claimed that he did not like to stand and be shot at without the ability to fire back, so the men in his unit sawed down the stock of a musket for "Little Johnny" Clem to carry. During the defense of Horseshoe Ridge at Chickamauga, his regiment was surrounded by Confederate forces. They were ordered to retreat, but Clem got lost in the chaos. Not wanting to be captured by the enemy, Clem ran like a "scared rabbit" until he reached a clump of woods. There, he caught his breath, but as he exited the woods, he bumped into a group of Confederate soldiers.

A Confederate colonel rode to him on horseback. "My, but you are a little fellow to be in this business," said the colonel. "But war is war, and I think the best thing a mite of a chap like you can do is to drop that gun."

Instead, Clem shouldered his sawed-off musket and shot the Confederate in the chest. The colonel tumbled from his horse, and the other Confederates opened fire at Johnny Clem, who fell face down and pretended to be dead. Four hours later, the battle was over. Clem stood up, brushed himself off, and discovered three bullet holes in his forage cap.[61] He then returned to the Union line, happy to be alive.

Now, depending on which report you read, the Confederate colonel was either killed outright or survived his wound and eventually recovered. You can tell the story any way you'd like, but despite the conflicting reports, it sounds like he survived. According to *The New York Times*, after the war, John Clem learned about the colonel and wrote him a letter. "When I heard that I had not killed that Confederate officer, it was the best news I ever got,"[62] Clem said years later.

After the Battle of Chickamauga, John Clem was promoted to sergeant and became the youngest soldier to officially hold that rank. Clem fought through the remainder of the war and was wounded twice.

John Clem was only eighteen years old when Ulysses S. Grant became president in 1869. Somehow, he managed to get a personal audience with Grant to ask for a favor. Clem wanted to become an officer in the United States Army and applied to West Point but failed the entrance exam.

"Mr. President," Clem said, "I wish to ask you for an order admitting me to West Point."

"But why not take the examinations?" Grant replied.

"I did, Mr. President, but I failed to pass."

"That was unfortunate," Grant said. "How was that?"

"Why, Mr. President, you see I was in the war, and while I was there, these other boys of my age were in school."

"You were in the war?" I wonder what was going through Grant's head as he talked to this kid. John Clem was only eighteen, and the war had ended four years earlier.

"Yes, Mr. President. I was in the war four years."[63] Clem went on to share some of his war experiences with the president, who was deeply impressed with the young man. Seizing his chance, Clem then asked again for a letter of admittance to West Point.

"I can beat that scheme," Grant replied. "And you won't have to go to West Point at all. I will make you a second lieutenant of regulars right now."[64]

Grant wrote a letter and instructed Clem to deliver it to the secretary of war with the instructions to commission Clem as a second lieutenant in the United States Army. Grant thought the kid had learned more on the battlefield than he would in the classroom.

Clem married and then eventually remarried after his first wife passed away. His second wife was the daughter of a Confederate veteran, and Clem used to joke that this made him the most "united American."

At the time of the reunion in 1913, Colonel Clem was still in active service in the regular army. He was promoted to major general on his retirement two years later.

John Clem was only eleven at the time of the Battle of Gettysburg and wasn't present during the fight. Henry Parker of the 137th Pennsylvania Infantry claimed to be the youngest man to carry a rifle in the Battle of Gettysburg. He attended the reunion with his discharge papers to support his statement. He was thirteen years old in 1863, which made him sixty-three in 1913. He made it through the Gettysburg campaign without a scratch but claimed to have been wounded three times in the Battle of Petersburg and that all three shots hit him at the same time.[65]

But there could be an even younger veteran. George McGowan was fifty-eight years old in 1913, which meant he was only eight at the Battle of Gettysburg. He claimed to have fought all through the war. While at the reunion, he was introduced to General Felix Robertson of Texas, the youngest brigadier general in the Confederate army. Robertson looked at McGowan and assumed he was the son of one of the veterans. "No, Sir," McGowan said. "I was at Malvern Hill, and Tatum, the Wilderness, and many other battles throughout the war."

Robertson didn't argue and said, "I beg your pardon. Let's shake, comrade."

Just a quick side note: I think "Tatum" was shorthand for the Battle of Antietam, which took place on September 17, 1862. It was the single bloodiest day in American history, with more than twenty-two thousand soldiers killed, wounded, or missing in just one day.

Dan Doherty wasn't the oldest vet, nor was he the youngest, but he did have the distinction of traveling the farthest to the reunion. Doherty lived in Alaska, and it was estimated that he had traveled approximately five thousand miles to reach Gettysburg.[66]

The Grand Reunion was everything the name implied. It was a friendly mingling of fifty thousand veterans of the Confederate and Union armies, a renewal of old acquaintances, the formation of new friendships, and reminiscing about the days long past when those who now embraced as comrades had once done their best to kill each other. These informal gatherings mattered most to the elderly veterans. These men had demonstrated their bravery fifty years earlier, and they had little interest in the governors, congressmen, and other distinguished citizens who traveled from every corner of the country to speak at the reunion.

Some veterans came to Gettysburg to reunite with old comrades, but others arrived with a mission. One such man was Henry M. Fitzgerald, a Union veteran from Chicago, who went straight to the Confederate camp in search of the tents belonging to the Twentieth North Carolina Infantry.

Fitzgerald had a deep connection to the first day's battle of July 1, 1863, when the Twentieth North Carolina played a pivotal role in the attack on Oak Hill. That day, Union forces held their ground until the early afternoon, when Confederate troops launched a fierce assault, eventually forcing them to retreat through the streets of Gettysburg. By nightfall, Lee's army had gained the advantage but at a steep cost to both sides. Today, Oak Hill is home to the Eternal Light Peace Memorial, but in 1863 it was the site of some of the fiercest fighting on the battle's first day.

During the chaotic struggle, the Twentieth North Carolina's regimental flag became the prize of an intense skirmish. Colonel Charles Wheelock of the Ninety-Seventh New York Infantry managed to seize the banner and, in a bold display, waved it high to taunt the North Carolinians. His antics caught the attention of General Henry Baxter, who ordered him to send the flag to the rear. Wheelock, however, refused. Instead, he dramatically cut the flag from its staff with his sword and continued to wave it in defiance. The provocation was too much—the Confederate soldiers opened fire. The man standing beside Wheelock dropped dead, a bullet straight through his skull. Suddenly realizing his bravado had made him a prime target, Wheelock thought better of his boastful show and retreated to safety.

But the flag's story wasn't over, and here is where it gets really interesting. As the battle raged, Wheelock passed the captured banner to a private in the Ninety-Seventh New York. A Confederate soldier, determined to reclaim it, locked eyes with the man now carrying the flag. Amid the gunfire and chaos, he aimed his rifle and demanded the return of his regiment's colors. The Union private refused. The Confederate lunged, grabbing hold of the flag, and the two men wrestled violently, each refusing to let go. The flag was ripped in two during the struggle, torn from corner to corner.

As the battle intensified, both men scrambled away—each clutching half of the flag as they rejoined their respective lines. Later, when the Confederate soldier examined his prize, he counted twenty-seven bullet holes in his half. The flag had been brand new that morning—by day's end, it had already been baptized in blood and battle.

Fifty years later, Henry M. Fitzgerald entered the Confederate camp looking for someone from the Twentieth North Carolina. Captain John D. Irvin's ear perked up when he heard the call. Irvin later wrote, "I introduced myself to him, and after a while, he asked me if we lost our flag the first day. I told him we lost it but later recaptured our half of it."[67] Irvin then informed Fitzgerald that he was the color bearer for the Twentieth North Carolina.

"The color bearer!" Fitzgerald said. "That's better than I hoped for."[68] With a sly smile, he asked, "Did you ever wonder what had become of the missing half of your regiment's flag, Captain?"

"Why, that's the puzzle of the regiment's history," responded Irvin. "We lost the flag in the morning of the first day's fighting, and in the afternoon, we got back the staff and half of the colors, with twenty-seven bullet holes in it. But in the fight for possession, some Yank got hold of the flag and tore it in two. We've never known what became of it."

"The other half is at my home in Chicago," answered Fitzgerald, "and as soon as I get home, I'm going to return it to you."[69] He said, "I wanted to return it to some member of your regiment but hardly hoped to give it back to the very man I took it from."

Imagine their surprise when they realized they had been the two soldiers wrestling over that very flag in the midst of battle—neither knowing, for fifty years, what had become of the other or the missing half. But instead of resuming their fight, they did something much better. The two old veterans sat together, sharing stories and laughing at the strange twist of fate that had reunited them. What had once been a symbol of division was now a token of reconciliation—returned not in war but in friendship.

Time had done more than heal old wounds; it had turned former enemies into comrades bound by history.

Many old soldiers who attended the Grand Reunion traveled to Gettysburg by train, sitting upright inside the passenger cars. Unfortunately, some returned home lying down inside wooden caskets in the freight car.

In 1863, these veterans were young men who stood tall and moved with all the ease of youth. They were seasoned soldiers who could make thirty-five miles a day on a forced march in the broiling sun while carrying their haversack, canteen, dog tent, rifle, and ammunition. In 1913, those same men were back on the battlefield again, but this time they moved with shaky steps and stooped shoulders. Fifty years earlier, they had barely felt the effects of the sun, but now that same sun punished their old bodies.

On June 30, Augustus Brown from Livermore Falls, Maine, became the first casualty of the Grand Reunion. Brown dropped from exhaustion within an hour of arriving by train from New England. He was taken to one of the field hospitals and died soon after. His body was placed in a coffin and shipped back home. He was seventy-one years old.[70]

John Reynolds from Portchester, New York, dropped dead while walking across the field in the Great Camp. An ambulance was summoned, but it arrived too late. He was sixty-nine years old. Later that same day, Otto Stam from Almond, New York, was found dead in his tent.[71] He was seventy-five years old.

These men fought and survived the Battle of Gettysburg, only to die on that same field fifty years later.

The Confederate army retreated on July 4, 1863, leaving behind close to forty thousand dead and wounded men. An unknown soldier from New Jersey wrote this account of what the battlefield looked like on that day:

> *Upon the open fields, like sheaves bound by the reaper, in crevices of the rocks, behind fences, trees, and buildings; in thickets, where they had crept for safety only to die in agony; by stream or wall or hedge, wherever the battle had raged, or their waking steps could carry them, lay the dead. Some, with faces bloated and blackened beyond recognition, lay with glassy eyes staring up at the blazing summer sun; others, with faces*

> *downward and clenched hands filled with grass or earth, which told of the agony of the last moments. Here a headless trunk, there a severed limb; in all the grotesque positions that unbearable pain and intense suffering contorts the human form, they lay . . . and over all, hugging the earth like a fog, poisoning every breath, the pestilential stench of decaying humanity.*[72]

The burial parties got to work and did what they could to inter the bodies as quickly as possible for sanitary reasons. For the sake of time, Confederate and Union bodies were buried where they fell and sometimes occupied the same graves. Burial trenches were dug, and often the hole was only ten inches deep, leaving the feet and heads partially exposed—a more permanent solution was needed quickly.

A seventeen-acre field was acquired beside the Evergreen Cemetery, and the Soldiers' National Cemetery was established. Thirty-five hundred bodies were relocated to the new cemetery, and many of the dead were listed as unknown.

On November 19, 1863, the Soldiers' National Cemetery was dedicated. Edward Everett was the keynote speaker, delivering a two-hour speech to fifteen thousand people. Afterward, President Abraham Lincoln gave "a few appropriate remarks." Lincoln's speech was only ten sentences long, took two minutes to deliver, and was met by very mixed reviews. A reporter from *The Chicago Times* wrote, "The cheek of every American must tingle with shame as he reads the filly, flat, and dishwatery utterances of a man who has to be pointed out to intelligent foreigners as the President of the United States."[73]

However, Edward Everett, whose two-hour speech preceded Lincoln's, was quite impressed. The day after the dedication, he wrote the president, "Permit me also to express my great admiration of the thoughts expressed by you, with such eloquent sensibility and appropriateness, at the consecration of the Cemetery. I should be glad, if I could flatter myself, that I came as near to the central idea of the occasion in two hours as you did in two minutes."[74]

Lincoln's speech, which is now known as the Gettysburg Address, is regarded as one of the greatest speeches in American history:

> *Four score and seven years ago, our fathers brought forth on this continent a new nation, conceived in Liberty and dedicated to the*

*proposition that all men are created equal. Now we are engaged in a great civil war, testing whether that nation, or any nation so conceived and so dedicated, can long endure. We are met on a great battle-field of that war. We have come to dedicate a portion of that field, as a final resting place for those who here gave their lives that that nation might live. It is altogether fitting and proper that we should do this. But, in a larger sense, we can not dedicate—we can not consecrate—we can not hallow—this ground. The brave men, living and dead, who struggled here, have consecrated it, far above our poor power to add or detract. The world will little note, nor long remember what we say here, but it can never forget what they did here. It is for us the living, rather, to be dedicated here to the unfinished work which they who fought here have thus far so nobly advanced. It is rather for us to be here dedicated to the great task remaining before us—that from these honored dead we take increased devotion to that cause for which they gave the last full measure of devotion—that we here highly resolve that these dead shall not have died in vain—that this nation, under God, shall have a new birth of freedom—and that government of the people, by the people, for the people, shall not perish from the earth.*

The president dedicated the cemetery to the fallen Union soldiers, while the Confederate dead lay forgotten in shallow graves on the battle-field. They had been abandoned by their countrymen when General Lee ordered the retreat back to Virginia and were initially ignored by the Union army. Since the Northern army was in charge of the field, the Union dead took priority over the Southern dead. Eventually, the dead Confederates were buried in shallow trenches across the battlefield, close to where they fell.

For nine long years, the Confederate dead lay in the fields of Gettysburg. Many of these fields were still actively farmed, meaning horses and plows would often till the ground and disturb the bodies. The local farmers were so hampered by the dead Confederates in their fields that they threatened to gather the bones and grind them into fertilizer.[75]

When word finally reached the South that their fallen heroes lay neglected in distant fields, an association was formed with a singular, solemn purpose—to bring them home. Funds were raised, and laborers were sent to unearth the dead, sifting through the soil in search of names and identities long lost to time. But after nine years beneath the shallow soil, little remained. Most were impossible to recognize, reduced to a simple, heartbreaking label: "unknown." For three long years, the work continued. By the end, 3,320 soldiers made the final journey south. The bones of 2,935 were laid to rest in Richmond, Virginia, at Hollywood Cemetery, in a quiet corner now called "Gettysburg Hill."

Yet not all were found. Some still remain beneath the battlefield, their resting places undiscovered, their stories unfinished. Even into the twentieth century, bones continued to surface from the soil—mute reminders of the cost of war. Historians believe that anywhere from a few dozen to several hundred Confederate soldiers still lie beneath the fields of Gettysburg. So when you walk those grounds, remember—you tread on sacred earth.

When the veterans returned in 1913, they stepped onto a battlefield that still bore the scars of their suffering. Time had softened the landscape but not their memories. Forty thousand men had fallen there, and for those who survived, every step was a reminder of a brother, a father, a son who had not.

One of the most visited places during the Grand Reunion was the Soldiers' National Cemetery, where 3,664 graves stand in solemn rows, both marked and unmarked. From its ridge, the cemetery overlooked the vast Great Camp, as if watching over the men who once fought and bled there. Each headstone bore a tribute to two flags: the Stars and Stripes and the banner of Pennsylvania.

At dawn, frail and weathered old soldiers rose on aching limbs, leaning on canes and crutches, and made their way up the hill. Some stood in silence. Others traced the names on the stones with trembling hands. From sunrise to sunset, they lingered, searching for the final resting place of lost comrades. It was more than a visit. It was a pilgrimage of grief, memory, and love.

Walter H. Blake shares a sad story in his book *Hand Grips*. While walking through the cemetery, he encountered an old Union soldier standing over a grave. The soldier knelt, with tears in his eyes, as he brushed some soil off a tombstone with the name "William Henry Scott" chiseled into it. The old soldier said to Blake:

> *"After the first days fighting, I was badly wounded, and they carried me away to a hospital. Next to me was a young Southerner—a native of Georgia—one of Longstreet's boys. We two chummed up as we lay in that hospital during the days that followed the battle, and he told me his name was William Henry Scott. He told me of his plantation down south, and I told him about my home close to New York. We liked each other, and lying on those two cots side by side we grew to love each other, and we promised when each got better that we'd come and visit one another. Then we parted. I went home, and he stayed behind to get well, as I thought. But he never came to see me, and try as I would, I couldn't get in touch with him. I waited, and waited trying often to get news about him, but I waited, always hoping, believing that I'd see him, and then I came down here, and I hoped I'd see him here. And here he is—here he is." Then the veteran pointed at the tombstone, hung his head, and cried.*[76]

This heartbreaking story resonates with me, and I'd like to believe it is true. Unfortunately, no one named "William Henry Scott" is buried in the Soldiers' National Cemetery in Gettysburg or the adjacent Evergreen Cemetery. Confederate soldiers were not permitted to be buried in the National Cemetery, although it is believed that a few may have been placed in unknown graves by mistake. There were two Confederates buried in the Evergreen Cemetery, but they were later reinterred into unmarked graves to prevent vandalism, and their names were lost to time.

Still, this doesn't necessarily mean the story is false. Many of the stories recorded by Walter Blake can be verified through newspapers and other sources, making it unlikely that he would fabricate such a sentimental tale when so many accurate accounts were readily available. So why would he invent this one? Here's my hypothesis (and I reserve the right to grow out of this opinion): I think Walter Blake may have witnessed this event first-hand, but he may not have had a notepad to write down the details. Then, when he had time to put pen to paper, he may have misremembered some of the information, like the name. William Henry Scott is a collection of three common names and may have been an unintended amalgamation. But who knows for sure? I'll let you decide for yourself as to whether this story is true.

The cemetery wasn't the only place where old soldiers gathered to mourn. One of the most visited memorials was the equestrian statue of General John F. Reynolds, standing in solemn silence over the Gettysburg landscape. Born in Lancaster, Pennsylvania, in 1820, Reynolds was a skilled officer and one of the most beloved figures in the Union army. His death came just an hour into the battle when he was struck down at McPherson's Ridge while leading from the front.

Even as the fighting still raged, the *National Republican* newspaper published an obituary on July 2, 1863, mourning Reynolds's loss with reverence: "He was heroically brave and generous, cool in action, alert in movement, and quick in perception. He was thoroughly manly and noble—among the finest of soldierly characters developed by the war. Leading the advance, he was yesterday struck down, mortally wounded. He died as he would have chosen to die, battling for his country's unity and life. The war has not had a nobler victim."[77]

The following day, the same paper described his death in vivid, heartbreaking detail:

> *While personally, gallantly leading the first bayonet charge . . . General John F. Reynolds received a wound which, in less than an hour's time, resulted in death. The missile which robbed us of one of the brightest ornaments of our army, as well as one of the bravest and most useful members, was the sharp-pointed Minnie rifle ball, it having entered the back of his neck, coming out at the temple.*
>
> *Thus died the gallant soldier, bravely up-holding the honor of his country, upon the soil of his native State, and within less than fifty miles of his own beloved home.*[78]

Reynolds was admired not just for his tactical skill but also for his character. He led from the front, shared the burdens of war with his men, and treated them with dignity. To many, he embodied the ideal Union officer. His loss was not just a strategic blow—it was deeply personal.

At the 1913 Grand Reunion, a quiet pilgrimage unfolded each day at his statue. Veterans came not for the ceremony but for remembrance. They stood in silence, laid wildflowers gathered from nearby fields, and sometimes bowed their heads. By the end of the week, the statue's base was buried beneath fading blooms. Those who visited left with tears in their eyes, still mourning the general who had earned the deep love and loyalty of his men.

Hugh Mellen of Fairport, New York, returned to Gettysburg for the first time since the battle. At seventy-four years old and crippled from his wounds, he was determined to see the Gettysburg Lincoln Train Station—the same station where President Lincoln had arrived before delivering the Gettysburg Address. Due to his age and injuries, Mellen struggled to reach the second floor, but with the help of two friends, he managed to make the climb. "This is the most interesting place in the world to me,"[79] Hugh Mellen said, and then he embarked on his tale:

> *I was wounded in the arm early in the morning of July 1st and was forced to leave my regiment, the One Hundred and Forty-seventh New York. I was taken to a temporary hospital on the second floor of this building. This is the very spot. From this very window, several hours afterwards, I should think it was about 10 o'clock, I saw General Reynolds shot from his horse. The disaster occurred on the Chambersburg Pike about 100 yards from this station.*
>
> *Then the Union force fell back, and the Rebels took possession of the town. For two days, I was a prisoner in this station, and then, learning that I could walk, I was marched at the point of a bayonet to the courthouse and imprisoned there. However, the next day the Confederates retreated, and I was free again.*
>
> *I have yearned for years to get back to this spot, but was unable to do so before today. All these later years, I have feared that the old station had been demolished, so you may know how glad I was when I saw the familiar building upon my arrival.*[80]

This is a compelling story, but it should be taken with a grain of salt. While researching this book, I stood at the spot where Reynolds was killed and then went to the Gettysburg train station to look out from the second-story window—just as Hugh Mellen claimed to have done. Today, modern buildings obstruct much of the view, and even if those weren't there in 1863, several ridgelines still interrupt a clear line of sight. The distance between the station and McPherson's Ridge is also considerable. If Mellen truly did see Reynolds fall, the general would have appeared no larger than a speck on the horizon—far too small to be identified with certainty. I don't doubt the core of Mellen's memory, but it seems more likely he saw someone else get shot off a horse during the battle and later assumed it was Reynolds once he heard the news.

I can't say this with absolute certainty, but if you ever visit Gettysburg, I encourage you to stand at both spots and decide for yourself whether Hugh Mellen truly saw General Reynolds fall—or if he may have witnessed someone else's tragic end.

On June 30, 1913, the vets were served three square meals. Oatmeal and milk, fried ham, boiled potatoes, bread, butter, and endless cups of coffee for breakfast. "Dinner" was the biggest meal of the day and was served from noon to 1:30 p.m. Today, we would call that lunch, and it consisted of roast beef with gravy, mashed potatoes, peas, tapioca pudding, bread, and all of the coffee and iced tea they could drink. Supper was served from 5:30 p.m. to 7:00 p.m.; today, we call that dinner. This meal consisted of pork and beans, fried potatoes, cucumbers, pickles, and even more coffee.[81]

As the sun melted into the horizon and the heavy heat of the day began to ease, the Great Camp settled into a quiet hum of evening activity. The men who had spent the day wandering the battlefield trickled back, dusty and tired, but eager to share stories of where they'd been and what they'd seen. Campfires flickered to life at the ends of the company streets, sending tendrils of smoke curling into the night sky.

Then came the music. A fife's high, clear notes cut through the evening hush, soon joined by the steady beat of a drum, the mournful drawl of a harmonica, and the lively twang of banjos and guitars. The songs carried across the camp—old, familiar tunes that had once lifted spirits on long marches or in the quiet between battles. The musicians played until one by one, the old soldiers let out tired sighs, tipped their hats, and made their way to their tents, leaving only the most stubborn among them to carry on.

The day had started in a whirlwind of confusion. Too many men, too few tents—an overwhelming tide of veterans surging into the camp. But as the sun crossed the sky, order found its way into the chaos. The thick humidity and smothering heat had driven some away, but those who endured found good company and an easy camaraderie that only shared hardship can forge.

For many, stepping back onto the battlefield brought an odd kind of comfort. The war itself had long since faded into history, but surrounded by those who had lived it, the memories felt understood in a way that no one back home could truly grasp. Sleep didn't come quickly. A lack of cots kept some awake; for others, it was the sheer joy of rediscovering an old friend or someone they hadn't seen in fifty years. Around the fires, they laughed, reminisced, and let time slip away.

As the night deepened, the murmured voices grew softer, giving way to the steady rise and fall of snoring, although conversation never entirely faded. And when the first pale light of dawn crept over the horizon, some old soldiers were still there, leaning in close to the last glowing embers, speaking in low voices, unwilling to let go of the past.

5

# July 1—Tuesday

The sun had yet to break over the horizon, and the trees stood in silhouette against the faint glow of the approaching dawn. But even in the dim light, movement could be seen—shadows shifting through the tall grass, the murmur of voices carrying in the pre-dawn hush.

Most of the old soldiers were back in their cots, snoring, but a group of old Confederates was already on the march, retracing familiar ground, searching for the spot where, half a century before, they had stood in formation. Their boots crunched softly over the earth as they made their way to Spangler's Woods, the very ground where Pickett's Charge had gathered for its doomed assault. And when they finally reached it, one of them threw back his head and let loose the Rebel Yell.

The sound cut through the early morning silence like a knife, raw and piercing. Then another joined in, and another, until the whole company was crying out, voices rough with age but still carrying the fire of youth. The yell rose and swelled, echoing across the empty fields, loud enough to be heard all the way back at the Great Camp, where some men sat up in their tents, startled awake by a sound they had not heard in fifty years.

"What in thunder is that?" demanded a startled Union veteran as he rolled off his cot.[1] The Rebel Yell had been psychologically terrifying during the war, and hearing it again after an absence of so many years brought it all right back. He rubbed his eyes, drew aside the tent flaps, and stared into the darkness.

And as if answering the call of the past, a fife and drum were found. The first few notes of "Dixie" rang out, and, without hesitation, the veterans took up the song. Their voices wove together, cracked and weathered but full of pride, filling the battlefield with a melody that had once marched them into war. The sun, just peeking above the trees, cast long golden rays across the fields, lighting up the men as they sang—a moment of brotherhood and history come alive once more:

I wish I was in the land of cotton,
Old times there are not forgotten;
Look away! Look away! Look away! Dixie Land.
In Dixie's Land, where I was born in,
Early on one frosty mornin',
Look away! Look away! Look away! Dixie Land.

I wish I was in Dixie, Hooray! Hooray!
In Dixie's Land I'll take my stand
to live and die in Dixie.
Away, away, away down south in Dixie.
Away, away, away down south in Dixie.

As the final notes of "Dixie" faded into the warm morning air, the echoes of the past seemed to hang there for just a moment longer. But the battlefield was no longer a place of division, and as the old Confederates returned to camp, a new sound rose to meet them.

From the tents of the Great Camp, the Boys in Blue stirred, rubbing sleep from their eyes and stretching weary limbs. And then, with a cheer, they called out to their former foes—not in anger, not in rivalry, but in camaraderie. The years had washed away the bitterness, leaving only the shared understanding of men who had survived what so many had not.

As the Confederates drew nearer, the deep boom of reveille guns shattered the morning's stillness. The camp sprang to life, stirring like a mighty beast awakened from slumber. At headquarters, an enormous American flag was hoisted to the top of the pole, snapping in the breeze as the first rays of sunlight caught its red, white, and blue.

Then, clear and strong, the first strains of "The Star-Spangled Banner" rang through the air. Men rose from their tents one by one, shaking off the last remnants of sleep. Voices joined in, some deep and steady, others cracked with age but full of pride. Johnnies and Yankees sang together, their voices swelling into a mighty chorus that carried across the camp and beyond:

O say, can you see,
By the dawn's early light.
What so proudly we hailed
At the twilight's last gleaming?
Whose broad stripes and bright stars,
Through the perilous fight.
O'er the ramparts we watched,
Were so gallantly streaming?
And the rockets' red glare,
The bombs bursting in air,
Gave proof through the night,
That our flag was still there.
O say, does that star-spangled banner yet wave,
O'er the land of the free and the home of the brave.

It was reported that "practically the entire camp, Johnnies as well as Yankees, were lustily singing the hymn."[2] And what a way to start the day—beneath the rising sun, on the fields where they had once fought, now standing together in song.

Soon after, the kitchen fires roared to life, sending rich, mouthwatering smells drifting across the Great Camp. Fresh bread, sizzling bacon, and the earthy aroma of coffee, the very lifeblood of the old soldiers. By 6:30 a.m., most of the veterans were already lined up, tin plates in hand, waiting eagerly for their morning meal. The kitchen attendants ladled out generous portions, though now and then a grumble would rise from the ranks if a plate looked too lean. A glance at a veteran's hardened expression was usually enough to convince the servers to add just a little more.

Breakfast on July 1 was nothing if not practical, designed to keep a man regular and ready for the day ahead. The spread included stewed prunes, boiled rice, fried liver, bacon, fresh bread with butter, and, of course, gallons of coffee.[3]

Each man was given a pint, but the veterans worked their charms to get a little more.

"Now, sonny, I always was a great hand at coffee, and I want you to fill that up to the little rim there."

Sometimes the server would protest, claiming his pitcher was running low, but the old soldiers knew better. They'd seen those tricks before. There was always more coffee somewhere.

"Never mind, sonny, there's plenty more where that came from. I earned that coffee right here on this ground 50 years ago today."[4]

These comments never failed to produce the desired effect.

With breakfast finished and the sun climbing higher in the sky, the veterans were left to their own devices. They had the morning to do as they pleased: roam the fields, swap stories, or sit in the shade with another cup of coffee until the afternoon, when the formal ceremonies would begin inside the Great Tent.

Many veterans slipped back into their old habits as they adapted to camp life. Throughout the Civil War, both sides had mocking nicknames for each other. The origins of these nicknames are unknown, but both sides consistently used them during the conflict. If you hailed from the North, it was common to refer to Confederates as "Johnnies" or "Johnny Reb," with "Reb" short for Rebel. Conversely, if you were a Confederate, you'd typically refer to Northerners as "Billies," "Yank," or "Billy Yank," with "Yank" short for Yankee. And so, in 1913, if you donned blue, you were called "Billy Yank," while those in gray were known as "Johnny Reb."

During the day, William G. Mitchell, a veteran from New York City, stumbled on another habit from wartime. He encountered a Confederate and asked, "Got any 'baccy, Johnny?"

Without missing a beat, the old Confederate replied, "Got any coffee, Billy?"

The quick response caught William Mitchell off guard. "No, but I'll get you some." Right then and there, Mitchell hatched a plan. He went into town and bought dozens of little packages of coffee beans. On his way back to camp, he sought out anyone with a gray uniform and asked, "Hey Johnny, got any 'baccy?"

"Got any coffee?"

Mitchell reached into his pocket and pulled out a package of coffee. The Confederate was a bit surprised but clearly amused. An exchange took place, and Mitchell walked away with a big smile and a black pigtail twist of tobacco. When Mitchell returned to the New York camp, he was loaded down with fine Southern tobacco to share with his friends.[5]

During the war, it was common for the Yanks, who had an abundance of coffee but no tobacco, to trade with the Johnnies, who had no coffee but a surplus of tobacco.

A similar story occurred between William Hotchkiss of Alabama and J. D. Williams of Pennsylvania. Both men were on picket duty on different sides when they encountered each other during the Battle of Petersburg. A trade ensued after the standard questions: "Got any 'baccy?" followed by "Got any coffee?" Williams handed over some coffee beans, but the fighting started back up before the transaction could be completed, and both men hurried back to their own lines.

Fifty years later, at the Grand Reunion, Hotchkiss sought out Williams until he found him. "Do you remember that trade at the Petersburg spring?"

Williams nodded in remembrance. "Well, I didn't give you enough tobacco that time," Hotchkiss said. "Here it is."[6]

Throughout the morning, the former enemy armies met on the battlefield. Instead of firing muskets and stabbing bayonets into one another, they met with handshakes and smiles. *The Evening World* newspaper described it like this:

> *They met laughing through their lips, out of eyes centered along wrinkles, but smiling, meeting with short steps. "Hello, Johnny. Been going over your route down?"*
>
> *"Hello, Yank. What command was you in?"*
>
> *"Ninth New Jersey."*
>
> *"Why, you cussed old fool, wonder if you was the one that got me?"*
>
> *"Don't know, Johnny, but if I was, I hope you got my ear. Let's go see where we were first hurt and find out if we were near together."*[7]

Arm in arm, they would go off exploring the battlefield.

Helen Longstreet spent the night sleeping on a pile of straw, but she didn't allow this minor inconvenience to slow her down. She had a job to do. The *New York Tribune* called her "as fresh and enthusiastic as if she had stepped from a Fifth Avenue hotel." She returned to the Great Camp and had breakfast with the veterans. This was the perfect time to rub elbows with the old soldiers and hear their stories.

She sat next to an old Confederate and asked about his missing leg. "It's moldering up on Emmitsburg Road," he said. "The gloomiest hour of my life was not the fight or the surrender; it was the black night which followed Pickett's Charge. I always knew after that defeat was only a question of time, and I was glad when the useless bloodshed was over."

Helen pointed at the enormous American flag flying above camp and said, "Oh, isn't it glorious! How could you look on the old flag and know its meaning and fire on it?"

The old Confederate said, "I didn't stop to think so much about what we were fighting about. My land and my people called to me. They were in trouble. It was about the same as if it had been my mother. Right or wrong, I would rush to her rescue." He then pointed to Old Glory and said, "That is my flag, the flag of my fathers, the flag of my country, and my children's flag forever."[8]

Helen thanked the old man for his time and moved on. The day was already heating up, and she wanted to head down to the Rogers House before the temperature peaked. She had promised to call on Dan Sickles; now was as good a time as any.

She walked down the Emmitsburg Road to the Rogers House and found Sickles holding court on the porch. An endless line of veterans waited on the lawn to shake Sickles's hand. Helen committed the scene to memory while waiting her turn. Here he was in the flesh, the living legend himself, in all the faded glory that time wears into a man. Sickles sat on a padded rocking chair with one pant leg pinned up around his missing leg, while a pair of crutches leaned against the house within easy reach. A good officer is always dressed for the occasion, regardless of the weather. He wore a shirt, tie, vest, and jacket with some military ribbons pinned on for good measure. On his head, he wore a felt officer's hat wrapped in gold cord, wireframe glasses, complete with an unlit cigar sticking out of his mouth. As they came up to introduce themselves, Sickles would chat with the old soldiers, shake their hands, and, if asked, sign an autograph.

Miss Wilmerding, Sickles's (*cough-cough*) housekeeper, was hovering nearby. She kept a watchful eye on the general to make sure the crowds weren't demanding too much of him. She recognized Helen Longstreet standing in line and introduced her once she reached the front. On hearing her name, Sickles straightened his back, and he reached for his crutches.

(*Top*) "This is where the Rogers House stood." The same location in 1913 and (*bottom*) in 2025. During the Grand Reunion, General Dan Sickles stayed in the house. The house is gone, but the trees remain. (*Top*) reproduced from the *Fiftieth Anniversary Report*; (*bottom*) photographed by the author, 2025.

With their aid, he rose on his one good leg and bowed deeply to Helen. He said, "What a splendid and noble enemy [your] husband was."

The two exchanged pleasantries, and Sickles settled back into his chair. But he didn't miss the opportunity to point out where he had lost his leg, just a short distance from where they talked. But that's a story we'll get to later . . .

Before the Grand Reunion, Helen and Sickles had exchanged correspondence. He knew she was reporting for the newspapers and needed a space to work from. Sickles had promised to set aside two tents for her use. However, when she arrived, Helen went to the Great Camp headquarters and was disappointed to find no arrangements had been made for her. She explained her difficulty finding lodging, but Sickles cut her short. "Didn't you get the telegram I sent you?"[9]

"Why, no," Helen replied.

"I sent you a telegram some days ago," General Sickles replied, "informing you that Carr's Brigade will have a tent for you the moment you reach Gettysburg. The tent is now at your disposal."[10]

Helen's face reddened. Her arrival had been anything but smooth. After a frustrating afternoon, she had slept on a pile of straw. If only she had headed to the Rogers House first, she could have avoided the entire ordeal.

Without waiting for a response, Sickles summoned an associate from Carr's Brigade, who escorted Helen to her quarters directly behind the house. Helen found the tent suitable for her needs and sent someone to gather her belongings. Once settled in, Helen spent the rest of the day interviewing old soldiers and the evening clacking away at her typewriter inside her new quarters.

The day was shaping up to be a hot one. By 10:00 a.m., it was already ninety-two degrees[11] and quite humid. By the time the formal program began, it was even hotter. "The pitiless glare of a sun that sent the mercury bubbling over the hundred mark and made clothes a burden and a bath only a delusion."[12]

The formal ceremonies kicked off on Monday at 2:00 p.m. inside the Great Tent. The weather was sweltering, but that didn't keep fifteen thousand people from cramming inside the giant circus tent. Every seat was occupied long before any of the speakers took the stage. The afternoon's theme was "Veterans Day," aimed at welcoming the old soldiers back to the battlefield. There were quite a few speeches lined up on the agenda.

A good speech is important because it is a powerful tool for communication, persuasion, education, and inspiration. It can shape opinions, drive change, and leave a lasting impact on individuals and communities. However, with all that said, we'll be deemphasizing the speeches at the Grand Reunion. I don't mean to imply that they weren't important; they certainly were, but I'm much more interested in what the veterans *did* at Gettysburg rather than what was *said* at Gettysburg. After all, actions speak louder than words.

If you're eager to read the speeches, I recommend the book *Fiftieth Anniversary Battle of Gettysburg Report of the Pennsylvania Commission.* This book meticulously records every speech given in the Great Tent during the Grand Reunion. While I won't showcase them all, I'll share a few highlights to give you a taste of the festivities.

Colonel James M. Schoonmaker presided over a packed tent and received a welcome so fervent that his face flushed with pleasure. As chairman of the Pennsylvania Commission, much of the Grand Reunion's organization was owed to his tireless efforts, and the veterans were letting their appreciation be known.

Around one thousand Confederate veterans were in attendance, and although those in blue far outnumbered the men in gray, what they lacked in numbers they made up for in lung power.[13] Secretary of War Lindley M. Garrison and Governor John Tener of Pennsylvania also took to the stage to welcome the old soldiers back to Gettysburg.

Afterward, Alfred Beers, the head of the Grand Army of the Republic (GAR), spoke to the crowd:

> *The great bulk of men who served on either side cherished no personal animosity toward each other. Each did his duty as he saw it. Today, the veterans of the North salute the veterans of the South with a feeling of joy in their hearts that the conflict is over and that they can meet each other as brothers. Let then, those who wore the blue and those who wore the gray devote every effort to swell the chorus of peace and goodwill.*[14]

When Governor Tener stood to speak, a voice shouted from the rear of the tent: "Texas says 'hoorah' for Tener!" Fifteen thousand men leapt to their feet and gave Tener three resounding cheers for all he did to make the Grand Reunion a success.[15]

Once the crowd settled down, Tener said, "We meet on this occasion to participate in a ceremony that stands unmatched in all recorded time; for nowhere in history have men who opposed each other in mighty battle thus come together in peaceful reunion fifty years thereafter."[16]

When Governor Tener finished his speech, General Bennet H. Young, commander in chief of the United Confederate Veterans (UCV), rose slowly and bowed to Tener. "In recognition of your splendid hospitality, we propose to give you that which no one else in the world can give—the Rebel Yell!" One thousand old Confederates leapt out of their seats, swung their hats around their heads, and let out a terrifying battle cry. The Rebel Yell was described as a fierce, high-pitched, banshee's wail meant to terrorize the enemy and rally the troops in battle.

Although the Rebel Yell raised the roof of the Great Tent, the old Confederates' lung power wasn't what it had been in 1863. However, the sound was still unmistakable and evoked memories of battles from the distant past. Many of the Union veterans cheered along, but it was also noted that the colored veterans in attendance looked on in silence and listened to the Rebel Yell without responding to it.[17]

The formal program on the first day lasted around two hours—just long enough to include some speeches by notable people, but not so long that it put the old soldiers to sleep. After General Young's speech, the band played "America," and the audience was dismissed.

The Great Tent was available before and after the formal exercises for mini-reunions and could be partitioned with canvas dividers to give each group its own section. However, many groups chose to relocate their reunions to different parts of the battlefield. The Great Tent could hold close to fifteen thousand people, but there was minimal air circulation. *The Washington Times* noted, "The big canvas auditorium shuts off all the air, and its interior is like an oven."[18] As a result, several veterans fainted during the speeches and were moved to hospital tents to recover.

Major Hess, who was in command of the field hospitals, was astonished that more veterans hadn't succumbed to the heat. "A surprisingly hard bunch of old men," Hess said. "We have something like 2,000 beds on the field, and the 400 beds in the central hospital here would have sufficed. However, this is promising to be a blazing afternoon, and you cannot tell what will happen. I think the old men are holding up marvelously well, considering their advanced age."[19]

On July 1, 1913, almost sixty thousand veterans were in camp. The Great Tent, where the official program was held, could accommodate fifteen thousand people. If fifteen thousand were inside the Great Tent listening to speeches, what were the other forty-five thousand veterans doing? They were engaged in informal meetings from one end of the battlefield to another.

But battlefield tours, studying monuments, and long speeches weren't the only activities available to the old soldiers. One of the significant points of interest was the Gettysburg Cyclorama.

In 1879, Paul Dominique Philippoteaux was commissioned to paint an immense, 360-degree cyclorama depicting Pickett's Charge. It is 377 feet long and 42 feet tall, and a wonder to behold. The painting showcases the moment when the Confederate forces pierced the Union lines at the

Inside the Great Tent. Reproduced from the *Fiftieth Anniversary Report.*

Bloody Angle. If you look only at that one section, it is easy to see how the Southern troops could prevail. But as you scan along the horizon, the fuller picture is revealed, and thousands of Union reinforcements are rushing to repulse the Confederates. The Southerners may have pierced the line, but the achievement was extremely short-lived. This event became known as the high-water mark of the Confederacy—the pinnacle moment when the battle had yet to be decided—and Philippoteaux captured that dramatic snapshot perfectly.

Philippoteaux spent several weeks at Gettysburg sketching the battlefield and interviewing General Winfield S. Hancock of the Union army, along with other survivors, to gather their perspectives on the battle. A team of artists under Philippoteaux completed the painting in a year and a half. They used almost five tons of oil-based paint to depict twenty thousand men and horses.

In total, four cycloramas of the Battle of Gettysburg were commissioned. Of the four original paintings, three were destroyed. One was cut into pieces and sewn into tents by Native Americans on a Shoshone Reservation. Another was lost in Sioux City, Iowa, when a tornado lifted the roof of the cyclorama building and shredded the painting. The last one was burned in a warehouse fire.

The popularity of cycloramas was short-lived. Once Thomas Edison introduced the moving picture, interest in cycloramas quickly waned. The surviving painting was left to rot in a shed for many years before someone remembered it and thought it might serve as a unique curiosity for the Grand Reunion.

In September 1912, construction started on a new cyclorama building on Baltimore Street in Gettysburg, directly across from the Soldiers' National Cemetery entrance. It was finished just in time to welcome visitors for the 1913 Grand Reunion. During that time, many veterans from both sides of the battle visited the cyclorama. Over the decades, the Gettysburg landscape had changed, and their memories had faded. Because of this, many veterans found it easier to identify their positions on the painting than on the battlefield itself. The painting was so lifelike that many war veterans wept on seeing it.

A reporter from the *Boston Evening Transcript* observed the audience's reaction to the cyclorama. One young man stared at the painting with wide-eyed wonderment. "I would have given almost anything in my power to have been there!" One of the old soldiers who heard the remark laughed. "Well, I was there, and I would have given a good deal not to be there!"[20]

One old soldier who was visiting the cyclorama with some friends pointed to a specific portion of the painting and said, "You see that puff of smoke. Just wait a minute till that clears away, and I'll show you just where I stood."

Helen Young attended the Grand Reunion alongside her father, Reverend Jesse Bowman Young, a former officer in the Pennsylvania Volunteers. Immersed in the historic event, she later wrote about her experiences, capturing a poignant moment between two former enemies standing before the cyclorama painting.

"What brigade were you in?" asked a Union veteran.

"Barksdale's," came the Southern reply.

A shiver must have run down the Union soldier's spine at the name. He extended his trembling hand. "I was in the Second Division, Third Corps, when you drove us back across the fields."

Fifty years earlier, Barksdale's Brigade had charged through the Peach Orchard on July 2, 1863, smashing into the men commanded by that crazy bastard, General Dan Sickles. William Barksdale was mortally wounded during the assault, but not before almost wiping out his opponent.

Half a century later, the Union man looked into the eyes of the foe who had once sent him into retreat. Time had softened the sharp edges of war. He tightened his grip and said, "Shake again."

Helen Young wrote,

> *They stood there silently for a moment, the heart of each too full for speech. Then the Confederates rallied. "We're all comrades now," he said. "When the invitation of the Governor of Pennsylvania to come to Gettysburg was given to our commander . . . and when that invitation was read, we rose in a body. You couldn't have held us down! We've come here to pledge our loyalty to our country, and we mean it!"*

Another Confederate chimed in. "Yes. We want to have good feelings everywhere, and we want you fellows to help us."

The veteran from Barksdale's division turned back to the painting, his voice thick with emotion. "I'm trying to locate my division. We were off here someplace. See, you can just see our men coming in on this side—and over here in these woods, I lost a cousin."

"Tears streamed down his cheeks as he spoke, and the eyes of all of us were wet,"[21] Helen Young recalled.

Many veterans who stood before the cyclorama left with their hearts full and their eyes damp, swept up in the echoes of a battle that had once divided them but now bound them together through their shared trauma.

After the Grand Reunion ended, organizers were unsure what to do with the cyclorama. The building that housed the massive painting had been intended as a temporary structure, but they decided to keep it open as long as there was interest. As it turns out, there was enough interest to keep the building open for another fifty years.

In 1962, the National Park Service built a more permanent home for the cyclorama in Zeigler's Grove, right on the battlefield. This new location was just a stone's throw from the very scene depicted in the painting. In 2003, that building was closed, and the painting was cut into long strips and removed. The cyclorama underwent a $13-million restoration, a meticulous project that took several years to complete. Once fully restored, the painting opened to the public at its current location in the Gettysburg National Military Park Museum and Visitor Center. With the relocation complete, the building in Zeigler's Grove was no longer needed and was demolished in 2013.

If you've never seen the cyclorama, I highly recommend taking the trip to check it out. It's magnificent! It's a bit like seeing the Grand Canyon. A photo doesn't do it justice; you must experience it in person. If you want to learn more about this incredible painting, I strongly recommend the coffee-table book by Chris Brenneman and Sue Boardman titled *The Gettysburg Cyclorama: The Turning Point of the Civil War on Canvas.*

The previous chapter examined the sharp response of the Vermont veterans to the sight of a Confederate flag being paraded through the Great Camp. Yet, at the reunion itself, the Vermont camp was pitched right beside the Confederate camp, ensuring frequent and sometimes unexpected encounters. One such meeting left behind a memorable story.

Colonel Henry Clark of the Thirteenth Vermont Regiment enjoyed spending time with the old Confederates. He admired their badges, especially those given by the Daughters of the Confederacy, and wanted to take one home as a souvenir. He invited a Johnny Reb into his tent, and they had a great time together. After discussing the war from top to bottom, Clark said, "Hey Johnny, I want to buy one of your badges as a souvenir."

The Confederate responded. "Oh, I can't sell them."

"Why not?"

"Because I can never obtain another."

"What if you lose one?" Clark said.

"Oh, if we lose one and can prove that we lost it, we can obtain another," the Confederate said.

"Lose it then, lose it!" Clark said.

The old Confederate was enjoying his time with the boys from Vermont and didn't know what to do. He wanted to keep his badge and give a gift to his newfound friend. After thinking it through, he made up his mind and walked away. As he did, the badge "slipped" off his shirt and fell to the ground. Once the Confederate was out of sight, Clark scrambled to retrieve the badge. He then slipped it into his pocket for safekeeping.

A little while later, a few old Confederates returned to the Vermont camp, with their eyes searching the ground. Clark asked what was going on and discovered that one of the vets had lost his badge. Imagine that.

"Where did you lose it?" Clark asked.

"Oh, around here,"[22] one of the Confederates said.

Clark generously helped the old Confederates look for the lost badge, but it was never found.

Throughout the week, various veteran organizations were assigned time slots to hold mini-reunions inside the Great Tent. But the Confederates weren't about to make that mistake. The previous day's official program had already taught them a hard lesson—the Great Tent was less of a refuge and more of a furnace. Some of the older soldiers had even collapsed from the stifling heat.

The Confederates may have lost the war, but they were no fools. So instead of roasting under the canvas, the veterans from Maryland, Virginia, West Virginia, Missouri, Texas, and the Carolinas gathered for a general reunion behind the mounted guns on Confederate Avenue. And it was a stroke of genius. The Great Camp offered no escape from the relentless sun; its only shade was inside the tents, which retained heat like an oven. But Confederate Avenue? That was lined with tall, leafy trees, their branches casting cool shadows and inviting a refreshing breeze. Before long, it became the go-to gathering place for anyone looking to swap stories without melting in the process.

Reporters counted at least four bottlenecked locations where itinerant preachers were addressing congregations of Confederates. So many veterans crowded around that it was almost impossible for vehicles to drive down the avenue with any speed.[23] Chaplain after chaplain stood up to address the crowd. Dozens were led to the "mourner's bench," and shouting, singing, and loud prayers were heard. It was a gospel revival right there on the battlefield.

"Oh, it's a good enough camp meeting," said an old Confederate. "But it ain't real life-like. There's no women here and no religion ain't complete without the women folk."

Absalom Amaker was a seventy-year-old North Carolina veteran leading one of the gospel services. He enlisted in the Confederate army at the age of eighteen and served for four years. During the war, he participated in fourteen major engagements, was wounded twice, and lost his leg. Soon after the war, he met his wife, became a Baptist minister, and earned his living by hobbling behind a plow horse and working on the farm.[24]

With the Confederate cannon behind him, he led the veterans in a rendition of the "Veteran's Last Song," with lyrics written by Civil War chaplain John Lozier. This song was a favorite among old soldiers and was often sung at veteran gatherings in the early twentieth century.

I am standing on the summit
Of a century of years
That has measured the life of our nation,
And I sabered down the mountain
A flood of blood and tears
That was shed for our country's salvation.
And I see a mighty legion, who for a nation's life
Would forfeit young manhood's fresh glory,
And I see a mighty legion who pitted in the strife

Now sleeping in garments stiff and gory.
And we're going soon to meet them in the bivouac of the soul,
As the shadows around us give warning,
And I want to see my comrades when the angels call the Roll,
All are ready for inspection in the morning.
We were boys when we enlisted, and these wrinkled brows were clear,
And our eyes where not dimmed in their vision,
And the frost that never melts had not fallen on our hair,
And our step had not lost its precision.
But the years have built their terraces on every comrade's brow,
And age made our weary limbs quiver,
And the frost was falling thick and we landed ever quick
To the camp that is over the river.
And we're going soon to meet them in the bivouac of the soul
As the shadows around us give warning,
And I want to see my comrades when the angels call the Roll,
All are ready for inspection in the morning.

Absalom Amaker added his own twist to the song by incorporating lyrics from the hymn "When the Roll Is Called Up Yonder," by James Black. The refrain is, "When the last roll is called up yonder, I'll be there." This was sung repeatedly until Amaker called a Union veteran to his side and said, "Let's change it to 'When the last roll is called up yonder, we'll be there.'" The revised song brought tears to many eyes.

When the song concluded, Reverend Amaker called on the assembled Confederates to kneel in prayer, fervently asking for the preservation of the re–United States of America.

Let that sink in.

Here stood a gathering of Confederate veterans—men who, half a century earlier, had taken up arms, shed blood, and watched their comrades fall in a desperate bid to break away from the Union. And yet, in this moment, with tear-streaked faces and trembling voices, they prayed for the very nation they had once fought to dissolve in blood.

Don't underestimate the significance of this transformation. Many of these aging soldiers had lived long enough to regret the choices of their youth and recognize the cost of war, not just in lives but in the soul of a nation. Perhaps they sought reconciliation in their twilight years, not only with their former foes but also with themselves. And perhaps their prayer was as much for personal redemption as for the country they had once tried to tear apart.

After the service, a reporter interviewed Amaker. "I went through the entire war wearing this old gray uniform," Amaker said. "And held prayer in my tent every night. At the close of the war, I became a minister of the Gospel."[25]

Absalom Amaker was a Baptist minister for fifty-seven years and was married to his sweetheart for sixty-seven years. They had three children and eight grandchildren. Amaker lived to see his eighty-eighth birthday and died in 1930.[26]

Farther down on Confederate Avenue, a man in blue approached a man in gray who was reading from one of the bronze tablets posted along the road. The marker was for Lane's Brigade, who participated in Pickett's Charge on July 3, 1863. After exchanging pleasantries, the Southerner pointed to the marker and said, "I was in Lane's brigade. When we got over the wall there, we marched as if on parade, but I said to my comrades, 'Boys, we aren't going to make it. It's too far across.' Most of the boys didn't think that way, though. Out of our whole company, only three came back after the charge, and I was the only one unscathed."

"I saw you charge," said the Union veteran. "I was in Sedgwick's corps in reserve and watched you come across."

The two old soldiers shook hands. "Aren't you glad you are here now?"

"Yes," agreed the Confederate.

"Now we can talk over and under the war," the old Union veteran said as they shook hands again.

Down the road a piece, the Maryland Confederates were relaxing under the shade trees on Confederate Avenue.

"My sakes, boys, but wasn't it hot here 50 years ago today?" Corporal Mettee from the Maryland camp said as he stood alongside the stone wall on Seminary Ridge.

"But it was every bit as hot, if not hotter, across yonder on Cemetery Ridge," said John Obernderfer of the Confederate Soldiers' Home at Pikesville.

Farther down on Confederate Avenue, several Confederate officers were dancing to the music of a fiddle player. This, in and of itself, is not that peculiar, but what makes this story interesting is the fiddler by the name of J. B. Boessinger from Richfield, Virginia. He was a member of the Forty-Fifth Infantry Regiment from North Carolina, and the extraordinary fact about him was that he had only one complete arm. He used his left arm to hold the fiddle and manipulate the strings, while gripping the bow beneath his knee to draw it across. This is a clever workaround for someone missing an arm. He played the old tunes—"The Arkansas Traveler," "Turkey in the Straw," and "The Mississippi Sawyer"—with such skill and vigor that it seemed impossible for his hearers to keep their feet still.[27]

More than once, a party of veterans coming from the train, dusty, worn out, and tired, would stop suddenly at the sound of his music, drop their suitcases in the middle of the road, and let their heels fly. Yee-haw! They would add whoops and the Rebel Yell to the music. It was said that at one point, the musical wizard had three brigadier generals dancing with the vim of men fifty years younger. At night, some Union soldiers strolled over to the Confederate camp and tried to shake a leg, but the Johnnies beat them every time.[28]

While many Confederate veterans enjoyed a pleasant time of fellowship under the shade trees on Confederate Avenue, not everyone shared their experience.

Miller H. Gary, a Union veteran from Paterson, New Jersey, had high hopes for the Grand Reunion but found only bitter disappointment. Arriving at the Great Camp on Sunday night, his enthusiasm quickly faded. By Tuesday morning, he was feeling unwell—sick from the heat, sick of the crowds, and sick to his stomach from the food. Exhausted and irritated, he left before the formal exercises in the Great Tent even began. He had nothing positive to say about his time in Gettysburg and wasted no time finding a reporter to voice his complaints.

According to *The Morning Call* newspaper, Gary had expected more comfortable accommodations, imagining wooden floors inside the tents and cozy beds. Instead, he slept on a grass floor and had to borrow a coat to pad his cot. His dissatisfaction extended to the food as well:

> *We were given a tin cup and a tin plate and had to go from one tent to another for our eatables, and then after getting enough on our plate and coffee in our cups, we had to go back to our own tents and sit on our beds as we ate . . . I simply couldn't eat the things they gave us, and there*

*were many others who also turned away disgusted, for some of the ham was no longer fresh.*[29]

Gary had looked forward to reuniting with old comrades and visiting tent to tent, but he felt too ill to enjoy it. Deciding he'd had enough, he returned home to Paterson on Tuesday afternoon, where he immediately called for a doctor and was confined to bed with a fever. His interview was published the next day, alarming families back home who feared their elderly fathers and grandfathers were suffering at the Grand Reunion.

Halmage Post was another Union vet from Paterson, New Jersey. He was forced to go back home on account of his poor physical condition. Once home, he picked up the newspaper and was surprised to see Miller Gary's interview. What he read bothered him so much that he called up a reporter to give his take on the Grand Reunion. His headline was "This Veteran Was Satisfied," with the subtitle "Says the Food at Gettysburg Was Great and There Were Blankets in Plenty." Post took the time to refute all of Gary's claims; he had a much more realistic expectation of what it would be like to camp on the old battlefield:

*Of course, we were not fed on song birds' tongues, and such other slender dishes, but what we received was good and substantial, plenty of it and no one to tell you when to stop. All our meals were served at the proper time and universal satisfaction, so far as I could ascertain, as expressed in every quarter. For instance, ham and eggs, mashed potatoes, rice, bread, and coffee don't make a poor breakfast and the manner in which it was cooked and served would have done credit to our first-class New York restaurants. At dinner, prime roast beef headed a long list of eatables and the gravy—why it simply flowed from the kitchen and was the finest I ever tasted.*

Post went on to talk about the tents:

*That other talk about being lodged uncomfortably and poorly housed was clap-trap. Naturally, I didn't have time to talk with the some fifty thousand "vets" in camp, but those with whom I chanced the chat seemed to have no complaints on this score. There were blankets and blankets and then some more. Each soldier was allotted two of them, and if any veteran wasn't able to secure any, it seems to me that it was his own fault.*[30]

Post concluded that he would still be at the Grand Reunion, enjoying more roast beef and gravy, if it weren't for his old, troublesome legs.

Halmage Post wasn't the only one offended by Gary's interview. Every day, stacks of newspapers were delivered to the Great Camp, and many veterans eagerly read them to stay informed about news from home. One such veteran from Paterson, New Jersey, picked up a copy of *The Morning Call* and was outraged by Miller Gary's statements. As the newspaper circulated among the men, the frustration grew until Captain John T. Miller decided to take action by writing a formal protest:

*To the editor of The Call:—We, the veterans in camp at this place, have been informed that in the issue of your paper of July 1, 1913, there appeared an article that stated that the veterans in camp were not receiving proper treatment and which we, the veterans from Paterson, N.J., desire to deny: and at a meeting of said veterans, the following was unanimously adopted:*

*"Whereas, We have heard that false statements have appeared in The Morning Call relating to the treatment we have received and that said article stated that we were lying upon the ground without shelter or blankets with not enough to eat, and whereas, the above statements are a tissue of falsehoods."*[31]

Captain Miller's letter expressed gratitude to the government and the state of Pennsylvania for their generous treatment of the veterans at Gettysburg. He insisted that the food was excellent, and they slept comfortably in good, dry tents. His statement was intended to reassure friends and family back home, easing any concerns the original article may have caused. Twenty other New Jersey veterans signed the protest letter while still camped on the battlefield, and it was sent to *The Morning Call*, where it was published a few days later.

This response highlighted the divide in perspectives at the Grand Reunion. While some veterans, like Gary, found the conditions unbearable, others deeply appreciated the efforts to accommodate them. The conflicting accounts reflect the range of experiences at Gettysburg, shaped by personal expectations, health, and resilience.

Speaking of food, supper on July 1 featured a hearty spread of corned beef, sweet potatoes, sliced tomatoes, and fresh bread; no meal was complete without a cup of coffee.[32] Whether the food was delicious or downright dreadful depended entirely on who you asked, but most seemed content enough to eat it.

I'll let the reader decide which version of events they believe. As for me, this confirms what I've always known—we New Jersey folks have a long, proud history of being absolute pains in the neck.

On a more serious note, the long days of excessive heat proved too much for some old soldiers. Allan Albert from Washington, DC, was seventy-five years old and suffered from heart trouble. He didn't want to sleep on a cot in the Great Camp, so he rented a room at a private residence in the town of Gettysburg. After enjoying the day at the Grand Reunion, he retired to his room on Monday evening and suffered a stroke.[33] He died the following afternoon on July 1, becoming the fourth casualty of the Grand Reunion. His body was shipped home to Washington, DC, and he was interred in Arlington National Cemetery.[34]

Later that same day, Christopher Yates of Latrobe, Pennsylvania, died due to the extreme heat, and Edgar Bigsley from Wisconsin was found dead in his tent from exhaustion.[35]

However, not all the deaths from the reunion occurred in the camp. John Hermence from Wellsville, New York, left Gettysburg because of the heat. He departed on a train and stood on the outdoor platform, getting some fresh air. As the speeding train traveled near Canton, Pennsylvania, Hermence fainted and fell onto the railroad tracks. He died instantly.[36]

William Brawner and William Page were the first Confederate veterans to arrive in Gettysburg, and, in a gesture heavy with symbolism, they were given the keys to the city. For a few days, they lingered in town, waiting for the Great Camp to open, before relocating to the Confederate section of the Maryland camp, the very ground where Charles Mettee had raised the first Confederate flag. Once settled, there remained a deeper task: to confront their past. They returned to Culp's Hill, where, on July 2 and 3,

1863, they had fought with youthful fury. But they were not alone. By their side were Union veterans, men who were once enemies but now quickly becoming friends. Together, they walked across the battlefield that had forever changed their lives.

To provide some background, Culp's Hill is a heavily wooded rise, gentle on one side but rugged and steep on the other, scattered with large boulders and exposed rock outcroppings. It's more of a bump in the landscape than a towering mountain, reaching only around six hundred feet above sea level. Even so, high ground is always valuable in war, and Culp's Hill became a fiercely contested piece of real estate during the three-day battle.

Maryland, though a slave-owning state, never seceded from the Union. It remained deeply divided, its people split between loyalty to the North and sympathy for the South. Marylanders took up arms on both sides of the conflict, and at Gettysburg they faced each other as enemies on Culp's Hill. Some historians debate whether these regiments exchanged direct fire or fought in close proximity, but one thing is sure—the war fractured Maryland, leaving wounds that would endure long after the last shots were fired.

Despite Maryland's complex status, its Confederate veterans were granted a rare honor. In 1886, the Second Maryland Infantry was allowed to erect a monument on the Gettysburg Battlefield—the first of its kind for any Southern state. Modest in design, the monument's presence sparked controversy. Northern veteran organizations decried it as an "intrusion on sacred soil." Yet, as time passed and reconciliation efforts grew, resistance softened. Following the success of the 1913 Gettysburg Reunion, a second Confederate monument was approved, a symbolic gesture of reconciliation that paved the way for others in the years to come.

Brawner and Page made their way to Culp's Hill, where the Second Maryland Infantry's monument stood—the only Confederate regimental memorial on the battlefield at that time. It's a four-sided obelisk, approximately eight feet tall, with inscriptions that briefly describe the actions taken by the Second Maryland during the battle:

> Advancing from Rock Creek about 7 p.m. July 2nd
> Occupied the line of works
> at this point and held its
> position until next morning.

On the morning of July 3rd
the battalion . . . charged under a fire in front, flank and rear
to a stone planted 100 yards west from this monument.

William Page walked up to the monument, placed his hands on the cold marble, and wept. The two aging Confederates, faces streaked with tears, leaned on each other for support. As they gazed over the now-tranquil landscape, the echoes of battle remained vivid. The ground beneath their feet had once been soaked in blood, the air thick with smoke and the cries of the dying. Their Union companions stood in solemn silence, listening as the men recounted the horrors they had endured.

For Page, the memories were especially painful. He had fought at Gettysburg alongside his brother, Washington, and their close friend William Brawner. The three were inseparable, calling themselves "the Three Musketeers." They had begun their service together in the First Maryland Infantry. However, two units bore the same name—one Union, one Confederate—so the Southern regiment was redesignated as the Second Maryland Infantry.

The fight for Culp's Hill began on the evening of July 2, 1863, when General Robert E. Lee launched coordinated attacks on both ends of the Union line. Confederate general Richard Ewell ordered an artillery barrage to weaken the federal defenses. As darkness fell, Southern troops advanced. Initially, they gained ground, pushing back Union forces. However, the steep, wooded terrain and encroaching nightfall slowed their progress. The Union, under General George S. Greene, swiftly reinforced their position, constructing breastworks that provided them with a crucial advantage.

The battle descended into chaos. Gunfire flashed in the darkness. Men stumbled through the trees, unable to distinguish friend from foe. The confusion led to deadly friendly fire, as soldiers unknowingly shot at their comrades.

An unnamed soldier later recalled an act of mercy amid the carnage:

*It was after dark on the second day at Gettysburg when Gen. G. H. Stuart's brigade wrested a line of works from the enemy on Culp's Hill. Many of the enemy fell as they retreated. . . . Some of them suffered severely from thirst, and their cries for water were piteous. The moon was bright, and the position was in a large oak woods. Among those*

> *put on the skirmish line from Company A, Second Maryland regiment . . . was Wm. Taylor, from Georgetown, D.C., who occupied a position immediately on my right. I was somewhat perplexed to understand why the enemy's pickets just in front of us fired so much until Taylor called to me, "I've been trying to go to that fellow out there, but every time I get from behind my tree, they fire at me." At length, just after they had fired at him, he called out: "You fools, I am just trying to give one of your own men some water." Notwithstanding that he had been driven back at least a dozen times, he made another essay, and this time, to the credit of the enemy, he was not molested. He went to the man, who lay considerably nearer to his own friends than to us, and returned safely. Such an act of humane heroism . . . should not go unmentioned.*[37]

Such a small gesture of compassion stood in stark contrast to the brutality surrounding them.

At dawn on July 3, five Union artillery batteries fired on the Confederates, pinning them down for thirty minutes in preparation for a Union counterattack. Instead, General Ewell ordered his men to charge. This included William and Washington Page, William Brawner, and the rest of the Second Maryland Infantry. As soon as the Three Musketeers stepped forward, Washington Page was shot through the heart. He died almost instantly. Brawner and Page were stunned, but they were ordered on and had to leave their fallen brother behind. The Confederates surged up the hill again and again, but each time they were repelled. After seven hours of relentless combat, the Confederates were forced to withdraw.

And Culp's Hill remained firmly in Union hands.

The Civil War is often remembered as a conflict in which brother fought against brother, and nowhere was that more true than on Culp's Hill. Colonel Wallace of the Union First Maryland later wrote, "The 1st Maryland Confederate Regiment met us and were cut to pieces. We sorrowfully gathered up many of our old friends and acquaintances and had them carefully and tenderly cared for."[38]

The human toll on Culp's Hill was devastating. The Confederates lost approximately 2,800 men; Union casualties numbered around 1,000. Of the 470 men who had marched into battle with the Second Maryland Infantry, only 226 survived. Washington Page's body was never recovered.

Like so many others, he was likely buried in a mass grave on Culp's Hill, close to where the Second Maryland Infantry monument stands today.

Not all losses were human. The Second Maryland Infantry had a beloved mascot, a black dog named Gracie. She had marched with the men into battle, and when they charged Culp's Hill, she led the way.

In an after-action report, Union soldier Samuel P. Bates described the scene:

> *Suddenly, the quiet was broken by a yell bursting from thousands of lungs, and the next instant, their gray lines emerged in sight, dashing madly on. Singularly enough, they were preceded a few yards by a rabid dog, with vengeful eyes and teeth, yelping and sounding defiance. They had scarcely come into easy musket range when the men in blue along the line sprang to their feet and poured in a deliberate volley. The shock was terrible. The oncoming force was staggered and, for a moment, sought shelter behind trees and rocks, but obedient to the voices of their officers, they struggled on. . . . They did what the most resolute could do, but it was all in vain. . . . Broken and well-nigh annihilated, the survivors of the charge staggered back, leaving the ground strewn with their dead and desperately wounded.*[39]

Samuel P. Bates noted the presence of a "rabid dog" preceding the Confederate charge, but to the boys of the Second Maryland, that was their loyal mascot. Gracie was described as an average-sized black dog and was so well loved that she was allegedly added to the muster roll.

Not much else is known about Gracie. It's believed that she was female, but Union general Thomas Kane wrote a brief description of Gracie and referred to the dog as a more generic "he." Kane wrote that Gracie "came in among the Boys in Blue. . . . At first, some of my men said, he barked in valorous glee, but I myself first saw him on three legs between our own and the Men in Gray."

Mortally wounded by gunfire, Gracie licked a soldier's hand before collapsing. Kane ordered her to be honorably buried, declaring her "as the only Christian-minded being on either side."[40]

Fifty years later, at the Grand Reunion, Maryland veterans—Union and Confederate alike—found themselves camped side by side. On the evening of July 1, they held a joint reunion, gathering as former enemies to share memories of their war experiences. Around 350 veterans attended, discussing the positions they once held on Culp's Hill. The newspapers reported the meeting: "The gathering was marked by a general spirit of good fellowship."[41] Yet the unspoken weight of loss hung over them. It's easy to imagine them reflecting on the tragic loss of life, including William Page's brother and Gracie the dog. Perhaps they also recalled moments of shared humanity, like William Taylor bringing water to the wounded.

Time had softened the bitterness of war, but the cost of those seven hours on Culp's Hill could never be undone. However, the Maryland reunion did a lot of good. It ultimately led to the establishment of the Gettysburg Memorial Association of Maryland, which embraced both Union and Confederate veterans as members. This Memorial Association continued to bridge the divide between the former enemies.

General Andrew C. Trippe, perhaps sensing the somber mood hanging over the Maryland camp, decided it was time to lighten things up. After all, what's a reunion without a bit of storytelling?

Wounded on Culp's Hill back in 1863 and captured by the Union, Trippe recounted his time as a prisoner of war recovering at Widow Weibel's house. Though the battle was brutal, he made it clear that the real ordeal began after the fighting stopped.

"The Widow Weibel was a terror," he declared. "I was more afraid of her than I was of the regiment of the Yankees."

After spending two months under her care, Trippe was certain that some wounds never truly healed. Even fifty years later, the memory of Widow Weibel still sent shivers down his spine. During the reunion, Trippe revisited the old widow's house, standing outside like a man confronting his past. With a grin, he told his fellow veterans, "You boys don't know how glad I am that I'm not there today as her guest!"[42]

Even after all those years, some battles—especially the ones fought under a strict caretaker's watch—were best left in the past.

As the Maryland reunion was winding down, some Confederates weren't quite ready to call it a night. They plotted to "capture" some of their Northern brothers. They then joined the Virginia camp and proposed invading the camps in Pennsylvania and New York.

"We propose to take them by surprise just as we did in the 60s," said John Obernderfer, "but instead of throwing them into prison on short rations, we shall extend to them a hearty clasp of the hand, with an expression of peace and goodwill. Won't that be fine?"[43]

While they were still organizing, a regiment of like-minded Union vets infiltrated the Confederate camp. As soon as the Southerners saw them coming, they rushed forward, surrounded them, captured them, and dragged them back to their tents to swap stories from the war.

One of the more interesting topics of conversation the former enemies shared concerned fear. "You Johnnies had us scared at the second battle of Bull Run," said Captain John R. Porter from the Forty-Eighth Pennsylvania Volunteers. "You made us run once."

"Well, I reckon you had us scared, too," John Obernderfer said.

"We were both badly scared," replied Captain Porter.[44]

A reporter from the *Times-Dispatch* wrote:

> *There's not a man in camp apparently . . . who does not admit that he was scared to death every time he went into battle. . . . All this talk about veterans bragging is rot. Very candidly, they tell you that even the most seasoned campaigners are always ready to die of fright. Hearing them talk would excite wonder as to how a single battle ever happened to continue after the first volley.*

Luther Ferris from the 179th New York Infantry said, "When I went to war, my old aunt said she would pray for me every day. I said, 'Aunt, you pray, and I dodge, and between the two, I'll come back alive.' I don't know whether she prayed, but I dodged, and here I am. Every man dodges, and if he says he doesn't, he's a braggart."

An unnamed Confederate who had survived Pickett's Charge was terrified every step of the way. "If he says he wasn't afraid," he observed, "the truth is not in him."[45]

The old soldiers did more than talk about being afraid. They told jokes and pulled pranks, and you might be surprised to hear this, but not every story told around the campfire was true. Many veterans shared tall tales that grew in exaggeration with each passing year. And here's where the talk of fear gave way to false bravado.

"I ain't seen a Reb yet who didn't charge Round Top and take it all by himself," said a Southerner visiting the Pennsylvania camp. "No, I ain't seen a yank who didn't break up Pickett's Charge by his own self,"[46] replied a Pennsylvania vet as they shook hands.

One of the old veterans from Massachusetts was quick to point out the baloney: "I've come to the conclusion that if the Johnny's had had 100 such fellows as some of them say they were, we'd never have won here, and if we had had 100 of such fellows as some of my comrades say they were, we'd have wiped Lee's army off the face of the earth." This man was a plain talker and didn't see the need to elaborate on his own story. He had lost his leg during the Battle of Gettysburg.

> *I was hit by a piece of shell, and that's about all I know about it. I didn't lick the Johnnies with one hand behind me, like some of my comrades. I just keeled over and was carried to the rear, and I have never set eyes on the place again until yesterday, when I went over to see the spot where I was wounded. And I never expected to see it again, but I am satisfied.*[47]

Meanwhile, a Union fife and drum corps tramped up and down the streets of the Confederate camp. They played the old military tunes as only the fife and drum can. They shook hands and threw their arms around each other, while some gave short speeches and expressed their feelings of friendship. The veterans cheered the musicians on, and many were brought to tears by the Union vets playing the Southern battle songs.

To liven up the crowd, one of the fifers, John Morris, called out to an old Confederate, "Come out here, kid, and we'll dance the Turkey Trot."[48] Then the two old soldiers, who shot at each other fifty years ago, danced together.

The fife and drum corps kept this up for hours and visited practically every Rebel tent.

The old veterans weren't the only ones to flock to Gettysburg. Tourists came in droves, attracting entrepreneurial people looking to make a quick buck by selling souvenirs. Among these were photographers. What tourists wouldn't want a photo of the old soldiers back on the battlefield, especially if they could get into the picture with them? Philip Myers was just eighteen during the reunion and took a summer job as a photographer's assistant. Years later, he wrote down his recollections of the reunion.

"We went to Gettysburg late in June," Myers wrote, "but by the time we arrived, the town was overflowing with thousands of visitors. We considered ourselves fortunate to bivouac in the hayloft of a barn on the edge of town." Russ Lewis, the photographer Myers was working for, picked Devil's Den for his base of operations, so Myers spent the days scrambling up and down the rocks around Devil's Den, posing people and tending to the technical needs of the camera.

By the time night fell, he was exhausted, but he often found it hard to sleep due to the heat. So, each night, the two men sat in the doorway of the hayloft and looked out on the tented city. Myers recalled it:

> *One by one, the lights in the tents were extinguished, the singing ceased, and an eerie calm embraced the encampment. A brilliant moon created soft radiance as, at eleven o'clock, a bugler at nearby headquarters broke the silence with the hauntingly melancholy notes of Taps. When the last plaintive notes of that somber call had faded, he was followed by another trumpeter farther off, then by another still more remote, and another, until it was impossible to tell if the notes we heard were real or imaginary.*[49]

The night was a hot one. The air was still, and the humidity was oppressive. The night before had been cool, and extra blankets were needed to keep the chill away, but this evening was just the opposite. It was sticky and uncomfortable, making for brutal sleeping conditions. To add to the discomfort, blue streaks of lightning flashed across the sky, and distant thunder rumbled across the land. Many veterans buttoned down their tents in anticipation of a coming storm, but doing so only added to their misery by trapping the heat inside. Thankfully, it didn't last long. Soon the skies cleared, and the tents were reopened. With the threat of rain gone, many veterans found the tents too hot to sleep in and moved their cots out into the company streets.[50] It wasn't much better, but it was better than nothing. Since sleep was scarce, many elderly soldiers stayed awake all night, chatting around the campfires.

The five hundred incandescent lights strung along the company streets cast a golden glow across the sea of canvas tents. The crackling embers of a thousand campfires sent sparks drifting off into the inky sky. Old men stared into the flames and conjured up the ghosts of yesterday to a soundtrack of crickets and tree frogs. Off in the distance could be heard the plucking of a banjo, and in another area, the soul-stirring vibrato of a violin, but frequent bursts of laughter often drowned these out.

Besides providing a break from the relentless sun, the evenings allowed the old soldiers to share the day's adventures. N. Roberts from Stewartville, Missouri, entertained the veterans with his chance encounter. "I met a Yank here a little while ago who declared he recognized me as the rebel who had shot at him three times during the fight here," he said to a circle of veterans. "I apologized to him for my poor marksmanship and said I was sorry that I had not done a better job."[51]

As the night wore on, the music faded, the talking quieted to soft chatter, and the snoring in the tents grew louder.

With the sun down, the Great Camp was a beautiful place to be. The men from Vermont described it like this: "At night, the grandeur and beauty of this camp was beyond description. Lighted by electricity, it presented a scene, to those who saw it, that will ever be remembered, one that the lapse of time will not from their memory efface."[52]

Walter Blake from Vineland, New Jersey, described it like this:

> *When dusk came, a fairyland sprang up. It beggars all description. The vast canvas city burst into brilliancy. It became as light as day. Seen from the ridges on either side of the camp, the dazzling arc lights appeared to have set on fire the night's sky. They radiated against the tower of the Bloody Angle and shot dizzying shafts of brilliance far into the shadows around Round Top.*[53]

Joseph Trax was one of the more curious attendees of the 1913 reunion. He was described as an interesting relic: "He's a droll talker, brimming over with patriotism, and can spout war from dawn until sunset." Trax served as George Armstrong Custer's orderly during the Civil War and took great pride in that fact, telling everyone he met. He also wore an enormous, flaming-red necktie that all of Custer's men wore at reunions.

But that wasn't the most interesting thing about Joseph Trax. When attending parades and reunions, he brought with him two very curious items. The first was a little brass cannon roughly two feet long. The second was a suitcase filled with gunpowder. Because of this, Joseph Trax was known as "the man with the cannon."

Trax referred to his gun as the "Custer Cannon" in honor of his former commander. The cannon was a composite of Civil War souvenirs and was described as a unique instrument of "noise."

Over the years, Trax collected a cartload of souvenirs and trinkets from the reunions, and he never knew what to do with them. One day, inspiration struck, and he melted them all down to cast his little gun. He said it contained four pounds of brass buttons, three division bugles, four regimental bugles, two brass drum rams, forty-four US infantry buckles, thirty-six US cavalry buckles, two brass keys said to have come from Ford's Theatre in Washington, five spears of infantry flags, three eagles of cavalry flags, two eagles of division flags, thirty-three pairs of spurs, twenty-four copper cents, 104 Spencer carbine cartridges, thirteen caps from shells, four pounds of artillery harness buckles, five sleeve buttons, five metal cases from army service watches, sixteen army spoons, three gold dollars, and one cowbell. It also contained a piece of the lock from the Harpers

A group of old soldiers sit around the campfire and swap tales during the 1913 Grand Reunion. Note the electric lights strewn throughout the Great Camp toward the right of the image. From *Pictorial History of 1913* (Rahway, NJ: Quinn-Boen); courtesy of the Library of Congress.

Ferry railroad, along with twenty pounds of fragments of a bell picked up at Charles Town, West Virginia. Altogether, the gun weighed 252 pounds and was finely polished and engraved.[54]

Trax kept the cannon outside his tent and fired it at random intervals throughout the day. On the night of July 1, he almost caused a riot. He habitually fired the cannon first thing in the morning and at sundown. Before bed, he fired off the gun and reloaded it. Then he fell asleep.

A few hours later, he woke up, thinking it was dawn. He forgot that he had loaded the cannon the night before, so he added a second charge and lit the fuse. The cannon fired off a tremendous blast that thundered through the camp, and hundreds of veterans were jolted from their sleep. It was only 3:00 in the morning, and the awakened veterans shook their fists and cursed up a storm! Some of the Confederates let out the Rebel Yell, while others raised hell for being awakened.

Trax was unfazed by the chaos he had created. He said, "A cannon shot is like a good stiff drink to the Southerner. It rallies them. A musket shot doesn't affect them one bit, but a cannon shot brings them all around like hornets."[55]

Meanwhile, in his tent on the other side of camp, Lieutenant George S. Patton wrote a letter to his wife, Beatrice. "Yesterday, we were out all morning doing park policemen work. And in the afternoon, I distributed some 7900 blankets to vets. They are a disgusting bunch, dirty and old, and of all the people who 'God loves.' One old hound has been beating a drum ever since he got here. Two others have a small cannon which they fire as often as they can."[56]

Was Patton referring to Joseph Trax and his Custer gun? It's hard to say for sure. However, one thing is clear: Lieutenant George S. Patton was not impressed with the old soldiers. Expecting to find dignified veterans eager to discuss battle strategy, he was disappointed, remarking that "the best of them were only damed malitia men and did not no [know] much."

Late in the evening on July 1, Brigadier General Hunter Liggett, the military commander of the Great Camp at Gettysburg, learned the hard way that sometimes your own rules can come back to bite you. To ensure the aging veterans could sleep undisturbed, Liggett had ordered that no motor vehicles with their blinding headlights and rumbling engines would be allowed into camp after 10:00 p.m.

Fast-forward to nearly 1:00 a.m., and who should roll up to the gate but General Liggett himself. Unfortunately for him, his own rule was being enforced with military precision. The guard on duty, an armed private with a firm grip on orders and no idea who he was speaking to, refused to let Liggett's car through. Rather than pull rank, the general, perhaps admiring the private's dedication or just too tired to argue, accepted his fate. He meekly turned his car around and parked it far outside the camp. He then stumbled more than a mile in the darkness to his headquarters.[57]

A few hours later, Brigadier General Liggett snuck out of camp, only to arrive *again*—this time with all the pomp and circumstance befitting his status. A seventeen-gun salute marked his "official" entrance, as if the previous night's hike of shame had never happened.

6

# July 2—Wednesday

On July 2, the formal exercises in the Great Tent started at 2:00 p.m. It was Military Day, and the speeches focused on the past and present members of the armed forces. Major General John Brooks of Pennsylvania said:

> *Comrades of the Army of the Potomac, after 50 years, we are gathered here with the Army of Northern Virginia, not as foes but as friends. . . . Comrades, it seems to me, as it seems to many, that our Republic has been destined to convince the world that the language of the Constitution that all men are born free and equal was not an idle boast. . . . Let us not fail to remember that "united we stand, divided we fall."*[1]

Sergeant John Scarborough of North Carolina had fought for the South and became his state's school superintendent after the war. He referred to himself as a "Reconstructed Rebel" and spoke about improving racial relations. During his speech, he said:

> *Where did the negro come from? He was not here by his own free will; he was brought here by the greed of the white man. We owe it to our negros in North Carolina . . . and to ourselves, to make the best citizens out of them, and the man whose business it is to improve the conditions of the negro by education and uplift them is the important teacher of the land. I've great sympathy with the negros, and my business is largely with*

> *them. I talk to him in his schoolhouse as I talk to the white folks in their schoolhouses. We must show to him that we are his friends and tie him to us with hooks of steel, and he will reward us for what we do for him . . . God help us to be true to our manhood and our womanhood, help us to live right and treat other people right, and try to help hold up every man who is trying to better his condition in this good land, and only then can we have a clear conscience towards our fellow men. . . . And I want to say to the men and women here that we owe it to the black men and the black women and the black children to make them the best citizens the material will allow. That is the way that I feel about it, and that is the way that I believe that we can accomplish what we desire if we really want him to be a good citizen.*[2]

This was followed by a reading of Abraham Lincoln's Gettysburg Address. "Four score and seven years ago, our fathers brought forth on this continent a new nation."

Before the next speaker could take the grandstand, a severe thunderstorm swept over the Great Camp, bringing the program to a temporary halt.

Meanwhile, across the six-thousand-acre battlefield, veterans gathered in little groups and large crowds holding mini-reunions. Around 3:30 p.m. on July 2, 1913, an unexpected rainstorm struck, giving the veterans the scare of their lives. It came out of an ominous-looking bank of clouds, like an unforeseen attack from the enemy. The rolling thunder was deafening and reminded the veterans of the cannonading guns from fifty years earlier. It also reminded the old soldiers of what life was like under field conditions.

Thousands of old soldiers found themselves on an exposed battlefield, with no trees, tents, or roofs to hide under. For some, the nearest shelter was miles away, and they were drenched to the skin long before returning to camp. Union and Confederates showed how gracefully they could retreat in the face of an overwhelming force. The 124th New York Regiment had intended to hold a reunion at Devil's Den, for it was there that they got into the action on July 2, 1863. The thunderstorm broke as the festivities began, and the mini-reunion was called off. They huddled for shelter on the lee side of the immense boulders of Devil's Den while the lightning flashed around them, crashing into trees and casting strange light across the big stone piles.[3]

Back in the Great Camp, five thousand tent flaps were wide open when the storm hit, and it was almost impossible to get them all closed once the downpour began.[4] Old soldiers from North and South scrambled into the closest tents, regardless of whom they belonged to, and barricaded themselves inside with all the haste their tired legs and feeble hands could make. Instead of huddling around campfires, the veterans huddled around tentpoles, trying to keep them from blowing over in the sudden wind. A more energetic man might dash outside to tie the flaps down and pull the ropes tight while the older men waited inside. Once the tent was secure, they would take stock of who was around them. But not even the rain could dampen their spirits, and the old veterans found themselves making new friends with whomever they were with. Once they were out of the elements, the thunder sounded like sweet music to their ears, a fitting celebration of the great battle.

Due to the sudden downpour, Charles N. Smith from New York found himself occupying a tent with a group of Texans. As usual, they began discussing the battle, and it was soon discovered that they were near each other on July 2, 1863. Smith shared his perspective on the battle:

> *We were rushing to the relief of Sickles, who was in the Peach Orchard, badly pressed by Hood. On our way, we noticed General Warren hastening in from Little Round Top. He rode to the head of our column and spoke earnestly to General Weed, our brigade commander. General Weed immediately retraced his steps, with the 140th New York in the lead, and got to the foot of Little Round Top. There, a battery was trying to ascend the hill, but the horses were unable to make progress over the boulders on the steep hill. We helped unhitch the horses, and, taking hold of the harness, we dragged the guns into position on the top of the hill.*
>
> *As we reached the apex, we saw the Texans coming up. It was a hard climb for you, but you, Johnnies, were coming fast. Then, our officers ordered a bayonet charge, leading the charge themselves with unsheathed swords. You kept a-coming, and soon we had it hard and heavy, hand-to-hand, clubbing and bayoneting. You didn't get up there, but you were mighty close to it and made a desperate fight.*[5]

The Texans listened intently as Smith recounted his version of events. When he finished, they eagerly shared their perspective.

Their story painted a dramatic scene—their boys had stormed in from Chambersburg along the Emmitsburg Road, charging into battle with relentless determination. They crashed into the federal line, driving the enemy back, seizing five artillery pieces, and pushing forward until they were nearly at the crest of Little Round Top. But there, entrenched cannons and 2,500 Union soldiers stopped their advance.[6]

Although these memories were shaped and refined over the course of fifty years, one Texan among them had a more contemporary view of the battle. H. Watters Berryman shared a letter he wrote to his mother on July 9, 1863, detailing the conflict near Little Round Top. His letter is printed here in full.

> *Dear Mother, Sister, and Family: it is the will of God that Newt [a brother of Berryman] and myself are permitted to write you all again, bearing the news to you of our good health, but it is not so with all. Poor Mort Murphy [of Alto, Texas] was killed in making one of the most gallant charges ever made by the First Texas. It was on the second day of July at the great battlefield of Gettysburg, Pennsylvania. Lieutenant H. N. Jones and Wiley House (both of Crockett County, Texas) fell at the same place. We have eight or 10 wounded out of our company.*
>
> *Newt [Berryman] was wounded in the head. He was right by my side. It knocked him down. I thought he was killed, but he jumped up and went to fighting harder than ever. I tried to persuade him to leave the field, but he would not leave. He told me if every man left for a slight wound, we would never gain a battle. He was struck a gashing blow on the forehead by a minie ball.*
>
> *The Texas brigade, after the big fight on the second, was moved up on the extreme right of the battlefield to protect our right flank, as the enemy was trying to turn it. We had not time enough, but to put our skirmishers—I was one—when a brigade of Yankee cavalry came charging upon the gallant First Texas. As I was in front, cavalry came very near running over me, but I jumped behind a stone fence and held my position. I killed a Captain and wounded a Lieutenant. They were both trying to rally their men, who were in the greatest confusion. I took five*

*or six prisoners, all of whom had six-shooters. I got only one pistol, as we were expecting another charge, and I didn't have time to take all their arms. I pointed to the rear and told them to git.*

*I ran up the line to the regiment to find old company I, which had been removed to the extreme right of the regiment during my absence on skirmish. I soon found them, all mixed up with Yankee cavalry, cutting and slashing in every direction. I ran towards them as fast as possible. All the boys had fired off their pieces, and the Yankees would not give them time to load, so the boys were using the butts of their guns. Moore killed one with a rock, Newt managed to reload his gun. There was a Yank cutting one of the boys over the head with a sabre when Newt ran up and blew his brains out. About this time, we had disposed of the regular Yankees. They left their horse blankets, rations, and all accoutrements to be enjoyed by the victorious First Texas.*[7]

What a brutal account of close-quarters combat! Yet fifty years later, these same men shared a tent during a rainstorm and discussed the details of the battle. By all accounts, it was a friendly meeting between former foes. There was no yelling and arguing, just a handful of old soldiers eager to share their experiences during the war.

The First Texas fought fiercely at Gettysburg and achieved their objectives by capturing the ground around Devil's Den. They had 426 men; during the battle, 29 were killed, 46 were wounded, and 22 were either missing or captured.

Elsewhere in the Great Camp during the storm, the more active veterans in the Maryland camp hurried to assist the aged and feeble, helping them unroll and stake down their tents. It was a busy half hour for Captain Hoffman on the Union side and Corporal Mettee on the Confederate side. "Soldiers must not mind a little thing like this," said Corporal Mettee. "Think of what we went through on this field 50 years ago; hardship goes with the lives of soldiers."[8]

Some of the veterans said the roaring in the heavens sounded perfectly natural. "It rained bullets on us this hard on July 2nd, 1863, as it rained water today. But we prefer the rain of today to that 50 years ago,"[9] said John L. Obernderfer of the Pikesville Home in Maryland, as he reflected on the downpour.

The thunder and lightning lashed out for twenty minutes, while the rain lasted over an hour. Despite the chaos it caused on the field, the storm was a blessing at the end of the hottest day of the reunion; it brought a refreshing drop in temperature and, more important, lowered the humidity.[10]

Before the storm hit, ambulances had been rushing over the field and through the streets of Gettysburg in an almost ceaseless stream to pick up men who had dropped from the heat. It had been a hard day for the orderlies and medical staff in the field hospitals, but the storm and the sudden drop in temperature gave them a chance to catch their breath.

Once the storm passed, an unusual activity took place. Local boys and women rushed to the battlefield in search of relics from the war. Even after fifty years, a harvest of bullets could be collected after a heavy storm washed away their hiding places; apparently, this was a recognized Gettysburg cottage industry.[11] Many of the bullets were quickly resold by entrepreneurial individuals to the very soldiers who had fired them in the first place.

With the storm over, the speeches in the Great Tent resumed. Lieutenant Governor Roswell Burchard of Rhode Island said, "May none but Him who rules the thunder and holds the lightning in His hand, put asunder the hearts of the two great armies who are reunited here today."[12]

To conclude the program on Military Day, the children and grandchildren of the generals from both sides were introduced. These were the sons and grandson of General Longstreet, the grandsons of General Pickett, and the daughter and grandchildren of General Meade. As they were individually called forward, three cheers went up by the Blue and Gray. Afterward, a benediction was given, and the audience was dismissed for the day.[13]

Various reunions were held in the Great Tent until 6:00 p.m. The Third Regiment Infantry National Guard of Pennsylvania Band (NGP) then performed a concert at 8:00 p.m.

With the storm behind us, it's time to return to the tale of that crazy bastard, Dan Sickles.

After murdering Philip Barton Key in cold blood, in broad daylight and right in front of the White House (and getting away with it too!), Sickles declined to run for another term in Congress. He returned to New York City to live a life in quiet obscurity.

Oh, please. That was never in the cards.

Sickles was an egomaniac of the highest order, and when the Civil War broke out in 1861, he saw it as his golden opportunity. He did what any self-respecting lunatic with political connections would do: He raised three thousand men and appointed himself their commander. With a bit of help from President Abraham Lincoln and some backdoor politics, his nomination was pushed through. And just like that, Sickles became a brigadier general. Let's pause for a moment and appreciate this: With a stroke of a pen, a man with zero military experience became a leader of an army. What could go wrong?

By the time he swaggered into Gettysburg in July 1863, Sickles had been promoted to major general, commanding ten thousand men in the Union army.

What follows is an overly simple version of the events during the second day's battle. If you'd like to learn the full details, I highly recommend Harry Pfanz's book, *Gettysburg: The Second Day* (1998).

On July 2, 1863, the Union army positioned itself along the natural contours of the Gettysburg landscape in what would become known as the fishhook formation. This defensive line began at Culp's Hill on the right flank, ran through Cemetery Ridge in the center, and extended to Little Round Top on the left flank. When viewed from above, the army's arrangement resembled a giant fishhook, providing them with high ground, a continuous defensive line, and the ability to reinforce positions quickly. All combined, it gave the Union a significant advantage in battle.

General George Meade was in overall command of the Army of the Potomac and saw Sickles for what he was: a rank amateur playing soldier. Meade's *very clear* order was to stay put, hold the line, and let the Confederates come to them.

But Sickles was, well, Sickles. And he didn't like the view from his assigned position. So he took it upon himself to move his entire corps one mile forward, completely unsupported and isolated from the rest of the Union army.

After marching his men into an exposed position, Sickles and his officers took a brief detour to evict the Trostle family from their own home. The Trostles had just settled in for a nice, peaceful dinner when they suddenly found themselves evicted "for their own safety" by a military takeover. As soon as the family was out of sight (and probably still processing what the hell just happened), Sickles's staff did what any self-respecting soldiers would do: They sat down and enjoyed the still-warm dinner their unwilling hosts had prepared, because, hey, leading men into battle is hungry work.

Meanwhile, over on the Confederate side, General James Longstreet couldn't believe his luck. He and his men were marching toward Little Round Top, and they hadn't expected Sickles to serve himself up on a silver platter. Longstreet wasted no time and opened fire at 4:00 p.m., launching one of the bloodiest assaults of the battle at the Wheatfield and Peach Orchard.

The result? A complete disaster for Sickles.

The Ninth Massachusetts Battery was ordered to hold the Trostle Farm at all costs. Seeing this, the Confederate Twenty-First Mississippi Infantry targeted the horses pulling the artillery to keep them from maneuvering their cannon. As Sickles's corps was getting torn to shreds, he rode around like a lunatic, trying to rally his troops.

That's when a twelve-pound cannonball smashed into his leg.

At this point, I'll let the man himself tell you what happened. Just keep in mind that Sickles had fifty years to refine and perfect his story:

> *At first, I did not know I was hit. My thoughts . . . were solely on the battle, so I am unable to tell exactly at what point I was struck. It was somewhere between the peach orchard and the wheat field. I made the discovery that I had been hit as I was riding back from the immediate front to my headquarters flag. I felt my foot was wet and damp. I looked down and found that my knee and leg were also wet and damp. I slipped my leg over the back of the horse and saw that I was bleeding a great deal. Then I knew my leg was badly fractured—it later turned out to have been fractured both above and below the knee.*

Let's pause for a moment. The muzzle velocity of a twelve-pound cannonball was around one thousand feet per second. And Sickles didn't feel it? Just for fun, I looked up the stats on softballs, which are only a shade smaller than a cannonball. A good softball pitcher can throw around sixty-five to seventy miles per hour. Now, picture taking a line drive to the leg at seventy miles per hour. You'd feel it. You'd probably invent new curse words on the spot. Now crank that up: A twelve-pound cannonball moving at one thousand feet per second is actually screaming along at 682 miles per hour. And we're supposed to believe Sickles didn't notice? Either the man had a godlike threshold of pain or he was talking straight out of his backside. Personally, I'm betting on the backside.

Sickles continues:

> *Instantly, I slipped from my horse's back and sent for a surgeon. I was still bleeding a great deal and saw that I would bleed to death before the arrival of the surgeon unless something was done. So I ordered one of my staff to take a small strap from his blanket and buckle it about my leg. The strap was pulled into a tight tourniquet, and the rapid flow of blood was stayed.*[14]

Chaplain Joe Twitchell claimed to have witnessed the incident and said, "It was after the fight had been going on about half an hour . . . that the general was shot below the knee. It came from so squarely in front that it didn't touch his horse, but it tore his leg all to flinders."[15]

Chaplain Twitchell helped drag Sickles from the battlefield and brought him to a field hospital. Regardless of his boasts, Sickles must have been in excruciating pain, but that didn't stop him from encouraging his men as he was carried from the field. Sickles chomped on a cigar and called to his men: "Give them hell, boys!"

Ultimately, the Third Corps was decimated, with more than four thousand men killed or wounded, and was forced from the field, leaving behind 116 dead horses on the Trostle Farm. Sickles's idiotic move nearly lost the battle, but it delayed Longstreet's troops just long enough for the Union to secure Little Round Top. Despite the carnage, Sickles insisted for the rest of his life that he had saved the Union army.

General Meade never agreed with Sickles's assessment. He said, "Sickles' movement practically destroyed his own corps . . . and with what results? Driving us back to the position he was ordered to hold originally. . . . If this is an advantage—to be so crippled in battle without attaining an object—I must confess I cannot see it."[16]

Ouch.

Later, a surgeon inspected Sickles's shattered leg, and the prognosis was not good. But that was just fine with Sickles. He may have lost a leg, but he gained a story that he would tell for the rest of his life. He went on to boast that "the doctor said before they amputated the leg that not even one of my sturdy constitution could have stood the terrific loss of blood."[17]

Sickles was anything but modest.

That night, Sickles's leg was amputated. But being the absolute crazy bastard he was, he refused to let them discard the severed appendage. Instead, he had it shipped in a small coffin to the Army Medical Museum in DC with a note saying, "With compliments from General Sickles." Sickles knew the museum was on the hunt for medical curiosities, and he figured his shattered leg would make the perfect exhibit.

Despite losing a limb, Sickles was still the ladies' man, and he knew how to woo the women. For the rest of his life, Sickles regularly visited his amputated leg, often bringing a lady admirer along to regale her with the story of how he had singlehandedly saved the Battle of Gettysburg.

Sickles's shattered leg bones are still on display at the National Museum of Health and Medicine. But just for the record, I don't think it's a romantic place to bring a first date.

Dan Sickles had some famous friends and was acquainted with the American author and humorist Mark Twain. In his autobiography, Twain described Sickles as "a genial old fellow; a handsome and stately military figure."[18] A few pages later, Twain writes about visiting Sickles in his home:

> *Now, when we sat there in the general's presence listening to his monotonous talk—it was about himself, and is always about himself . . . I noticed then, what I had noticed once before, four or five months ago, that the general valued his lost leg away above the one that is left. I am perfectly sure that if he had to part with either of them, he would part with the one that he has got.*[19]

To add another caveat to the story, Sickles was a personal friend of President Abraham Lincoln. After his leg was amputated, Sickles was immediately taken to Washington, DC, where he reported directly to the president about his actions at Gettysburg *while* the battle was still being fought. No doubt, his version of the story would go on to taint Lincoln's view of the battle, as he felt that Meade hadn't done enough to destroy Lee's army and allowed the Confederates to escape.

Once Sickles's wound healed, he requested to rejoin the Union army and take back his old command, but General Meade refused. He had grown tired of Sickles's antics and said he was no longer fit for command due to the loss of his leg. This sparked a bitter rivalry between the two men that lasted for the rest of their lives. However, Meade died nine years after the battle, while Sickles lived another forty years beyond that. This meant that Sickles outlived most of his critics and ensured that his version of events was the one people remembered.

In 1897, he even received the Medal of Honor; his citation said, "Displayed most conspicuous gallantry on the field vigorously contesting the advance of the enemy and continuing to encourage his troops after being himself severely wounded."[20] This only reinforced Sickles's view that what he did at Gettysburg was perfectly justified. Historians still debate whether Sickles was a hero or an unhinged lunatic who nearly doomed the Union army. But one thing's for sure—he was one crazy bastard.

At the Grand Reunion of 1913, Helen Longstreet was going through the Great Camp when she overheard an alarming rumor—Dan Sickles had finally kicked the bucket. Concerned (or maybe just curious), she trudged through the blistering heat to the old Rogers House, where she stumbled on a scene straight out of a dark comedy.

Word had spread like wildfire, sending a swarm of eager reporters rushing to confirm the supposed demise of the ever-dramatic general. But instead of a corpse, they were greeted by none other than Sickles himself, very much alive and well.

"There is a rumor about the camp," one reporter began.

"I've heard enough of those rumors," Sickles grumbled.

"But this one, General, is to the effect that you are dead."

Sickles scoffed and chomped on his cigar. "Well, it's not so; they have been trying to make me dead for a long time, but I think I'll be here when a lot of my enemies are under the sod."

The disappointed reporters slunk away with their big scoop ruined, but, just like Sickles, the rumor refused to die. Sickles, ever the man of action (or at least of dramatic gestures), hauled himself out of his chair and demanded to be driven over to camp headquarters to set the record straight.

Marching into General Hunter Liggett's office, Sickles wasted no time. "I want you to know, sir, that there was a rumor about that I was dead. That story, sir, is a damned lie."

"I believe you thoroughly, General," answered General Liggett. He opened a drawer in his desk. "I have both Scotch and bourbon, which shall it be?"

Sickles grinned, proving that even false death reports couldn't kill his sense of priorities. "A little of both."[21]

And so, with a drink in hand and his supposed death thoroughly debunked, Sickles declared to the press, "This reunion has put new life and vigor into me. Despite the intense heat, I feel younger, stronger, and more vibrant each day of my stay."[22]

Nothing—not rumors, rivals, or even death—could keep Dan Sickles down.

Sickles eventually returned to the Rogers House and found Helen Longstreet still waiting for him. She watched as he settled himself back onto the rocking chair on the porch and placed his crutches within easy reach. Only then did she say to him, "General, I have written an article about you for publication."

Sickles was apprehensive.

She then read aloud several pages of the loftiest tribute to the old corps leader. Here's an excerpt:

> *Sickles had come back to Gettysburg unheralded. He couldn't help coming. It was his victory. It is his field. The dim-eyed boys in gray and the maimed heroes in blue gather about him, to touch his hands reverently. They have forgotten the trials and tribulations of the twilight years of the citizens. Sickles is in the saddle once more. . . . Today, Gettysburg skies bend softly above him. Her skies are great and free. They shelter him. In the saddle once more, the men who fought with him and the men who faced him salute the old commander on Gettysburg field.*

Her article continues in a similar vein, heaping accolades on Sickles that he doesn't deserve. And I'm sure Sickles ate up every word. It validated everything he had been saying for fifty years. He probably sat back in his rocking chair with a self-satisfied grin, puffing on a cigar and nodding as if the heavens had finally acknowledged his genius. When she said, "It was his victory. It is his field," it must have been music to his ears. He'd likely quote it for the rest of his life—casually weaving it into conversation whenever possible. "You know, they say Gettysburg is my field," he'd remark as if it were an undeniable fact of history. And weirdly, he wouldn't be far from the truth. (But we'll get to *that* toward the end of his story.)

In short, he'd interpret this flowery tribute exactly as it was meant to be: confirmation that, in his mind, Dan Sickles wasn't just a general—he *was* Gettysburg.

Helen Longstreet wrote her newspaper articles with heroic grandiloquence, which is a fancy term for fancy language. Her writing was overly dramatic, featuring a poetic mix of sentimentality and highfalutin rhetoric. It aimed to stir emotions, depicting its subject in mythical proportions. But that sickeningly sweet language makes my eyes roll and smells like something you'd find in a cow pasture. Helen blew so much smoke up Sickles's rear that it was a wonder she hadn't proposed renaming the town *Sicklesburg*.

A group of veterans cheer at the Rogers House. General Dan Sickles is seated next to Eleanor Wilmerding, with Helen Longstreet in profile beside her. Courtesy of the Library of Congress.

Meanwhile, around fifty of Sickles's old soldiers had gathered on the lawn to listen to the dramatic reading. Helen's words moved the old general, and tears flowed down Sickles's cheeks. The old soldiers with him doffed their hats and wept, their tears soaking the ground that their blood had once drenched.

Once Sickles regained his composure, he got back to the task at hand, which was to greet the old soldiers who had crossed the battlefield to greet him. Sickles claimed to have shaken the hands of "2000 men, women, and children" on July 2, 1913.

"Hundreds of the 'rebs' have walked the weary and dusty three miles to and from their camp to shake me by the hand and assure me that all sectional differences were buried at Appomattox," Sickles said. (A quick reminder that Appomattox was where General Lee surrendered his forces to General Grant, marking the unofficial end of the Civil War.)

Sickles addressed the old Confederates, "Brother, I was too busy fighting you fifty years ago to make speeches. But now I want to say to all of you who have come to this hallowed spot that I am proud of you, proud of your section of the country, and proud to bear the title of 'American' with you."[23]

One of the Confederates was Captain Jesse A. Pack from the Thirteenth Mississippi Infantry. His regiment had fought directly against Sickles at the Peach Orchard. Pack traveled from Mississippi to attend the Grand Reunion and had a wonderful time. He and other members of his old brigade were given a special invitation by the Massachusetts veterans, whom they had tangled with fifty years earlier. While the other veterans were lodged in tents in the Great Camp, the Massachusetts men had rented a large wooden house in the center of the battlefield and invited Captain Pack to stay with them. When Captain Pack first approached the house, he was greeted with "Halloa, Johnnie, come right in and make yourself at home, for we are awful glad to see you."

Captain Pack responded, "All right, Yank. That's what I'm here for."

Captain Pack recognized the building as soon as he saw it; it was where the Mississippi men and the Massachusetts men had clashed during the fight, and the walls were still riddled with Minié balls. Pack said that during the battle, he and some others rushed to the well in the yard to get water to quench their thirst and refill their canteens. He claimed it was the coldest and best water he had ever tasted. At the reunion, Captain Pack couldn't wait to return to the well and drink the water again. He quickly did so and claimed it was just as cold and sweet as it had been fifty years earlier. Pack spent quite a bit of time at the old well during the reunion; he said it reminded him of an old friend.[24]

While hanging out at the well, Pack met Helen Longstreet. At first, he didn't recognize her, but once she gave her name, Pack bowed deeply and expressed his pleasure at meeting her.

"Aren't you glad it was settled the way it was?" she asked.

"Yes, ma'am, I am," he replied. "That is, if you mean the whole war."[25]

He then showed her a Pennsylvania Grand Army of the Republic (GAR) Post badge on his chest. He had exchanged it with a Union veteran who now wore his Confederate badge.

Captain Pack was given a cozy, well-furnished room on the second floor of the Rogers House, right above Dan Sickles. Over the week, Pack and Sickles hit it off, spending plenty of time together and becoming fast friends. Pack said Sickles was incredibly gracious and welcoming to the former Confederates. He even took photos with them.

Some Massachusetts men had brought their wives and daughters along, and these ladies ensured the aging Southern veterans were comfortable and well cared for. Meals were served on beautifully set tables, piled high with delicious food. Their hospitality didn't go unnoticed or unappreciated by the Confederates.[26]

During the day, General Sickles could often be found sitting on the porch of the Rogers House, just a few hundred feet from the very spot where he had lost his leg. Veterans gathered around him in a steady stream, eager to make his acquaintance and shake his hand. No one showed more admiration than the old Confederates, who clasped his hand so often and so firmly that it must have ached by the end of the day.

When the Confederates met Sickles, one said to him, "God bless you. I'm glad the time has come when it is possible for such a thing as this to come about."

"You must go out on the field," one of the old Confederates insisted, "and have your picture taken with us."

Sickles, ever the dramatic one, gave a wistful sigh. "I'm afraid I'm hardly equal to the task, though I appreciate the compliment," he said, casting a longing look at the battlefield like a man reminiscing about lost youth and maybe his lost leg.

"Shucks! Lend a hand, boys!"[27]

Before Sickles could protest, the Confederates took matters into their own hands. With the enthusiasm of men half their age, they hoisted the one-legged war hero onto their shoulders, and off they went—a parade of grinning, old soldiers, carrying Sickles like some battle-scarred royalty.

They made their way to the monument, marked the very spot where he had been wounded, plopped him down onto his good leg, and clustered around for a photo. The photographer, likely suppressing laughter, captured the moment for posterity. Then, with the same careful coordination (and perhaps a bit more wheezing), they scooped Sickles back up and paraded him back to his rocking chair on the Rogers House porch.

I can imagine the mix of amusement and mild horror in the eyes of Miss Wilmerding, Sickles's ever-watchful (*cough-cough*) housekeeper, who no doubt stood by with a disapproving glare and a mental note to scold Sickles later.

Afterward, General Sickles boasted that he had posed for at least forty cameras while lounging on the porch of the Rogers House. It was the first and last time the enemy had ever captured him for a photo op.

The town of Gettysburg was teeming with humanity. Incoming trains brought in thousands of veterans, family members, and other visitors, making it impossible to make headway through the streets. General traffic would have been at a standstill without the Pennsylvania State Police directing traffic. It was reported that the city had never seen so many visitors. Crowds of men and women, including veterans, stood in line for hours at the local post office, waiting to buy stamps and send letters home.

The post office was so overwhelmed with letters that it couldn't process all the mail. Instead, they boxed everything up and sent it to York and Harrisburg for distribution. During the week-long reunion, seventy-five thousand pieces of mail passed through the post office, and the postal workers couldn't keep up with the demand; they claimed they were five days behind schedule.

Meanwhile, anything that could be sold was. In the town of Gettysburg, savvy locals sold water to thirsty tourists for one cent a glass or five cents with ice. Transportation to and from the battlefield cost as much as $1.50 a person, but a skilled haggler could negotiate it down to a quarter.

Unfortunately, not everyone was an honest businessperson. Many swindlers were present, hawking fake souvenirs to the visitors and trying to entice money from their pockets. "Antique" dealers were making a killing selling to the gullible. Flattened bullets, shells, cannonballs, old guns, and camp supplies that were never closer to the battlefield than the town square were sold to unsuspecting tourists for all sorts of prices.[28]

"This is the very bullet that took General Reynolds's life—yours for just fifty cents!" or "For just one dollar, you can own a piece of the shell that took General Sickles's leg!"

The old Latin phrase *caveat emptor* was alive and well at the Gettysburg Reunion: "Let the buyer beware!"

There were a lot of shysters in town trying to do whatever they could to part the visitors from their money. It became so bad that agents from the State Dairy and Pure Food Department visited Gettysburg and took samples of ice cream and soft drinks being sold on the streets. After analysis, it was discovered that some of the ice cream did not contain enough butterfat. The offenders were fined between twelve and twenty-five dollars each, but even more damning was that they printed their names in the local newspaper as a warning to the other residents. As soon as the word got out that they were performing these tests, at least fifteen ice cream stands packed up and left town.[29]

The general health of the veterans was considered remarkably good. Hundreds were treated in various hospitals, but the vast majority of cases were due to heat exhaustion[30]—what was then called "heat prostration." By the end of the week, 319 veterans had been treated for it. Luckily, with quick treatment, most were back on their feet in just a few hours.

However, the biggest culprit behind these medical cases wasn't just the brutal July heat; it was alcohol. Booze dehydrates the body, making the old soldiers even more vulnerable to the sweltering weather. Dr. Samuel Dixon, the state commissioner of health, made it clear: "Most of the many cases being treated in the Emergency State Hospital were directly traceable to over-indulgence in alcohol. Many cases of alcoholism also being noted in camp."[31]

Reverend Clarence E. Macartney, a Civil War enthusiast who wanted to attend the big event, saw firsthand how much the veterans enjoyed their drinks. When he arrived in Gettysburg, all the hotels were full, so he rented a cot in a resident's parlor. His roommates were a group of Virginia veterans who had ditched their hot canvas tents for a cooler night indoors. One of them, an old doctor, was happy to share his "prescriptions" from a tall bottle with his fellow vets. As Macartney recalled, "He kindly offered to 'prescribe' for us too, but we thought it was hot enough without kindling a fire within us."

Macartney also witnessed some heavy drinking on his train ride to Gettysburg. He recalled:

> *One of the many sad things is the ravages of the bottle. On the way down on the train, not a few of the old soldiers were exalting their bottles on high, and one grizzled veteran told me, when I warned him that too much heat and too much whiskey . . . would land him in the hospital, that he had vowed a vow not to drink any water until he got home. I doubt if he did. Many of the cases of sickness and collapse have been due to whiskey.*[32]

With so many veterans overindulging, the chief surgeon of the Great Camp asked all the bars in town to shut down for the duration of the reunion. They refused; the bar owners couldn't resist the opportunity to make a buck from all of the visiting tourists.[33] They did agree to a small compromise—closing at 11:30 p.m. and not reopening until the next morning. It wasn't ideal for the bar owners, but with the flood of tourists in town, they weren't exactly struggling for business.

One of the favorite pastimes of Civil War enthusiasts is the "what if" game, and it goes something like this: "What if Great Britain had sided with the Confederacy?" A lengthy discussion would then ensue regarding an alternate timeline that never took place, but anything is possible with the "what if" game. "What if Lincoln lived?" or "What if Longstreet had gone 'to the right' at Gettysburg?" or "What if General Hooker was in command of the Union army instead of Meade?" These are fun questions to entertain, and armchair warriors across the globe have strong opinions on the matter.

The biggest "what if" game of the Civil War (in my opinion) is "What if Stonewall Jackson was at Gettysburg?"

Thomas Jonathan "Stonewall" Jackson was an enigmatic general in the Confederate army. He was well known for pushing his men harder and longer than other commanders, which allowed Jackson and his men, nicknamed the "Stonewall Brigade," to show up in places they weren't expected. Jackson's greatest achievement also happened to be his last, and it took place during the Battle of Chancellorsville, just two months before the Battle of Gettysburg. I don't want to get bogged down in too many details, so I will oversimplify what happened at Chancellorsville.

From April 30 to May 6, 1863, the Union and Confederate armies clashed in Spotsylvania, Virginia. General Robert E. Lee pulled off a bold move. He split his army and simultaneously attacked the Union forces from two different directions. On the Union side, General Joseph Hooker was leading the charge against Lee. Meanwhile, Confederate general Stonewall Jackson and his brigade were making their way around the Union position.

Now, here's where things went off the rails. Jackson's movements were spotted by none other than that crazy bastard, General Dan Sickles, who was a total amateur tactician and completely misread the situation. When he saw Jackson's troops moving, he assumed the Confederates were repositioning, not preparing for a massive attack. Thinking he could throw a wrench in their plans, Sickles pushed his men forward into the gap Jackson had left. In reality, he only exposed the Union's right flank even more.

Surprise, surprise.

Meanwhile, Jackson kept going, circling around, and when he finally struck, the Union soldiers were caught entirely off guard. Most of them were cooking dinner or playing cards when the Confederates came crashing through the trees. Chaos erupted, thousands were captured, and, to top it all off, the Confederates got to enjoy the dinners their enemies had just been making.

But Stonewall Jackson wasn't done fighting and wanted to press his advantage. That night, he personally scouted the disorganized Union position to plan another attack. Unfortunately, on his way back, his own sentries failed to recognize him in the dark and opened fire. (This is one reason Civil War battles usually wrapped up by dusk—nobody wanted to risk getting shot by their own side.) Jackson was rushed to the rear, where doctors amputated his arm. Sadly, he died a week later.

As noted before, the greatest Civil War "what if" is "What if Stonewall Jackson lived and fought at Gettysburg?" This question has been argued up and down, left and right, even while the war was still being waged, and it still rages to this very day!

And so it was that Stonewall Jackson's ghost was alive and well at the Grand Reunion. "There would have been a different tale to tell at Gettysburg had Jackson been here 50 years ago," said Private James N. Small, a veteran from the Second Virginia Infantry, which happened to be a part of the Stonewall Brigade.

On the morning of July 2, 1913, Private Small sat in his tent, reflecting on the second day's fight, which centered around Culp's Hill and Cemetery Ridge. Private Small indulged in the "what if" game:

> *If Jackson had been here with us, we would have taken Culp's Hill, and there would have been no Battle of Gettysburg to celebrate today. I remember how the men of the brigade lying near Gettysburg smarted under their inaction the night before the second day's fight. It seemed that we were wasting time that was precious. We heard the Federal artillery coming up and were itching for orders to move. The brigade was on its way back to Gettysburg from Shippensburg, where we had stopped on our way to Carlisle. We laid all night within sight of Gettysburg. Jackson would've kept us going all night until we reached a position he would have picked out for an attack in the morning. He would have carried us to Culp's Hill and nothing would have stopped us until we reached the Heights. The men knew something was going wrong for I remember how we all said so. All through the brigade, men were saying, "what are we doing here? We've got to get going. Why not keep them going as we used to when Jackson was with us?" Had Jackson been in the campaign around Gettysburg the position of the troops would have been reversed for he would have taken Cemetery Heights, but then even if we had won at Gettysburg, we would not have won out in the end. The Federals had too much of an advantage on us. If they lost a man, they could put 10 fresh men in his place, for they had the world to draw on. If we lost a man, there was no one to take his place for drafting ranks were limited. And the majority of our men were young and inexperienced, poorly equipped, and still more poorly fed at times. We were half*

*starved, more often than well fed. It was not a body of soldiers, but a body of ragamuffins that surrendered at Appomattox.*[34]

Captain Pack from Mississippi said that every Union soldier he spoke with expressed the greatest admiration for General Robert E. Lee as both a man and a soldier. However, they all regarded Stonewall Jackson as the greatest commander the war produced or the world ever knew.[35]

As the veterans gathered at Gettysburg fifty years later, the echoes of Jackson's name still stirred debate, admiration, and longing for what might have been. The war was long over, but the past was never far away for these old soldiers.

Two Confederate brothers stood at the Copse of Trees at Gettysburg's high-water mark, soaking in the view from the Union side. They had survived Pickett's Charge and were back, decades later, to see it from a different perspective. Other men from Pickett's division were there too, but these two stood out—literally. Both were over six feet tall, standing straight despite their years. Their soft Southern drawls contrasted with the voices of the curious Northerners gathering around, eager to hear their story.

Now a Kentucky resident, Calvin Deering wore a white name tag pinned to his gray coat. His brother, Alexander Deering, had traveled from Richmond. Both had served in the Twenty-Eighth Virginia Regiment, and, despite fighting side by side, they hadn't seen each other in nearly forty years—until this reunion brought them together. When one heard the other was in Gettysburg, he sought him out.

Leaning against the iron fence at the Copse of Trees, they traced their regiment's path across the valley. Their gray coats drew attention, and soon people approached to shake their hands, ask questions, and listen to them. The brothers welcomed them all.

"I'm pleased to see so many of you," Alexander said with a smile. "Last time I was here, I didn't get close enough to recognize you."

Recalling his reception at the reunion, Calvin laughed as he shared his experience: "When I got into town, someone said to me, 'Here you come, Johnny, you'll have plenty here.' And I told him, 'Oh, I know that—I got plenty the last time I was here.'"[36]

(*Top*) Veterans from both the Union and Confederate armies pose at the High-Water Mark of the Rebellion Monument during the Grand Reunion. Courtesy of the Library of Congress. (*Bottom*) The same location in 2025, photographed by the author.

Calvin had been captured during the charge and now returned to the very spot where it happened. Though it had been fifty years, he had no trouble finding it.

After taking in the moment, the brothers headed off to visit General Meade's headquarters. Intrigued by their story, a group of Union veterans followed along, eager to hear more.

In the next chapter, we'll revisit Calvin Deering as we explore Pickett's Charge and the pivotal moments that shaped his journey.

Hundreds of little stories unfolded each day at the Grand Reunion, small moments that, while not monumental on their own, were captivating and full of character. These were the types of events that captured the spirit of the gathering—moments of nostalgia, reconciliation, and human connection. They didn't make headlines like the grand speeches or reenactments, but they left a lasting impression on those who experienced them. Here's a select highlight from July 2, a snapshot of those fleeting and yet powerful moments that made the reunion so special.

The old soldiers returned to Gettysburg for various reasons, but one man had a rather unusual motive. George Thorne, the chief clerk at the Harrisburg State Department, shared a funny but strange story about a visit from an elderly Union veteran. This particular vet had been carrying a bit of fifty-year-old guilt from the first day of the battle. He confessed to Thorne that he "succumbed to temptation" and swiped a bunch of onions from Thorne's garden near Seminary Ridge. After all these years, he wanted to repay Thorne for the onions and relieve his conscience. Thorne didn't care about the onions and turned down the money, but he did ask the old vet whether he knew the identity of the soldiers who had raided his eight beehives and stole all the honey. However, the old soldier was innocent of this crime. To the best of my knowledge, no one has ever confessed to that theft.[37]

Another story recounts a remarkable coincidence when two old soldiers crossed paths near where Armistead fell at the Bloody Angle. The old Confederate shared his experience from that fateful day as an old Union veteran pushed through the crowd. "What's your name, comrade?" the Union veteran asked.

"John Carson of Burlington, North Carolina," came the response.

"What's that?"

The Union vet looked surprised, and the Confederate from Pickett's Charge repeated his name: "John Carson of Burlington, North Carolina."

The Union man reached out and took the Confederate's hand. "What a coincidence, for my name is John Carson too, and I come from Burlington, but it's Burlington, N.J."[38] It turns out that neither of these men had received a scratch during the battle and were directly opposite each other in the fighting. They were both so tickled by the coincidence that they walked a mile through the afternoon heat to the press tents to share the news with the reporters.

This story is interesting because it appears in another newspaper with slightly different details. *The Philadelphia Inquirer* covers a meeting between two men named John Caisan, also from Burlington, New Jersey, and Burlington, North Carolina. I assume these are the same men, and if you pronounce John Carson with a bit of an accent, it's easy to get John *Caisan*.

To add another fly to the ointment, *The Philadelphia Inquirer* also mentioned two "George W. Anthonys," one from Burlington, New Jersey, and the other from Burlington, North Carolina. The paper said,

> *Today the "Johnny" Anthony hunted up Anthony the "Yank" and then for the rest of the morning the man in gray and the man in blue sat under an American flag . . . and swapped war yarns of the great battles in which they had faced each other as deadly enemies half a century ago. Later, with equal magnanimity, the Northern Anthony visited his Southern friend in the Confederate camp, and there they held another reception among the men in gray.*[39]

I'm reasonably sure that the John Carsons of Burlington are the same individuals as the George Anthonys of Burlington. I have no idea how the newspapers got the names so incredibly different. It just reinforces that the newspapers don't always get it right. The reporters scrambled over the battlefield looking for the most interesting stories and didn't always take the time to fact-check every detail. But I'll leave it up to the reader to determine whether this was a single incident or two separate accounts full of coincidences.

Another story took place between two vets on the battlefield. While touring Culp's Hill, a Confederate with an empty sleeve approached a Union vet. During the conversation, the Southerner remarked, "I'd like to see the Yankee who shot my arm off."

"What regiment did you belong to?" asked the Union vet.

After exchanging more details, it became clear that the two men had stood face-to-face during the battle.

"Perhaps I shot you," was the Yankee's grim joke. "I was firing there."

And then the two veterans shook hands and went on to discuss the battle.

A similar story unfolded at the Bloody Angle. Augustus Washburne of Philadelphia returned to the high-water mark, standing once more on the very ground where he had fought fiercely in hand-to-hand combat during Pickett's Charge, where he had lost his arm. As he traced the spot where he had suffered a bayonet wound, he was shocked to find himself face-to-face with the very man who had taken his arm all those years ago.

Heart pounding, Washburne confronted the old Rebel. "Do you remember me?" he asked.

The veteran studied him in silence, his eyes narrowing as recognition dawned. Then, with a chuckle of disbelief, he exclaimed, "By gosh, you are the fellow!"

That old Rebel was James Burnett from Indiana. What could have been a tense moment instead became an unexpected bond. Within thirty minutes, the former enemies—once locked in brutal combat—laughed together like old comrades, calling each other "Jim" and "Gus."[40]

Alexander Hunter from Virginia was a popular guest at the reunion. He came into town wearing the same uniform and leather accoutrements he had worn fifty years earlier.

He was wounded at the Battle of Second Manassas, fought from August 28 to 30, 1862, in Prince William County, Virginia. After the battle, Hunter received a shell jacket that had initially belonged to another private in the Eighth Virginia Infantry who had been killed during the fighting. The fallen soldier's sister gave it to Hunter, who wore it for the remainder of the war. As a member of the Fourth Virginia, Black Horse Cavalry,[41] and Mosby's Rangers, Hunter was wounded twice while wearing the shell jacket.

By the reunion in 1913, the jacket was in tatters with a bullet hole shot through the sleeve. The leather accoutrements were all original issues, except for the belt, which he had scavenged from a dead Union soldier during the Battle of Gettysburg. He showed off his uniform to anyone who stopped long enough to look. Besides the uniform, people always asked Alexander Hunter about the Rebel Yell. He said, "I have often been asked about the Rebel Yell. I have always answered that we Rebs were savage with hunger, and men always holler when hungry."

Another story involving the Rebel Yell involved Captain J. C. Houser, an elderly Confederate soldier from Georgia. He climbed up Little Round Top and encountered more than one hundred Yankees. They had a lively time discussing the battle. By all reports, it was a lighthearted conversation, and everyone was enjoying themselves. They remembered the battle from long ago as they looked out on Devil's Den. One of the Union vets said, "Everything's here but the yell."

"Oh, that's here too," replied Houser. "Want to hear it again?"

The others nodded. "Then here she goes!" Captain Houser swung his old felt hat and let it rip. The reporter on the scene said that "one must hear it to appreciate it; cold type can't portray the . . . qualities that the peculiar yell can contain."[42]

When screamed by an advancing army, the Rebel Yell was the kind of sound that could make your blood freeze and your heart skip a beat. Now, imagine it coming from one lone person; somehow, it just doesn't have the same impact. It starts as a strange, throat-clearing noise, like someone trying to cough up a hairball while running up a hill. Then, without warning, it goes from zero to absolute chaos—a high-pitched scream that sounds like a deranged cat, an alarm clock, and an opera singer all crammed into a cannon. It's like the vocal cords of a person who has been yelling at the top of their lungs for too long, but somehow it gets louder with every breath, as if defying all laws of physics and good taste.

The Rebel Yell trailed off when Captain Houser finally ran out of breath. The Union veterans were quite impressed, but one of them spoke up. "Captain, let's hear it again."[43]

Old Houser graciously complied and gave the Rebel Yell, so long and so loud that he couldn't speak above a whisper for the rest of the reunion.

(*Top*) Four Union veterans pose at the statue of General Warren on Little Round Top during the Grand Reunion—note the approaching Confederate at the left of the 1913 photograph. Reproduced from the *Fiftieth Anniversary Report*. (*Bottom*) The same location in 2025, photographed by the author.

This next story captured the very essence of the reunion, spreading like wildfire across the country and finding its way into every major newspaper. It was the kind of heartwarming, symbolic tale that resonated deeply with a nation still trying to heal its past wounds. Two veterans—one in the blue of the Union and the other in the gray of the Confederacy—met downtown in Gettysburg. The scene was powerful: Two men who had once fought against each other now stood in the same place, sharing the same ground. They didn't just shake hands. They literally fell into each other's arms, overwhelmed with emotion, as though the weight of years of animosity, suffering, and loss had finally been lifted.

They spent the day together, touring the town, reflecting on the past and what they had endured. As they walked, their conversation shifted toward an idea that seemed to crystallize as they moved from one place to the next—a symbol of reconciliation, of burying the hatchet, *literally.* The two of them, hand in hand, made their way to a hardware store. They bought a hatchet, an ordinary object carrying extraordinary weight. It wasn't the tool itself that mattered, but rather what it represented: an end to conflict, a gesture of peace between two men who had seen the horrors of war up close.

They trudged a mile and a half to the battlefield, their pace steady, both men lost in thought. On arriving at the site of Pickett's Charge, where the bloodshed had been particularly fierce, they paused, feeling the weight of history in the air. Then they began to dig. They were not just making a hole; they were constructing a new type of monument. Once it was deep enough, they embraced, tears streaming down their faces as the reality of the moment struck them. And then, in a final, powerful act, they buried the hatchet in the ground, symbolizing the end of their personal conflict and perhaps the conclusion of the broader divisions that had torn their country apart.[44]

Newspapers across the nation reported the story of this emotional act. It perfectly captured the mood of the reunion—two men, once enemies, now united by their shared experiences of history and their country. Yet, despite the widespread attention this story received, the names of the two veterans were never recorded. Perhaps it didn't matter. The narrative had become so universally embraced that their identities seemed secondary to the broader symbolism. The names of these men were lost to time, buried like the hatchet they had placed in the earth. It evolved into a story not of two individuals but of a collective hope for healing and reconciliation that unfolded at the Grand Reunion.

Earlier in this book, we discussed the "Myth of the Uninvited Black Soldier," in which some modern scholars claim that the United States Colored Troops were intentionally excluded from the Grand Reunion. This is a false claim built on poor research. All honorably discharged veterans were invited, and it was up to each individual to decide whether they wanted to attend.

The Reunion Commission arranged for Black soldiers to attend, and approximately three hundred Black Union veterans attended. This was before the era of desegregation, so they were assigned their own section in the camp but were treated just like every other veteran. And according to the reports, they had a great time.

However, what the Commission hadn't anticipated was the arrival of Black *Confederate* soldiers.

Since no arrangements had been made for them, they were given straw beds and sent to sleep on the floor of the Great Tent. However, their situation quickly changed when a group of Tennessee Confederates discovered them. Recognizing their fellow Southerners, the Tennesseans brought them back to their own camp, rearranged their quarters, provided a separate tent, and ensured that they were well taken care of. This act of camaraderie led to the Tennessee Delegation being regarded as the most unified among the Southern groups.

The exact number of Black Confederates at the reunion is unknown, but we can make an educated guess. We know that the Tennessee Confederates gave them their own tent. At its maximum capacity, the tent was designed to accommodate twelve cots, and initially each tent was intended to contain only eight cots to provide the veterans with more space. However, extra cots were added once the camp began to fill up. Therefore, thinking about it logically, it's hard to justify giving one to two people their own tent. So, how many must have shown up to justify giving them their own tent? We may never know the answer, but I think it's safe to say that between four and ten Black Confederates attended the reunion.

To avoid controversy, let me be clear: I'm not claiming these Black Confederates were officially enlisted soldiers. They may have been enslaved individuals, teamsters, cooks, or body servants. The newspaper accounts report that they served the South during the war and attended the reunion dressed in gray Confederate uniforms. So, for simplicity's sake, we'll refer to them here as Black Confederates.

We don't have a complete list of the Black Confederates who attended the reunion, but we do know that Levi Miller was among them—and he may have camped with the Tennessee veterans.

Born into slavery on January 9, 1836, in Rockbridge, Virginia, Miller was a gifted orator and a respected preacher who lived his life in accordance with his faith. Those who knew him held him in high regard. Described as a husky man, Miller was seventy-seven years old at the time of the reunion. Confederate veterans reportedly covered the cost of his transportation to and from the reunion.[45]

His presence—marked by his dark skin and gray Confederate uniform—drew significant attention, but his White comrades treated him with respect and camaraderie.

Here's some additional background on Levi Miller: In 1861, Captain John McBride acquired Miller as a servant from his brother, Robert McBride, who owned him. Miller was present for the battles around Richmond in 1862.

When Captain McBride was wounded at the Second Battle of Bull Run, Miller stayed by his side, nursing him back to health in the hospital. McBride recovered just in time to fight at Fredericksburg.

Levi Miller accompanied the Confederate army into Pennsylvania during General Lee's advance toward Gettysburg, remaining with the troops until they withdrew from the state. Despite being encouraged to desert, he refused and remained loyal to the Confederacy until the war's end. In a letter of recommendation, Captain J. E. Anderson of the Fifth Texas Regiment dispelled any doubts about Miller's loyalty to the South: "He was in the Pennsylvania campaign, and at New Castle and Chambersburg, he met several Negroes whom he knew, and who had run away from Virginia. They tried to get Levi to desert—but he would not."[46]

Captain Anderson continued:

*In the spring of 1864, we returned to Virginia and rejoined General Lee's army. At the Battle of the Wilderness, when in a desperate emergency, General Lee insisted upon leading the Texas brigade in a charge, the men refused to permit him to do so and, seizing the reins of his horse, compelled him to go to the rear, unable to bear the sight of his being killed before their eyes. In the furious fighting that followed, Captain McBride had both legs broken and was believed to be mortally wounded. This was early in the morning of May 6, 1864.*

*Levi Miller was at that time with the wagon trains and did not learn of the captain being wounded until he got to Spotsylvania Court House, where we arrived early on May 8. On the morning of the tenth, Levi brought a haversack of rations. In order to reach me in our temporary ditch and breastworks, he had to cross an open field for two hundred yards. As he was running at his highest speed the enemy's sharpshooters clipped the dirt all around him, but he came through untouched. I told him he must not attempt to go back until night, as the sharpshooters would be sure to get him. I directed him how to find the wounded captain, and as soon as it was dark, he was to rejoin and nurse him until he died.*

*At about two o'clock in the afternoon, I saw from the maneuvers of the enemy in our front, that they were getting ready to charge us. I told Levi he would gain his chance during the fighting. He asked for a gun and ammunition, which were given him, as we had a number of extra weapons. At about four o'clock, a furious charge was made. Levi Miller stood by my side, and man never fought harder and better than he did when the enemy tried to cross our little breastworks. We clubbed and bayoneted them off, and no one used his bayonet with more skill and effect than he. During the fight my men encouraged him by shouting, "Give them hell, Levi."*

*After the fight was over, one of my men proposed that Levi Miller should be enrolled as a full member of the company. I put the motion, and of course it was passed unanimously. I immediately enrolled him as a full member of the company, which roll I have yet in my possession. As soon as it was dark, Levi made his way to Captain McBride, who had been taken to a hospital at Charlottesville, Virginia. He faithfully nursed him until October, 1865, which was some time after the war closed. Captain McBride returned to Texas, where he died in 1880. He owed his life to Levi Miller's good nursing.*[47]

The original caption read, "Levi Miller, only Colored Confederate." His dark skin and gray uniform attracted considerable attention at the 1913 Gettysburg Reunion. Courtesy of Library of American History.

After the war, Levi Miller moved to Winchester, and, thanks to Captain Anderson's recommendation, he obtained a full pension from the state of Virginia.[48] Not much is known about his time at the Grand Reunion, but the papers indicate that he received considerable attention for wearing the Confederate uniform while visiting the battlefield.

Levi Miller died on February 26, 1921, and was buried in Lexington, Virginia. His headstone states, "Levi Miller 1838–1921 C.S.A" (Confederate States of America).

The Grand Reunion at Gettysburg in 1913 was meant to honor the Civil War veterans, a momentous gathering of old soldiers reliving past glories and remembering fallen comrades. Yet, in the midst of the commemoration, one group was notably absent from recognition—the women who had borne the war's heaviest burden on the home front. They had sent husbands, sons, and brothers off to fight, endured years of uncertainty, and mourned those who never returned.

Writing for *The New York Times*, Helen Longstreet lamented this oversight, noting that no provisions had been made for these women at the reunion. She feared their suffering and sacrifices would remain untold.[49]

Others shared her sentiment, including General Alfred Beers, commander in chief of the Grand Army of the Republic, who hoped that Gettysburg would take a deeper interest in the women of the North and the South. He advocated the creation of a national monument on the battlefield dedicated to the wives, mothers, sisters, and sweethearts who suffered untold anguish at home while their men fought and died in the war. General Beer's message was well received by the old soldiers on both sides of the conflict and heavily discussed throughout the reunion. Although the Pennsylvania Memorial does mention the vital role of women, the recognition that Helen Longstreet and General Beers advocated has never come to pass.

Helen Longstreet interviewed quite a few veterans at the reunion. One from Pennsylvania happened to live in Gettysburg. He took her to a broken old cherry tree near the Peach Orchard. Peaches weren't quite ripe at the beginning of July when the battle took place, but cherries were in peak season.

> *"It was right here," he said. "There was a brave fellow from Michigan that I was mighty fond of. We were resting after the repulse of Pickett's*

*Charge and wondering whether we would have to follow them Johnny Rebs back into Virginia. The young Michigan soldier was little more than a lad; dark-haired, dark-eyed, slender, and straight as an Indian. Them Michigan boys were great fighters.*

*"The Michigan boy soldier was the bravest of the brave. He talked to me a great deal about the sweetheart he had left behind. He told me of eyes blue as the heavens above, and the fair hair that held of gleams of sunlight and throat and cheeks like the magnolias we had picked away down in Old Virginia. The day of Pickett's Charge he had received a letter from the girl waiting for him back at home. We were mighty tired, but the stimulus of victory made me forget our weariness. The repulse of Pickett's division made us all feel that the end was in sight and that the Nation's flag would still wave over land and sea, with the start of every truant State shining in its undimmed blue.*

*"My Michigan boy friend and I were resting not far away from this old cherry tree. I picked a quart of cherries and traded them to him for three pieces of hardtack; as he was eating the cherries, a stray shell directed by the devil snuffed out the life of Michigan's boy soldier. I took from his pocket the picture of the little girl who was waiting in her faraway Michigan home and sent it back to her with a lock of the dead soldier's hair. It was the women who suffered most during the war, and I am sorry they are not here today."*[50]

Later, while walking down Emmitsburg Road, Helen Longstreet encountered a tired old veteran shambling down the road. Helen offered him her umbrella, but he refused. "Pshaw! I was fightin' up this road before you was born. I guess I kin stand a little sun now. But how I wish Jane was here. She had a harder time than I did enduring the war."[51]

Farther down the Emmitsburg Road, she encountered a faded old woman gazing out on the battlefield. She told Helen, "I couldn't help coming. Jim was killed along here somewhere. I think it must have been about here. He was just my sweetheart, but I told him that I would wait until he came back. I won't have much longer to wait now. He did not come back to me, but I am going to him."[52]

As Helen Longstreet walked the roads of Gettysburg, she encountered veterans and widows, each carrying their memories of the war. Some understood that the most profound suffering had not been on the battlefield but in the hearts of those left behind. Others wished their wives could be recognized for the hardships they had endured.

Though the war had ended decades before, its wounds lingered in the hearts of those who had waited, watched, and wept. While the battlefield was marked with monuments to the soldiers, the grief of the women who bore the cost of war remained largely unrecognized—a quiet sacrifice forever woven into the fabric of history.

While some at the Grand Reunion reflected on the sacrifices of those left behind, others found solace in reconnecting with former comrades—even those who had once been enemies. Among the many stories Helen Longstreet recorded was an unexpected reunion between two old soldiers, one who had fought for the Union and another who had once stood against him.

The battle for Fort Fisher in January 1865 was a brutal, unrelenting struggle. The fort was the Confederacy's last major coastal stronghold, and the Union forces were determined to take it. Amid the smoke and chaos, Sergeant Gerton of the 147th New York Volunteers found himself thrust into command when his captain fell wounded. The Confederates, now surrounded with no chance of escape, were ordered to surrender—but they weren't ready to go down without a fight.

Leading the Confederate defense was Captain Smith, a fiery young officer barely twenty-two years old, his defiance burning as fiercely as the cannons that had battered the fort. When Gerton demanded his surrender, Smith refused to comply. Instead, he did the unthinkable—he challenged Gerton to a duel.

Standing at a towering six feet, four inches, and weighing 225 pounds, Sergeant Gerton was a giant of a man. In contrast, Captain Smith was a slender boy. Gerton later recalled, "I could have overcome him with one hand. It would have been like tackling an infant, so I declined to fight the duel."

The war ended, the years passed, and the battlefield faded into memory, but the unfinished encounter between the two men remained.

Nearly half a century later, at the Grand Reunion in Gettysburg, both Gerton and Smith came searching—not for vengeance but for each other. When they finally met, Smith spoke first, his voice filled with the weight of time: "I came here to find that sergeant. I wanted to tell him before I answered the last call that I have lived long enough to be glad that I surrendered the fort to you."

Gerton, the once-mighty soldier now aged and graying, replied with solemn conviction:

> *Smith, I came here to find you and to tell you before I join our comrades on the other side, that I wouldn't fight that duel with you over your sword down at Fort Fisher because I knew I would have to kill you. I believed the day would come when you would be as ready to die for the American flag as you were willing to die then on the sword you had been given by the South.*[53]

Time had transformed them both. Once enemies, they now stood together as brothers, united by history, war, and the flag that had once divided them. Stories like theirs were reported across the nation, as veterans from both sides gathered to share memories of battles long past. Though they vividly recalled the hardships and horrors of war, there was no desire to rekindle old animosities. Instead, they chose to exchange their experiences, not as enemies but as men who had endured the same suffering—and were now ready to forgive, if not forget.

This spirit of reconciliation was evident in even the smallest gestures, such as the simple act of trading badges. As Helen Longstreet made her way through the reunion, she encountered an old soldier wearing a gray uniform and stopped to ask him a question: "Why would a Union man wear a gray suit?"

"Me?" he said, surprised. "I am not a Yankee. Fought under Longstreet, and I'm from Mississippi."

"Why do you wear that badge, then?" She pointed to the Fifth Pennsylvania Volunteer Infantry badge pinned to his chest.

"Why," he said, "a Yank came along today from the Fifth Pennsylvania and asked me if I'd trade badges with him, after we'd had a talk and found out where we were at Gettysburg. So we traded. He's wearing my badge now—Fifteenth Mississippi. Says he'll keep it as long as he lives."[54]

The spirit of reconciliation at the Grand Reunion was evident in numerous ways—through shared stories, exchanged badges, and the simple understanding that the past was best left behind. But while the old soldiers reflected on their experiences, another battle was being fought—not on the fields of Gettysburg but at Helen Longstreet's typewriter.

A syndicate of newspapers had hired Helen to cover the Grand Reunion, and her reporting was printed nationwide. She took her job very seriously and was often at her typewriter late into the evening.

"I find my work here very hard in this heat," she said. "Then I have an assistant with me who cannot help because she has become ill, and that makes my labors doubly hard. Do I like my work? Oh yes, and I mean to succeed at it."[55]

Helen had an assistant whose job was to take shorthand notes of interviews with the veterans, but she wasn't up to the task. Helen said:

> *I brought over a stenographer with me, a young woman who isn't used to the hardships of the camp. After being here for two days without food, she has departed and gone back home. I pleaded, I threatened, I implored. I said, "Your father was a soldier. He fought four years, sometimes on half rations, sometimes on no rations at all. Try to be his daughter. It is only four days we have to stay here, and you can always get lemonade."*
>
> *But she said she did not believe in war, anyway. She appeared on the scene in days of peace, and what she wanted most was not glory, but something to eat. So I am holding the fort alone, under Gettysburg's skies.*[56]

Helen Longstreet had come to Gettysburg determined to document the Grand Reunion despite her hardships. Between the relentless heat, long hours at the typewriter, and the unexpected loss of her assistant, she pressed on, determined to succeed. But her greatest stories didn't come from behind her desk—they came from the voices of the veterans themselves.

While spending time with General Dan Sickles, Helen Longstreet met a veteran from the Third Army Corps, who was vigorous despite being eighty years old. The veteran had traveled all the way from Washington State to see his old commander for the last time. He was wearing a uniform that was riddled with holes. Helen asked him, "Who shot those holes in your coat?"

"Longstreet's men," he replied, "as they attacked us, up this road, just 50 years ago today. I have not been back here since, but have come back here today to say that if the gray-coated fellows who swarmed over these hills and shot a few holes in my body couldn't keep the old flag down, there ain't nobody else that's going to be allowed to do it."

Helen then asked him, "What's the meanest thing you did during the Civil War?"

The veteran hung his head in shame.

> *I remember it well, I wish I could forget it. I am sort of ashamed to tell you about it, but I was hungry. Our troops were passing a modest farmhouse. An old woman sat on a side veranda. I did not have time for ceremony so I dashed into her kitchen on a quest for food. I didn't discover a bite, not even a lemon. I was mighty hungry, so I went out to interview the old lady. She was concealing something underneath her apron, which she uncovered with difficult reluctance—four fat hens. I took them all. I will never forget the old lady's face as she said: "there goes my last setting hens." It was a pretty sorry thing for me to do.*[57]

The veteran's story, a mixture of pride and remorse, was just one of many that colored the reunion. In the years since the war, these men had carried their experiences with them, and as they gathered in Gettysburg, they were not just remembering the past—they were coming to terms with it. The reunion provided an opportunity to reflect, confront old regrets, and find closure. For Helen Longstreet, it was a powerful reminder of the lasting impact of war, not just on the battlefield but also on the lives of those who lived through it.

July 1 was the high-water mark of the reunion, and by the next day, the armies of the Blue and Gray started to recede under the intense heat and the discomforts of camp life. The sun beating down on the canvas turned the tents into furnaces. The weather during the early days of the encampment was intensely hot, but the hottest day of the week was July 2. The thermometer inside one of the hospital tents registered 103.5 degrees Fahrenheit. Options were to stay under the sweltering canvas or suffer under the sun's direct glare. Neither offered much relief, and both led to much suffering.

General Hunter Liggett, in command of the camp, estimated that more than six thousand veterans left during the day and another one thousand more would depart by nightfall. Most of them had looked over the battlefield, shaken hands with old comrades, taken another glimpse at their old foes, and headed home. The men attending the camp were not sorry to see them go. The camp was crowded beyond capacity, and hundreds of old men were quartered in tents made for circuses, not for sleeping, while dozens of others slept on the ground. And although the cooks worked night and day, they struggled to keep up with the demand for food.[58]

A seventy-five-year-old veteran said, "I came here all the way from Oregon expecting to stay the entire week, but I couldn't stand it. I held on since Monday morning, but I had to give in, and I'm on my way home now. I have seen it, and that is all I wanted to make the long journey for. I can go home satisfied, but I'm sure I would've died if I'd stayed here."[59]

Another veteran said, "I came from Indiana, and I wish I was home. It was simply awful, and I never before experienced such heat. I'm going to get into a Pullman car tonight, and have the electric fan turned on, and kept going until I arrive home."

Another said, "I was told by my friends that it would be hot at Gettysburg, but I never imagined it would be so hot. I sweltered until I became so weak I could hardly walk, and some of the boys helped me to the station. Home for me."[60]

The officials at the Great Camp were prepared for everything. Although they didn't have enough tents to house all of the veterans, one of the things they had in abundance was coffins. The average age of the veterans was seventy-two years old. At that time, the insurance companies anticipated around 4,300 deaths a year for men in that age bracket. They estimated that 100 deaths a week, especially in the July heat, was not excessive.[61] With this number in mind, the camp officials had a specific tent dedicated to housing hundreds of coffins. The exact number of coffins seemed to change depending on who was asked.

"Those persons who sent 500 coffins to Gettysburg did not know the vitalizing and immunizing qualities of the Pennsylvania climate," says the *Public Ledger*. "Coffins are the last thing Pennsylvanians think about, and they never use them for their summer guests."[62]

Charles A. Shaffer was a member of the Pennsylvania House of Representatives from 1911 to 1922. As a government official, he was in charge of the embalmers sent to Gettysburg to take care of the anticipated one hundred dead veterans. However, the actual death toll never came close to the estimation, and as a result, they ended up shipping almost all of the coffins back to the company from which they were purchased.

According to *The Dispatch*, a Lexington, North Carolina, newspaper, five hundred coffins[63] were shipped to Gettysburg ahead of the Grand Reunion.

Dr. Robert Wesley Pyle, who happened to be both a veteran and a veterinarian, claimed that there were seven hundred coffins in the Great Camp. He claimed that "The survivors, when they pass the ghastly pile, only laugh and declare they will not need them for years yet, that they intend attending the next re-union."[64]

One of the veterans from New York said:

> *I got walking about in the hot sun until I grew very tired. And I thought of those 500 coffins that had been brought down to Gettysburg to take the old boys home in. It made me so scared that I told a friend about it. "Oh, take a drink," he said. "And forget about the coffins." I took one drink, and then I took another and before I knew it I had taken nine drinks, and the more drinks I took, the more coffins I saw, and then I thought it was time to quit, and it is me for the cool spot at home as soon as I can get there.*[65]

According to *The Gettysburg Compiler*, the number of coffins was greatly exaggerated. "There were not 100, or 200, or 500 coffins brought to this place. How many were ready, we have no means of knowing, but only one [train] car load of 57 coffins reached here and were unloaded at the commissary, the temporary morgue."[66]

A conflicting report spoke about an enterprising undertaker who was the only unhappy man at Gettysburg. He had allegedly "made a contract with the quartermaster to care for all dead veterans, and using some system of computation furnished by a life insurance company, he calculated that at least 450 would die during the week. Accordingly, he shipped that number of coffins to the camp and had a whole corps of embalmers on hand, but only eleven veterans died, and the undertaker lost money."[67]

Although most of the coffins weren't needed, a few of them were. Landes Travis was returning to the Hotel Gettysburg at 8:00 a.m. on July 2 when he suddenly reeled and fell onto the concrete sidewalk. Onlookers carried the veteran into the hotel lobby and summoned an ambulance. A doctor arrived and pronounced Travis dead on the spot. Landes Travis was sixty-eight years old.[68]

There was a second fatality on July 2 when Allen Diehl, a veteran from Arlington, Virginia, died from a cerebral hemorrhage induced by the extreme heat.[69]

Back during the war, army food had very little variety. Breakfast would consist of hardtack, bacon, beans, and coffee. What they called "dinner" we call lunch, and it consisted of hardtack, bacon, beans, and coffee. The last meal of the day was called supper, and once again it consisted of hardtack, bacon, beans, and coffee.

What is hardtack, you ask?

Hardtack was the original "energy bar" from the past, with zero taste and no enjoyment. It was a dense, rock-like biscuit made of flour, water, and a dash of salt, and it was only slightly better than going hungry. In fact, hardtack was better at breaking teeth than filling the stomach. Imagine chewing on a brick, only with less charm and more existential despair.

It was a staple for sailors and soldiers during long trips because it didn't spoil. It was pure carbohydrates but lacked protein, fat, fiber, vitamins, or taste. But if you needed something to keep you going for a few days when real food was scarce, then hardtack was your go-to. And sometimes the Confederates didn't even have that much, especially toward the end of the war when flour was hard to come by. Often, they were down to just cornmeal and watered-down chicory root as a substitute for coffee. There were even accounts of hungry Confederates boiling shoe leather for food! This was the ultimate "tough meat," and the only seasoning was desperation.

Fortunately, the food provided at the fiftieth reunion was on a whole different level. It was of good quality and plentiful, with enough variety to keep things interesting.

For most Northern veterans, Pennsylvania's hospitality was just business as usual—decent food, nothing to complain about, and nothing to rave about. It was just a meal.

However, Southern veterans acted like they had stumbled into a royal banquet. Having spent years surviving on hardtack, cornmeal crumbs, and wishful thinking, they were blown away by the sheer abundance of food. Many old Confederates were thin and relatively poor, and each meal was a feast fit for a king. They could even go back for seconds and thirds!

The menu for July 2, 1913, was as follows: For breakfast, the chow line served apple sauce, oatmeal, and milk, as well as fried eggs, fried bacon, hashed brown potatoes, fresh bread, hard bread, butter, and coffee. Not a bad-sounding meal. Dinner (which we would call lunch) was roast mutton, boiled potatoes, stringless beans, fresh bread, hard bread, butter, coffee, and iced tea. The evening supper consisted of ribs of beef, fried potatoes, peas, fresh bread, hard bread, butter, and coffee.[70] The ovens worked throughout the day, and the smell of fresh bread and coffee wafted over the camp. Many veterans topped off their meals with a cup of joe and a cigar.

Speaking of cigars, Philip Myers, the eighteen-year-old photography assistant, met a Union veteran who wanted a picture taken at Devil's Den. During the battle, the old vet had been up on Little Round Top, but he wanted a photo of himself at Devil's Den because "I want to see where that so and so who shot me must've been standing."

While setting up the camera, the old Yankee stood there puffing on a cigar, with one hand holding his cheek. Myers recommended against the unusual pose and said it would spoil the picture. The veteran explained,

> *I'm a-fightin' and a-yellin' at the top of my lungs when this bullet comes along and catches me right in the mouth. But what with yellin', my mouth is wide open, so it misses my teeth and comes outta my cheek. And when it heals, it doesn't close up tight. . . . There is still a little hole there. If I don't plug it with my finger, I don't get no draft on my smoke.*[71]

He then proceeded with a demonstration. The old veteran inhaled a puff from his cigar, pursed his lips tightly, and then blew a tendril of smoke out from the hole in his cheek.

As Myers watched the old soldier casually exhale smoke from his war-wound-turned-chimney, he couldn't decide what was more impressive—the man's survival or his commitment to a good cigar.

The Gettysburg veterans had plenty to do during their visit, but most of it involved standing around under the blazing sun. For those who preferred their history lessons with a side of shade, a trip into town to catch the 1913 silent film *The Battle of Gettysburg* was the perfect escape. Sitting in a cool, dark theater for an hour was a luxurious experience.

At a time when most films ran a quick five to fifteen minutes, this epic stretched to an impressive fifty minutes across five reels—a true blockbuster for its day. Directed by Charles Giblyn and Thomas Ince, the film was hyped as "the greatest motion picture in the world" and boasted a whopping $75,000 budget. The battle scenes featured nearly fifteen thousand actors, complete with exploding cannons, bursting shells, cavalry charges, and dramatic hand-to-hand combat.

Of course, the film also proudly advertised itself as "an accurate reproduction of the greatest battle of the Civil War." By "accurate," they meant it was filmed in sunny Malibu, California, because nothing says Gettysburg like palm trees and the Pacific Ocean.

The film premiered at the Walter Theatre in Gettysburg, just in time for the reunion. One review claimed, "No greater realism could be found than in the direct visualization of the horrible and yet sublime spectacle that went to make up the battles of Culp's Hill, the immortal charge of Pickett's Brigade, the breathless and heartbreaking hand to hand fighting at the Bloody Angle." And if the battle wasn't enough for you, the *Battle of Gettysburg* film also featured President Abraham Lincoln *and* a love story. As entertaining as this may sound, this movie has sadly been lost to time, and no copies are known to exist; only a few grainy clips have survived.

The film opened in Gettysburg on Friday, June 27, at 6:45 p.m. at Walter's Theatre. Admission was twenty-five cents. Peter Guibert, who walked to Gettysburg with a cartload of instruments, performed as a one-man band for the opening act.

A reporter from *The Spokesman-Review* saw the film and described it like this: "Facing defeat on the third day, General Lee gave the order to General Pickett to charge, and the brave soldiers followed their leader through a murderous rifle fire and a fierce cannonading until most of them were stretched out lifeless upon the field. This is the most heroic and sensational incident of the war history of the world and is shown in the film in all detail."[72]

Eager to escape the sun and witness the spectacle, a group of veterans from Virginia attended the silent film. When it reached the part about Pickett's Charge, many of the old soldiers wept as the actors retreated from the Bloody Angle. Even in the early days of cinema, sometimes a film could strike a little too close to home.

But while one film aimed for solemn historical drama, another took a more, shall we say, creative approach. With the reunion in full swing, filmmaker Frank Smith saw an opportunity to bring history to the big screen by making a movie right there in the middle of the Great Camp. So, while the veterans were touring the battlefield and viewing the monuments, the director brought in a camera crew and some actors and made a cheesy movie. It turns out that when you put a fake veteran in a camp full of real ones, the reviews can get brutal. One reporter wrote, "It has imported a German actor with gold teeth from New York to play the part of the Union veteran. There being fifty-five thousand real veterans in camp, the play actor veteran is greeted with loud guffaws whenever he appears in his wig."[73]

The film *United at Gettysburg* was released only a few weeks after it was shot. By today's standards, it is kitschy, with overly dramatic and unintentionally funny moments. It's clear that they tried hard to make a quality film, but it ultimately felt corny and second-rate. That said, it still offers some great footage of the reunion and may even contain a surprise of historical significance . . .

The story goes like this: An old Confederate soldier arrives at the fiftieth reunion and is met at the train by his daughter, who happens to be a nurse. Meanwhile, an old Union vet shows up (with gold teeth) and runs into his son, a major in the army. During the reenactment of Pickett's Charge, the Union veteran falls victim to heat prostration and collapses. An ambulance just happens to be driving by at that exact moment and picks up the downed vet. He's taken to a hospital tent, where the old Confederate's daughter just happens to be working.

Now, if you haven't already figured out where this is going, you clearly haven't seen enough bad movies. But hold on, it gets better.

Somehow the old Confederate ends up at the hospital tent, where his daughter is tending to the old Union vet. Just as the scene is winding down, guess who shows up? Yep, the Union vet's son. And, in a shocking turn of events, the Union vet is miraculously healed—just in time to go off on a battlefield tour with the old Confederate. This leaves the son and daughter behind and, of course, sparks fly. Because what's a reunion without a little romantic drama?

Now, here's where this silent film actually becomes interesting. The two old soldiers sit down and discuss where they were during the battle. There's a long—painfully long—fade to black, and suddenly they flash back fifty years earlier to the Battle of Gettysburg. Soldiers march into battle, fighting across open fields, while lobbing cannonballs at each other. There's even a cavalry charge.

And then, just like that, for no apparent reason, they call a truce in the middle of the battle. We see "younger" versions of the two old soldiers squaring off against each other across a field. With the entirely fictional truce in effect, they decide to get together and make a trade. One doesn't have any food, and the other doesn't have any tobacco. They shake hands and sit down to enjoy some conversation when, all of a sudden, the battle starts back up again, breaking up their party.

Since it's a silent film, a title card appears on screen with dialogue from the Confederate: "Don't shoot until I get behind my tree." The Union man agrees, waits for the Confederate to get halfway across the field, and then shoots him in the back. The Union man then approaches his adversary, who is wounded and begging for water. To add insult to injury, the Union man takes a long drink from his canteen. Once satisfied, he upends his canteen, pours all the water onto the ground, and walks away. What a dastardly thing to do!

The flashback ends, we're back in 1913, and the title card says, "So we meet again." When the old Confederate realizes who he's talking to, he attacks the old Union soldier. But then, just in the nick of time, the son and daughter, who have been having a wonderful time together, show up on the scene and pull the two old men apart. Later, the son and daughter reunite, and sparks fly as they gaze out over the battlefield from one of the observation towers.

Meanwhile, the two old soldiers meet one final time, reconcile, and wander off together as friends. They all live happily ever after! Although the film is cheesy, I do not doubt that a similar storyline played out repeatedly at the reunion with the veterans.

However, here's the surprising historical significance: The fight scenes set during the flashback may have been taken from the lost film *The Battle of Gettysburg*. If so, they represent some of the best-preserved footage from that movie. The battle scenes look epic. Wouldn't it be amazing if someone were to find an intact copy of that film in their attic? I know I'd love to see it.

The Boy Scouts were indispensable at Gettysburg. John Collins[74] from Elmira, New York, and a member of the Iron Brigade, was walking through the town when a horse, frightened by a passing motor car, veered into the sidewalk and knocked over the old soldier. A crowd of onlookers gathered, but five Washington Boy Scouts were passing by and jumped into action. They slipped through the crowd, and four of the scouts held the curious onlookers back by forming a "fence" around the fallen vet with their staves. The fifth scout ran off and flagged down one of the many ambulances at Gettysburg for such an occasion.[75] By the time a doctor arrived with the ambulance, the scouts had their first aid kits out and were already assisting the old soldier.

The Boy Scouts worked tirelessly during the reunion to support the veterans. At night, when the old soldiers would get lost finding their way around camp, they would cry out, "Oh scout, oh scout!" A twelve- or thirteen-year-old scout would run to help the old soldiers find their tents. The scouts would often carry the veterans' baggage, bring them food, and deliver cool cups of water. As one reporter wrote, "Isn't it true that these . . . boys in khaki are simply the grandsons and great-grandsons of the boys of fifteen who fought until their hearts stopped beating on this very field?"[76]

On the Main Street of Gettysburg, a tall, fine-looking old soldier collapsed from the heat as he walked with his friend. A couple of Boy Scouts grabbed him and laid him down in a doorway while they applied a restorative. In doing so, they opened his shirt, exposing a long, ugly scar that ran from his right collarbone across his entire chest. The scouts marveled at the scar while his friend explained, "He was in Greg's Cavalry on the day they fought the duel with Jeb Stewart's Cavalry while Pickett's Charge was being made. A rebel trooper slashed him with his saber. He was in the hospital two months, but he got well, and he has never been ill since the war. I can't account for Jim keeling over at this time, though."[77]

The heat did him in, but soon enough the Boy Scouts loaded the old vet into an ambulance and sent him to the hospital.

In May 1861, the Eleventh Pennsylvania Infantry was given a puppy named Sallie as their mascot. While the regiment was training, Sallie used to playfully run through the legs of the soldiers as they marched in formation, sometimes tripping them. As she grew, she learned her place and marched beside Colonel Richard Coulter at the front of the line. Because of this, she was sometimes referred to as "Dick Coulter's Dog." When the Eleventh Pennsylvania marched into battle, Sallie went with them, taking her position at the end of the firing line and barking furiously at the enemy.

She was a medium-sized American Staffordshire dog with bright hazel eyes full of fire and intelligence. She was active and quick, with remarkable endurance. Her knowledge of the individual members of the regiment was truly impressive. A whole corps might pass her by, but she knew her soldiers and never followed any others.

During the first day of the Battle of Gettysburg, she became separated from her regiment during their retreat from Oak Ridge and was presumed dead. Three days later, the men returned to Oak Ridge and found Sallie alive but weak, licking the wounds of her comrades and keeping a faithful vigil over the deceased.

Sallie recovered and stayed with the Eleventh Pennsylvania Infantry almost until the end of the war, when she was killed at the Battle of Hatcher's Run in February 1865. "Poor Sallie fell in the front line in the fight at the Run—a bullet pierced her brain," a soldier wrote in a letter after the battle. "She was buried where she fell, by some of the boys, even whilst under a murderous fire, so much had they become attached to the poor brute, who so long had shared with them the toilsome march and the perils of battle.

"Sallie's bark will no longer be heard at the head of the column—her tail is wagless, and the marques, shelter tents and blankets that knew her shall know her no more forever—for her there is no pomp and pride, and circumstances of glorious war."[78]

In 1890, the survivors of the Eleventh Pennsylvania unanimously decided to include a tribute to their canine comrade in their monument at Gettysburg. "The 11th Pa. has a grand monument to mark their line of battle," wrote a veteran. "A bronze soldier on top, looking over the field, while the dog, Sallie, is lying at the base keeping guard."[79]

The bronze statue at the top of the monument was cast in the likeness of Colonel Richard Coulter, the commander of the Eleventh Pennsylvania. Coulter died in 1908, so his son presided over the regimental reunion held in 1913. The monument to the Eleventh attracted much attention from veterans on both sides of the battle, particularly the part that shows Sallie lying down below her owner.

During a group photo, the survivors of the Eleventh Pennsylvania Infantry gathered around the monument, leaving enough room for the statue of Sallie to be included.

The Eleventh Pennsylvania Monument at Gettysburg is a popular site for visitors. The bronze statue of Sallie, the regiment's loyal canine mascot, has been touched so often that the patina on her head has worn away, giving it a different color from the rest of the statue. As a tribute, visitors sometimes leave dog treats beside her statue to honor her memory and the soldiers she stood with.

Everywhere you looked at the reunion, Union Blue and Confederate Gray mingled in a public display of peaceful camaraderie. However, that doesn't mean old rivalries had completely faded. On the night of July 2, an unfortunate incident at the Gettysburg Hotel shattered the illusion of perfect reconciliation.

Critics of the reunion often seize on this single event as proof that the so-called unity between former enemies was nothing more than hollow lip service—that the bitterness of war still smoldered beneath the surface, refusing to die even after fifty years had passed. Though the incident lasted only a few moments, it cast a long shadow over the spirit of the Grand Reunion.

The exact details remain unclear, with conflicting accounts of who did what and when. To make matters worse, the two individuals involved in the incident have similar names: Henry Baker and Warren Henry. I've done my best to organize the events chronologically to present a clearer picture.

Here's how the story unfolds:

Whenever two veterans met at the reunion, they would ask, "Where are you from?" This wasn't just small talk; it was battlefield diplomacy and a quick way to determine whether the person you were speaking with had shot at you during the war. Henry Baker was a gray-haired Union veteran from Springfield, Illinois, but when he was a young man, he often delivered mail to an attorney in town named Abraham Lincoln.[80] He never missed an opportunity to tell people this story. Why would he? It was like saying you once handed the Constitution to George Washington.

That evening, Baker strolled into the Gettysburg Hotel dining room just before 7:00 p.m., looking for a meal and some clever conversation. He was seated at a table with a few others, and, naturally, the question arose: "Where are you from?"

Baker lit right up. "Springfield, Illinois," he said, proud as ever, and he rolled out the story about delivering mail to Honest Abe. It made for a great conversation piece and usually got nods of approval.

But not this time.

He was seated across from a big man originally from Virginia but who now worked as an attorney in Camden,[81] New Jersey. (This supports my early statement that people from New Jersey are nothing but troublemakers.) This man was Warren Henry;[82] he was around thirty-eight years old and seated with his friend Malcolm Griffin. It's important to note that neither Warren Henry nor Malcolm Griffin was a veteran, though both of their fathers were. While Warren and Malcolm were having dinner at the Gettysburg Hotel, their fathers enjoyed the reunion in the Great Camp.

Warren Henry was spitting mad at Baker's praise of Lincoln. One newspaper described it like this: "The Virginian ripped out an oath about being the town of Lincoln, attaching two of the vilest epithets in profanity to the martyred president."[83]

Baker was shocked by the language. He looked around the room; there were ladies present, so he reprimanded Warren for using profanity in public. However, this only escalated the situation. Infuriated by the correction, Warren slapped Baker across the face. Baker stood up to defend himself and Lincoln's good name. He grabbed a nearby bottle and threw it at Warren.

And that's when the knife fight began.

Charles Ensor was a brakeman on the Pennsylvania Railroad, and he was enjoying his meal when "he saw Henry handling the old soldier roughly and raising a knife as if to stab him. Ensor threw a beer bottle at the knife, he testified, and was about to throw another when prevented by Malcolm Griffin."[84]

Meanwhile, Edward J. Carroll was a sergeant in the Quartermaster's Corps and was also dining in the Gettysburg Hotel when the incident occurred. He heard someone say, "Look what they are doing to that man."

Warren Henry was triggered. He whipped out a knife and started slashing at anyone close by. Tables were overturned and dishes crashed to the floor as people scrambled to get out of the way. Charles Ensor was stabbed six times by Warren, twice in the arm and four times in the back. Edward J. Carroll was stabbed in the left shoulder, and when he raised his hand to protect himself, Warren stabbed him in the hand. Meanwhile, Baker, the old veteran who had tried to protect Lincoln's honor, reeled back and managed to stay out of range of the knife, but during the ensuing chaos, someone kicked him in the leg and broke his ankle.[85] John D. Morgan, a Black waiter working in the dining room, tried to intercept Warren and stop the violence but instead received a stab wound just above his heart.

Warren made a mad dash for the door and, in the process, stabbed two more restaurant workers. Walter Setzler, another Black waiter, was stabbed in the chest, while J. B. Wineman, a hotel steward, was stabbed in the shoulder. Hayden Reinecker was a bellhop, and when he saw what was going on, he ran from the hotel and summoned the state police. As he was returning, he encountered Warren and received a knife wound to his left shoulder for his trouble.

The hotel had hired Harry Roat Jr. as a security guard. When he heard the commotion, he ran to the dining room and grappled with Warren Henry, receiving a slight wound to his hand. But Warren was a big man and cast him off and ran for the exit, with Roat in hot pursuit. As soon as Warren reached the street, he was confronted by Daniel Farber of the state police. Farber was stabbed in the arm and the chest before Warren was finally subdued. In total, eight people were cut or stabbed. Warren was then hauled off to the county jail.[86]

Fortunately for the eight who were attacked, none of the injuries were life-threatening, and the doctors soon had them patched up.

A conflicting story states that Warren's friend, Malcolm Griffin, was also stabbed in the melee. While sitting in his jail cell, Warren claimed complete innocence of any wrongdoing. He told an entirely different version of the events:

> *I was sitting with my friend, Malcolm Griffin, in the dining room, talking with him over a glass of beer. Someone behind my back reached over my shoulder and stabbed Griffin. I did not see the face of the assailant, and when I jumped up, all was confusion.*
>
> *I hit someone and knocked him down. It was the man who stabbed Griffin. The knife flew from his hand, and I picked it up. Instantly, there were cries of murder, and someone yelled, "Kill him!" They meant me. . . . When I started to get out, I was knocked down. I raced through the parlor and out on the street, the crowd following. My face was covered in blood. I did not stab anyone. . . . When someone in the crowd said, "Look, he has the knife," I was surprised. I did not know I had it. Griffin told me later that I had got into trouble for protecting him.*[87]

Warren Henry was tried in a court of law, and many people spoke up on his behalf, including Governor William Mann of Virginia and Governor John Tener of Pennsylvania. The judge ruled that Warren suffered from a "temporary aberration of the mind,"[88] and Warren walked out of the courtroom a free man. The verdict echoed another all-too-familiar case—where a crazy bastard got away with murder.

I'll leave it up to the reader to decide whether justice was served.

That wasn't the only negative incident that occurred. Philip Myers, the young photography assistant, wrote about another event during the reunion. Although relations between former foes were generally harmonious, heated disagreements did arise from time to time.

"One of the more serious ones took place in a restaurant near the Jennie Wade House," according to Philip Myers. "After violent words had been exchanged across the table, a Reb and a Yank had at each other, not with bayonets this time, but with forks. Unscathed in the melee of 1863, one of them—and I never learned whether North or South—was almost fatally wounded in 1913 with table hardware!"[89]

Philip Myers wrote his recollection of the Grand Reunion fifty-seven years after the event. I have often wondered whether his account of the fork fight was a time-twisted version of the knife fight. I have not found a second account to verify the fork fight, but that doesn't mean it didn't happen.

Regardless, the violence was widely condemned by the veterans from both armies and did not accurately portray the sentiments of those attending the otherwise peaceful reunion. T. H. Alexander was a Civil War veteran and a lawyer. When he heard about the knife fight, he strongly condemned the incident:

> *Such conduct throws the old soldiers into disrepute throughout the country, and it is not their fault. . . . As a body, the veterans of the North and the South are a fine body of heroes, and they should not be held responsible for the acts of a few of their comrades. But the public is mighty apt to say, "I told you so, they can't get together without fighting." Such sentiment is decidedly unfair.*[90]

Sadly, when people talk about the Grand Reunion, the knife fight is almost always brought up as proof of how old hostilities still existed within the hearts of the veterans. However, Warren Henry was not a Civil War veteran, and neither were any of his eight victims. The only veteran on the scene was Henry Baker, who escaped the knife but suffered a broken ankle during the scuffle.

Music has a way of stirring the heart and resurrecting long-forgotten memories. A bent old veteran from Virginia was taking a tour of the Northern section of the Great Camp when he heard the sweet sounds of "Dixie" being played a few tents away by a fifer of considerable talent. The old vet from Virginia stopped in his tracks and removed his hat. He straightened his crooked back and stood at attention until the song was done. Just where that song transported him to is impossible to know for sure. Afterward, he pulled a handkerchief from his pocket, wiped his eyes, blew his nose, and set off to find the fifer.

"Hello, Billy," he called as he found the fifer's tent. "Play Dixie for me again."

"Sure, I will, Reb," answered the old fifer. "You didn't get much chance to hear a concert 50 years ago tonight, did you?" Then the Northern fifer played for the Southern veteran for a good hour or so.

The music attracted a small crowd, and soon other veterans dropped by to visit. From farther down the company street, one of the old veterans said, "Why, that sounds like our old fifer, Jim Goldthorpe. Wait till I get my drum." He found his drum and then marched into the tent where the fifer played for the old Confederate.

"Why hello, Jim, thought you were dead long ago," the drummer said.

The fifer recognized his old comrade and said, "Where have you been all these years? Haven't seen you since '65."[91] And just like that, a Confederate fighter, a Northern fifer, and his drummer boy sat by the fire, played music, and enjoyed some nostalgic camaraderie.

As the sun slipped below the horizon, an old Confederate veteran lost his way while searching for his tent. He wandered past thousands of brown tents, trying to find the one he had slept in the previous night. The fading light made it difficult to read the street signs, and every tent looked the same. It was like searching for a needle in a haystack. Occasionally, he would pop into a tent and ask the occupants for directions. To explain how lost he was, he wandered into a tent on 21st Street, even though he was looking for a tent on 38th Street. One of the men from the First Minnesota Regiment saw him and invited the lost Confederate into their tent to rest for a bit.[92]

"Who were you with?" asked one of the Minnesota men.

"I belong to the Virginia outfit, the 28th."

"That would've been Oldmstead's forces," said the veteran from Minnesota.

"That's right," said the Confederate. "We met you off yonder, where the fighting was the thickest."

"Well, I'll be durned!" cried the Minnesotan.

"What do you make of that?"

Then, with a twinkle in his eyes, the man from Minnesota asked, "Do you know what became of your flag?"

"I don't," said the Confederate. "You see, I was with Armistead's Brigade, the one that got into the Yankee lines when Pickett made his charge. I don't know exactly what happened to the flag, but I think some of you Yankees got it."

"We did. I'm Captain T. H. Presnell of Company F. First Minnesota. We captured your flag, and it is now in St. Paul. We've got a spare blanket here, and you may have it. Come in and bunk with us."[93]

The old Confederate was worn out and gladly accepted. He sat down on an empty cot and made himself as comfortable as possible. They then talked over the battle for the next few hours, and somewhere in the conversation, these two ancient enemies became friends.

The old Confederate spent the night on a spare cot. The next morning, when he was getting ready to leave to find his own quarters, he looked at the men from Minnesota. As if to memorize every detail of the tent and its inhabitants.

"What is it, comrade?" one of them asked.

"I'm just thinking," replied the Confederate, "I'm sorry we lost that flag, but if we had to lose it, I'm glad it was you fellows who got it. You are pretty good people."[94]

With that, he said goodbye and left. But the story doesn't end there. We'll get into more detail on what happened to the flag of the Twenty-Eighth Virginia Infantry when we discuss Pickett's Charge in the next chapter.

Just a quick note on this story: The Minnesota vet mentions that the old Confederate fought under Oldmstead. However, I couldn't find any evidence of anyone named Oldmstead participating in Pickett's Charge. There was a Colonel Charles H. Olmstead who fought for the Confederacy, but he was stationed in South Carolina during the Battle of Gettysburg—not on that fateful field in Pennsylvania.

I also wondered whether "Oldmstead" might be a twisting of the name Armistead, since the flag capture occurred during Pickett's Charge and Lewis Armistead was a notable figure who fell in the fight. But the Twenty-Eighth Virginia Infantry was actually under the command of General Richard B. Garnett, so that connection doesn't quite line up, either.

That said, the rest of the story holds up well. The only real hiccup is the name. My best guess? A reporter at the time got it wrong, and the error stuck. It's a small detail but also a reminder of how easily facts can fall victim to human error.

That story is sometimes confused with a similar story about another captured flag.

The Fifty-Fifth Virginia Infantry was under the command of Colonel John M. Brockenbrough during Pickett's Charge. The Fifty-Fifth was on the far left of the Confederate attack and took intense fire from the Union artillery on Cemetery Ridge. This situation caused them to lag behind the other divisions. As they crossed the Emmitsburg Road, they witnessed the repulse of Pickett's Charge at the Bloody Angle. Here, the Fifty-Fifth faltered and fell back. Brockenbrough's Brigade was the first to retreat. While other regiments in Pickett's Charge endured horrific casualties, the Fifty-Fifth suffered only seven. Due to their poor performance, the Fifty-Fifth Virginia was ordered to defend the rear of the Confederate army as it withdrew from the Gettysburg Battlefield.

On July 14, 1863, at Falling Waters, Maryland, the Union cavalry attacked the rearguard, took five hundred prisoners, and captured the Fifty-Fifth Virginia Infantry's battle flag. Colonel William d'Alton Mann and the Seventh Michigan Cavalry captured the flag. Colonel Mann was then ordered to send the Confederate flag to Edwin Stanton, the secretary of war in Washington, DC. (Just for the record, Edwin Stanton was the lawyer who represented that crazy bastard, Dan Sickles, during his murder trial and got him off with the temporary insanity plea.) Stanton didn't think they needed another Confederate flag in Washington, so he presented it back to Colonel Mann to keep as a war trophy. Colonel Mann added some embroidery to the flag, which read, "BATTLE FLAG 55th Virginia Infantry, Captured, together with the entire Regiment, its Colonel included, and TWO PIECES ARTILLERY, by the 7th Michigan Cavalry, at FALLING WATERS, MD. July 14th, 1863. Presented to Col. W. D. Mann, 7th Michigan Cavalry, by Hon. E. M. Stanton, Secretary of War, August 22d, 1863."

Colonel Mann held onto that flag for fifty years. In 1913, he embraced the spirit of the reunion and offered it as a symbol of peace to his former adversaries. Colonel Mann's tent was set up outside the Great Camp on the lawn of the Lutheran seminary, where many of the important dignitaries were staying. Colonel William d'Alton Mann sent a message to the governor of Virginia, who had a familiar name: William Hodges Mann. As far as I can tell, they were not related. Governor Mann was thrilled to hear Colonel Mann's proposal, so on the evening of July 2, he and nearly every Virginian veteran in camp marched over to the seminary. They gathered in front of Colonel Mann's tent for a small ceremony, during which the colonel returned the flag and stated that the reunion would greatly help to eliminate any lingering hostility between the North and the South.[95]

Afterward, the Confederates returned to their section of the Great Camp, proudly displaying the flag the entire way. Soon word got out, and for the remainder of the reunion, many visitors stopped by to see the captured flag that had been returned.

Governor Mann then gave the battle flag of the Fifty-Fifth Virginia to Colonel Joseph Bidgood of the Thirty-Second Virginia Infantry. At first, this confused me; why return the flag to a man from a different regiment? It wasn't until I found Bidgood's obituary that everything fell into place. Here's an excerpt: "Because of Colonel Bidgood's knowledge of and experience in military affairs, Governor Mann made him secretary of Confederate Military Records, and for several years, he devoted his time to correcting and compiling the military history of Virginia as related to the War Between the States."[96]

Bidgood wanted to preserve the battle flag for future generations and donated it to the Museum of the Confederacy. In 2013, that museum merged with the American Civil War Museum in Richmond, Virginia, where the battle flag of the Fifty-Fifth still resides.

Leopold Wolf had already endured quite a journey before reaching Gettysburg. With no money for the $1.50 fare from Harrisburg, he walked the entire way, determined to join his fellow veterans at the Great Camp. But his luck didn't improve on arrival.

Exhausted from his trek, he crashed onto the first available cot, falling into a deep, much-needed sleep. By morning, he felt refreshed and eager to see familiar faces. "Now I want to go see the old boys,"[97] he said, stepping out into the bustling camp. The day was everything he had hoped for—reconnecting with old comrades, swapping stories, soaking in the reunion atmosphere.

But as night fell, trouble found him again. When he went to return to his tent, he realized he had no idea where it was. Thousands of identical brown tents stretched across the camp, and in the warm afternoon, he had left his coat behind in his rush to enjoy the day. That coat wasn't just for keeping him warm—it held his honorable discharge papers, the key to proving his service and securing a pension for his later years.

Panic set in.

Leopold Wolf had faced the brutalities of battle, grueling marches, and the many trials of war—but at that moment, finding his way home among a sea of tents felt like his most challenging fight yet.

With a sinking feeling in his stomach and clammy hands despite the heat, Leopold pressed on, his tired eyes scanning the endless rows of identical tents. Canvas stretched on in all directions, and each tent looked the same in the dim glow of lanterns. One lost coat amid a camp of five thousand tents was a literal needle in a haystack. He stopped men occasionally, asking whether they had seen a misplaced coat, but most were too exhausted or indifferent to provide much help. Some shrugged, some muttered half-hearted responses, and others shook their heads before vanishing into the darkness.

The temperature dropped the first few nights in camp, and most vets needed their blankets to keep warm. But on the evening of July 2, the heat was intolerable, and dozens of veterans moved their cots out of the sweltering tents and slept in the company streets, where there was a breeze. Leopold Wolf encountered several old soldiers sleeping on cots under the stars, but none of them knew what had happened to the lost coat.

As the night dragged on, his legs grew heavier, his breaths more labored. His mind raced: What if someone else had taken his coat? What if his papers were gone for good? He tried retracing his steps, but fatigue blurred his memory, making every path look unfamiliar. He wiped the sweat from his brow with a trembling hand, his body aching from the miles he had walked that day.

Still, he pressed on. His stomach churned with worry, his throat dry and scratchy, but none of that mattered compared to the gnawing dread of losing the only proof he had of his service. His past, his future, his dignity—all wrapped up in a coat he couldn't find. By the time the first hints of dawn painted the sky in soft shades of pink and blue, Leopold could barely stand. His knees wobbled, his vision blurred, and for a moment, he feared he might collapse right there between the endless rows of tents.

Just as he was about to give up, Lieutenant Thompson Lawrence spotted him. The old man was barely staying on his feet, staggering with fatigue. Lawrence rushed over, caught him before he could fall, and helped him to a seat. When Leopold explained what had happened, the lieutenant reassured him, "Let's get a doctor to you. Then we'll look up your coat and papers."

A doctor soon had Leopold feeling better, and he was assigned a new tent. The moment he lay down, sleep overtook him. Meanwhile, Lieutenant Lawrence and a few friends scoured the camp, searching for the lost coat and discharge papers. However, with so many tents and no clear way to distinguish between them, their search came up empty.[98]

Leopold Wolf's story is far from over, and we'll pick up the thread in the next chapter.

# 7

# July 3—Thursday

On the morning of July 3, the kitchens served up some stewed apricots, beef and vegetable stew, fried mush, fresh bread, hard bread, butter, and buckets of coffee.[1] Now, being from New Jersey, I had never heard of "fried mush" before, but apparently it's a thing out in the Midwest. It's an alternative to pancakes and waffles, based on fried cornmeal, and served with a sweet topping, such as syrup or honey. Although I've never had it, it sounds pretty tasty.

That morning, some Northern veterans were enjoying breakfast with some Southern veterans. Perhaps they were partaking of fried mush. Regardless, men from Massachusetts were walking by the tables when an old Confederate called out the usual question: "Where are you from?"

The Massachusetts man said, "From the North. What regiment are you from?"

"The 2nd Georgia," replied the Confederate. He then called out to another veteran marching by, "Where do you come from?"

"The 203rd Rhode Island," came the response.

The Confederate turned to his friend and said, "God knows what little chance we had if they got that many regiments from Rhode Island."[2]

This is a cute little quip that requires some context to be fully understood.

A typical Civil War regiment consisted of around 1,000 men. By the old Confederate's mental arithmetic, that meant Rhode Island—the smallest state in the Union, which had sent 203 regiments—must have enlisted more than 203,000 men. No wonder he was astonished. If the smallest state could put more than 200,000 men in the field, how many were the others raising? To put that number in perspective, General Lee commanded only 75,000 Confederates at Gettysburg. But the reality was far different. Despite the old soldier's math, Rhode Island supplied only around 25,000 soldiers throughout the war.

Everywhere you looked, the old soldiers of the Blue and the Gray were getting along. But just because the two old enemies were friendly toward each other didn't mean they didn't tease each other over the war's outcome. Two old veterans were posing for a picture, shaking hands over a cannon—one from the North and one from the South. While the photographer was setting up the shot, the Union man told the Confederate, "I'm mighty glad to do this, you know; but still, you know, we did lick you like hell."[3]

Across the camp, in a hospital tent, Leopold Wolf woke up feeling refreshed. He had walked all the way to Gettysburg and lost his only jacket and discharge papers in some random tent he could no longer find. But he took solace in the fact that someone was willing to help. Lieutenant Lawrence came to his rescue in his most desperate hour, took him to an aid station, and got him the help he needed. And so things were looking up for the first time in a long time, and Wolf felt optimistic. Maybe things would be okay after all.

He felt that way until his new friend gave him the bad news. Despite spending hours looking through the Great Camp, Lieutenant Lawrence could not locate his coat or honorable discharge papers. The old man was crushed. What was he going to do? He had no money and nowhere to go once the Grand Reunion ended the next day. Tears filled his eyes, but Lieutenant Lawrence reassured him. "We are going to get enough to send you back to Harrisburg; you won't have to walk there this time, and we're going to arrange to get you into the soldier's home there too."

"But what about my papers?"

"Your papers, you say; that's all right, we'll apply for duplicates. You're going to be alright for the rest of your life."

Leopold Wolf didn't know whether to laugh or cry from relief. Between his sobs and smiles, the old man shared his story:

*I haven't a living relative, and for years, I haven't had what I could call even a close friend. I'm 78 years old. I was born in Middletown, Pennsylvania. In 1856, I enlisted in the Third United States Cavalry, but within a year, was discharged from service on account of disability. Then the Civil War broke out, and I didn't know if they'd let me enlist or not, but they did, and in '63, I got into the 14th New York Cavalry. I served in the city and about there for another year and then was discharged again for physical disability. It was my head that was the trouble, and I was sent to the Asylum at Harrisburg.*

*After a while, I was sent to the soldier's home in Dayton Ohio, but my mind got worse and worse, I suppose, for they sent me onto the place for the insane at Washington DC, and there, after two years I was discharged as perfectly cured. I've never had any more trouble with my brain, but I was an old man by that time, and life became a struggle. For a while, I was in the almshouse in Harrisburg, but then I came out and tried again to make my own living, but it was a mighty hard job. But then I heard about this reunion, and I was determined to come on. I didn't know I could get transportation, so I walked the whole way and I did it too. But I never thought I'd get here sometimes. I didn't doubt it, and now everything is going to be alright. I'm going to get duplicates for my lost papers, and the lieutenant is going to get me into a home. I am thankful.*

Many of the men who had known Leopold Wolf in the past, including one who had known the old soldier almost his entire life, corroborated his story.[4]

Walter Blake tells an interesting story in his book *Hand Grips* about a chance meeting between some Confederates and an old Black man. Back then, they used many derogatory terms, so I will take some creative liberties with the language to make it more suitable for a twenty-first-century audience.

The story goes like this: One day, an old Black man was sitting under a tree in the New Jersey section of the Great Camp. While he was relaxing in the shade, a group of old Confederate soldiers was marching by when they saw him and stopped in their tracks.

"Howdy do, boss!" the old Black man straightened up and saluted the Southerners. Walter Blake claims that there was a "score" of Confederates present. A "score" is an old-fashioned term for twenty. So quite a few Southerners gathered around Samuel Thompson, the Black man from Mount Holly, New Jersey. Thompson was described as a giant of a man who dwarfed the Southerners.

One of the Confederates walked up to Samuel Thompson and shook his hand. "We all are glad to see you," he said. "And we all want to shake hands with you and to say we have some old boys back at home just as big as you."

"Indeed, you have, Boss," Thompson said. "Indeed, you have."

After this, each of the twenty Confederates stepped up to Thompson and shook his hand. They exchanged pleasantries, and some went so far as to slap him on the shoulder in camaraderie before the group marched off toward their next destination. Walter Blake described it as an "incident that made some of the Northern boys sit up and take notice."[5]

According to the myth, Black veterans were not invited to the Grand Reunion, and in the written account, Samuel Thompson is never described as a veteran or wearing a uniform. Because of this, many critics and supporters of the "Uninvited Black Soldier" myth claim that Samuel Thompson must have been one of the cooks working in the camp kitchens. That's one possible theory, but I have another.

While writing this book, I have conducted a fair amount of research; many times, it has led to dead ends, while at other times I have struck gold.

Samuel Thompson is a fairly common name, and I couldn't find any additional information on him at first. However, thanks to the Find a Grave website, I discovered a lead. It turns out that there was a Samuel Thompson, born in Burlington County, New Jersey, back in 1842, who served in the Twenty-Second US Colored Infantry in the Second New Jersey Brigade. The Twenty-Second was formed in January 1864 and marched into Virginia, where they fought at Petersburg and against the Confederate defense of Richmond. The men of the Twenty-Second also had the distinction of being some of the first Union soldiers to enter the city after it fell. As the war ended, the Twenty-Second was honored to march through Washington, DC, in President Abraham Lincoln's funeral procession.[6]

Samuel Thompson died on April 8, 1937, which makes it possible that he attended the Grand Reunion in 1913. He is buried at Mount Moriah Cemetery in Hainesport, New Jersey. I live in Burlington County, New Jersey, and can testify that this cemetery is on the very outskirts of Mount Holly, the same town Blake claims Thompson is from.

I can't 100 percent say that the Samuel Thompson that Walter Blake wrote about is the same Samuel Thompson buried in the Mount Moriah Cemetery. Still, I think it's reasonable, possible, and highly probable that the two are the same person. If so, we can add another name to the roll of United States Colored Troops (USCT) members that attended the Grand Reunion and also add another nail in the coffin against the myth that says Black veterans were not invited.

Assuming Samuel Thompson was a Union vet and not a civilian cook, there's one other interesting thing to note: According to Walter Blake's account, Thompson was hanging out under a tree in the New Jersey section of the Great Camp. This means he may not have been relegated to the colored section of the Great Camp and may have stayed with his New Jersey peers. However, it's impossible to know for sure.

In October 2023, my wife and I visited Mount Moriah Cemetery to pay our respects. There we found Samuel Thompson's final resting place along with twenty other USCT gravestones nearby. Many of those veterans were still alive in 1913. I can't help but wonder whether any of the other Black veterans joined Thompson on his journey to the Grand Reunion.

The third day of the reunion was called Civics Day, also known as Governors' Day, because eleven governors gave speeches inside the Great Tent. The first speech of the day was delivered by the former governor of Indiana, who was also the current vice president of the United States: Thomas R. Marshall. During his address, he said:

> *It would be vain to speak of right or wrong on this occasion. This celebration could only happen in America. Nowhere else in the world could men who fought as bitter foes 50 years ago meet and clasp hands in brotherly love as they are doing here today. The age will not come when in, any quiet burying ground, North or South, the Sons of the Republic yet to be born will forget to strew with flowers the graves of the blue and the*

*gray. This occasion wipes out the last of the Mason-Dixon line. As Bob Taylor once said, there is now no difference between the North and the South except cold bread and hot biscuits.*[7]

The governor of Minnesota, Adolph Eberhart, shared a joke with the crowd: "What an indescribable pleasure must be experienced by Vice President Marshall, who presides over the senate, to come here and look into the faces of so many honest men."[8]

The speeches were fine, but only a few will be highlighted in this section. Speaker of the House James Clark captured his audience with a message that should be repeated today:

*Cold must be the heart of that American who is not proud to claim as countrymen the flower of the southern youth who charged up the slippery slopes of Gettysburg with peerless Pickett, or those unconquerable men in blue, who through three long and dreadful days held these beetling heights in the face of fierce assaults. It was not Southern valor or Northern valor. It was, thank God, American valor. . . . Callous, indeed, must be the man who cannot find something to admire in the colossal, benignant character of Abraham Lincoln or in the splendid career of Robert E. Lee.*

*The soldiers of the North and the soldiers of the South were American freemen all, fighting like heroes for what they considered right. As such, I honor them. As such, I teach my children to cherish them.*[9]

The governors droned on for two hours, but very few of the veterans were there to listen. Although the reports vary, it is generally agreed that the attendance for Governors' Day was the lowest of the week. The Great Tent could strain to hold fifteen thousand people, but according to *The Boston Globe*, it held "an audience of perhaps 6000."[10] The civilian visitors to the battlefield found the speeches interesting, but the veterans had other places they'd rather be. Besides, they could always read the speeches later in the newspaper.

While the official program was still going on in the Great Tent, another event was getting ready to kick off a stone's throw away. For many veterans, this was their main reason for returning to Gettysburg. It was one thing to hear speeches about the nation's present peace and quite another thing to make peace with your past. But before we get to what happened in 1913, let's go back fifty years to find out what made it so significant in the first place.

Hundreds, if not thousands, of books have been written about the Civil War, and many discuss the infamous "Pickett's Charge." Because of this, there's nothing new I can add to the conversation, so I won't bother. Instead, I present two letters written shortly after the attack—one from the North and one from the South. Firsthand accounts are an excellent resource, often providing unique insights into the battle. Between the two of them, they offer a glimpse into that far-off day.

On the afternoon of July 3, 1863, General James Longstreet launched his charge against the Union line at Gettysburg. This is formally called "Longstreet's Assault" since he commanded the Confederate First Corps. It is also accurately referred to as the "Pickett-Pettigrew-Trimble Assault" since they were the division commanders under Longstreet. However, most people simply refer to it as "Pickett's Charge," and it remains one of the most iconic moments of the Civil War.

On the first day of the battle, the Confederates attacked on the left; on the second day, they attacked on the right; and on the third day, they were going to attack right down the middle. General Robert E. Lee planned to pierce the center of the Union line by first softening it up with a two-hour artillery barrage before sending in the infantry.

Sergeant Alfred P. Carpenter of the First Regiment, Minnesota Volunteers, wrote a letter to his cousin describing what it was like to weather such an intense artillery barrage in 1863:

> *We lay behind a ridge of land. All at once, the guns opened, and from morn until the middle of the afternoon, it raged with terrible violence.*
>
> *Flat upon the ground we lay, while the vertical rays of a July sun rendered the heat almost intolerable. To rise up was certain death, while flat upon the ground we were tolerably well protected . . . and very near to our bodies at times, one shell actually tearing the knapsack from a man's back as he lay face downward.*
>
> *There were over 200 guns at work in this part of the line, firing as fast as men could load them. The noise it produced; the whistling of solid*

*shot, the screeching of shells, the bursting of spherical case, the explosions of caissons, the roar of the place is indescribable. I can think of no adjective that will describe it. It must be seen, heard, felt, to be understood.*

It was rumored that the artillery battle was so loud that it could be heard all the way to Washington, DC. I don't know if that's true, but to make that claim, it must have been a bone-rattling experience.

Carpenter noted that the cannons "have become so heated that the cartridges explode before they can be rammed home."

Let's now switch over to the Southern perspective. General George Pickett was quite a prolific letter writer. On July 4, 1863, only one day after the battle, Pickett wrote a letter to his fiancée describing the disastrous charge that would forever bear his name:

*My letter of yesterday, my darling, written before the battle, was full of hope and cheer . . . when the men lay in the tall grass in the rear of the artillery line, the July sun pouring its scorching rays almost vertically down upon them, till one o'clock when the awful silence of the vast battlefield was broken by a cannon-shot which opened the greatest artillery duel of the world. The firing lasted two hours. When it ceased, we took advantage of the blackened field and, in the glowering darkness, formed our attacking column just before the brow of Seminary Ridge.*

During the artillery barrage, Pickett approached his commander, General James Longstreet, whom he referred to as "Old Pete." Pickett then goes on to describe Longstreet's anguish at the thought of sending his men to their deaths:

*I found him like a great lion at bay. I have never seen him so grave and troubled. For several minutes after I had saluted him, he looked at me without speaking. Then, in an agonized voice, the reserve all gone, he said: "Pickett, I am being crucified at the thought of the sacrifice of life which this attack will make. I have instructed Alexander to watch the effect of our fire upon the enemy, and when it begins to tell, he must take the responsibility and give you your orders, for I can't."*

*While he was yet speaking, a note was brought to me from Alexander. After reading it, I handed it to him, asking if I should obey and go forward. He looked at me for a moment, then held out his hand. Presently, clasping his other hand over mine without speaking, he bowed his head upon his breast.*

*I shall never forget the look in his face nor the clasp of his hand when I said: "Then, General, I shall lead my Division on."*

*I saw tears glistening on his cheeks and beard. The stern old warhorse, God bless him, was weeping for his men and, I know, praying too that this cup might pass from them. I obeyed the silent assent of his bowed head, an assent given against his own convictions—given in anguish and with reluctance.*

*My brave boys were full of hope and confident of victory as I led them forth, forming them in column of attack, and though officers and men alike knew what was before them, knew the odds against them,—they eagerly offered up their lives on the altar of duty, having absolute faith in their ultimate success.*[11]

Days later, on July 12, 1863, Pickett wrote another letter to his fiancée providing further details of the fateful charge:

*At about a quarter to three o'clock, when his written order to make the charge was handed to me, and dear Old Peter, after reading it in sorrow and fear, reluctantly bowed his head in assent, I obeyed, leading my three brigades straight on the enemy's front. You never saw anything like it. They moved across that field of death as a battalion marches forward in line of battle upon drill, each commander in front of his command leading and cheering on his men. Two lines of the enemy's infantry were driven back; two lines of guns were taken—and no support came.*[12]

Switching back to Union perspective, Sergeant Alfred P. Carpenter continued his letter to his cousin:

*We sprang to our feet and could then see what was up. On the opposite slope, a long line of rebel infantry was advancing, while a short distance behind them was a second line as support. Almost instantly, our*

> *whole line bristled with fresh artillery, which opened upon the enemy, making terrible havoc in their ranks. Wide gaps were opened, but were immediately closed, and the line came on in splendid order, down the slope, across the plain, over the ravine and are now halfway up the hill towards us.*
>
> *We had watched them all this time with the utmost impatience, scarcely able to restrain our fire, though knowing that at such a distance, it would be comparatively harmless. They are now within musket range and our infantry opens; men stagger from their ranks by scores, hundreds, thousands, but on they came like an inrolling wave of the sea.*

By the time the Confederates reached the stone wall at what became known as the Bloody Angle, they were in tatters. Despite this, a small contingent of Confederate soldiers managed to cross the stone wall, but their strength was fading fast.

Sergeant Carpenter continued:

> *They have gained a part of our line; the rest of their line is within a few rods of us, but torn, bleeding, decimated, but are determined not to yield, for they halt, plant their colors, and wait for their reserve to come up. Time after time, those colors fall, but are quickly caught up, until scarcely a man is left around them. Their support advances, but our artillery pour into them a fire that they reel, turn and fly.*
>
> *Our muskets became so heated we could no longer handle them. We dropped them and picked up those of the wounded. Our cartridges gave out. We rifled the boxes of the dead. Artillerymen from the disabled pieces in our rear sprang forward and seizing guns and cartridges from the wounded, fought by our sides as infantrymen. Many of the men became deaf and did not recover their hearing for a day or two.*

Carpenter concluded his letter, "It was a grand and terrible scene. I wish I could paint it to you as I saw and felt it."[13]

Meanwhile, Pickett described what he saw from his perspective:

> *Ah, if I had only had my other two brigades, a different story would have been flashed to the world. It was too late to retreat, and to go on was*

*death or capture. Poor old Dick Garnett did not dismount, as did the others of us, and he was killed instantly, falling from his horse. Kemper, desperately wounded, was brought from the field and subsequently taken prisoner. Dear old Lewis Armistead, God bless him, was mortally wounded at the head of his command after planting the flag of Virginia within the enemy's lines. Seven of my colonels were killed, and one was mortally wounded. Nine of my lieutenant colonels were wounded, and three lieutenant colonels were killed. Only one field officer of my whole command, Colonel Cabell, was unhurt, and the loss of my company officers was in proportion.*[14]

Across the field, General James Longstreet witnessed the consequences of his nod to Pickett:

*I dismounted to relieve my horse and was sitting on a rail fence watching very closely the movements of the troops. . . . Pickett had reached a point near the Federal lines. A pause was made to close ranks and mass for the final plunge. The troops on Pickett's left, although advancing, were evidently a little shaky. I was watching the troops supporting Pickett and saw plainly they could not hold together ten minutes longer. I called his [Colonel Freemantle's] attention to the wavering condition of the two divisions of the Third Corps and said they would not hold, that Pickett would strike and be crushed, and the attack would be a failure. As the division threw itself against the Federal line, Garnett fell and expired. The Confederate flag was planted in the Federal line, and immediately, Armistead fell mortally wounded at the feet of the Federal soldiers. The wavering division then seemed appalled, broke their ranks, and retired.*[15]

In another letter to his fiancée on July 6, 1863, Pickett brings an even more intimate look into the failed attack:

*Even now, I can hear them cheering as I gave the order, "Forward!" I can feel the thrill of their joyous voices as they called out all along the line, "We'll follow you, Marse George. We'll follow you—we'll follow you." Oh, how faithfully they kept their word—following me on—on—to their death, and I, believing in the promised support, led them on—on—on—Oh, God!*

*I can't write you a love-letter today, my Sally, for with my great love for you and my gratitude to God for sparing my life to devote to you, comes the overpowering thought of those whose lives were sacrificed—of the broken-hearted widows and mothers and orphans. The moans of my wounded boys, the sight of the dead, upturned faces, flood my soul with grief—and here am I whom they trusted, whom they followed, leaving them on that field of carnage.*[16]

These memories would haunt George Pickett until his death on July 30, 1875.

Although he did not mention it in his letter, Alfred Carpenter was wounded twice during the Battle of Gettysburg. He recovered and was sent down to Key West, Florida, where he was promoted to second lieutenant of the Second US Colored Infantry. While down there, he contracted yellow fever and died on October 18, 1864. Although he did not live to see the Grand Reunion, his nephew submitted Carpenter's letter to *The Baltimore Sun*, which was published during the reunion. No doubt, many veterans read his account while still camping on the old battlefield.

Pickett's Charge was a disastrous failure. It is often considered the turning point of the Civil War and the high-water mark of the Confederacy. Like a wave crashing on the beach, it reached its crescendo and quickly retreated. But if Gettysburg was considered the high-water mark of the Civil War, then the reenactment of Pickett's Charge can be regarded as the high-water mark of the Grand Reunion.

On July 3, 1913, the survivors of Pickett's Charge returned to Gettysburg to once more face their old adversaries. There had been many memorable moments at the reunion, but none quite so significant as the reenactment of Pickett's Charge, or, perhaps more accurately, Pickett's Last Charge.

This reenactment was not made by weekend warriors playing dress-up but by the same men who had made the charge fifty years earlier.

At the beginning of this book, I opened with a fictionalized account of the Pickett's Charge reenactment on July 3, 1913. In my telling, the aged Confederates march across the field, but instead of ending in solemn reconciliation, the moment unravels as old animosities resurface. What begins as a fragile gesture of peace collapses into a brawl at the stone wall, revealing that even fifty years after the war, bitterness and wounds still lingered just beneath the surface.

This fictional account has its origin in a mere footnote from the book *Crossroads: 1913* by Paul M. Angle, which said:

> *Years ago, the author heard from an old newspaperman . . . that at this point, several old Confederates, in their exuberance, jumped over the wall to embrace their former enemies. The Union response was instantaneous: "You sons-of-bitches, you didn't get over here in '63 and you ain't coming over now!" Fists flew, and only the presence of military police averted a riot. All my efforts to confirm the tale have failed, so I am forced to the conclusion that it is apocryphal. I wish it weren't.*[17]

You might've heard similar stories about a brawl at the Bloody Angle in 1913. It was the first thing I ever heard about the fiftieth reunion. But after digging through every account I could find, I have to agree with Angle—there's no proof. With thousands of spectators and dozens of reporters watching, any fight would've made front-page news. So, let's put that myth aside and get to what happened when the old enemies met again at Gettysburg.

Pickett's Last Charge started in different places, depending on which account you read. Some say the Confederates emerged from the woods at Seminary Ridge, just as they had in 1863. Others claim they were too frail for the whole march and started at the Emmitsburg Road, only around one thousand feet from the stone wall. Still others say they "charged" only the last hundred feet. Honestly, I think all of these are true. It just depends on when the eyewitness arrived. Some reports give a play-by-play of the event, while others just hit the highlights.

Major Thomas Holland was described as a tall Southerner who had commanded Company G of the Twentieth Virginia Infantry during Pickett's Charge. Holland claimed to have crossed the stone wall at the Bloody Angle and put his hand on Alonzo Cushing's battery. He accompanied General Lewis Armistead, using his sword to cleave a path before him. Together, Holland and Armistead reached the very apex of the high-water mark of the Confederacy before being cut down by the Union army. The two men were taken to a field hospital. Holland recovered, but Armistead didn't. At the Bloody Angle, a small monument notes where Armistead fell.

At the Grand Reunion in 1913, the Pennsylvania Commission asked Major Thomas Holland to survey the ground of Pickett's Charge. On July 2, he measured his starting point on Seminary Ridge to his end point at Armistead's monument at the Bloody Angle to be precisely 1,495[18] yards or 4,485 feet, just short of a mile. In 1863, the Confederates covered that distance in fifteen minutes, but in 1913 it took the old veterans almost ninety minutes to cover the same ground.

It's hard to tell whether the old Confederates made the full march over the 1,495 yards that Thomas Holland had calculated from the day before. But my guess is that they came close. After all, the easiest and most direct route from their camp to the Bloody Angle was to walk. So even if some formed up only at the Emmitsburg Road, they still had to walk there first.

The reporter for the Holyoke *Transcript-Telegram* witnessed 150 tottering old Confederates leaving their tents across the valley in the Great Camp and then forming into line.[19] The Southern section of the camp was located near Seminary Ridge, close to what is now called "Confederate Avenue."

Captain C. H. Mickie was in the Nineteenth Virginia Infantry, which was part of Pickett's Brigade. They lost 45 percent of their fighting men during the infamous charge. While waiting for the two-hour cannonade to pass, Captain Mickie was leaning against a sassafras tree on Seminary Ridge. Although they were well out of range of the enemy muskets, the Union artillery was crashing all around them. The order came, and as Captain Mickie marched across the field, he heard a cannon whistle overhead. He glanced back just in time to see the cannonball cut down the sassafras tree he had been leaning against.

Captain Mickie survived the charge and returned to Gettysburg in 1913. He showed some of his fellows the spot where he had been resting on Seminary Ridge and was amazed to discover that the stump of the sassafras tree was still there.[20]

Leaving behind the shade trees of Seminary Ridge, the old soldiers began their long march across the battlefield toward the Bloody Angle, almost a mile away. However, their path was not straightforward. Local farmers worked the land, and the dirt was plowed over with knee-high hay, fields of waving grain, and "great squares of buff-ripe wheat ready for the reaper."[21] The old Confederates wore gray uniforms, though some had removed their jackets and draped them over their arms. Many carried an open umbrella to shield themselves from the sun. They moved slowly and cautiously through the field. Many of the old men used canes and crutches to steady their march. Their course would take them through the hayfield and the edge of the Great Camp, where the Massachusetts men were situated. As they moved through the tents, many Massachusetts veterans came out to shake their hands, pat them on the back, and cheer them on.

Their pace was already slow, but it was further reduced with the arrival of the Union veterans, who came out to greet them. Although the Union vets cheered them on, "They did not neglect to chaff them either, and they got in return as good as they gave."[22]

I love how feisty the old soldiers were, and despite their age, they still took the time to bust each other's stones. Regardless of the delays, the Confederates crossed through the tents and onto the Emmitsburg Road.

In 1863, fifteen thousand men were involved in Pickett's Charge, but in 1913, only 150 survivors could make the journey. They marched in columns of four, carrying a tattered old flag, with a fife and drum playing "Dixie" to cheer them on.[23] I can't help but wonder what they were thinking about as they crossed that field in 1913. Were they thinking back to fifty years earlier, when they were young and victory seemed so close? Or were they thinking of their comrades who started the charge but never returned? Did they tremble at the memory of the cannonballs crashing around them and tearing great holes in the ground? Could they hear the chatter of the muskets as the Philadelphia Brigade fired into them? Or were they simply in the present, happy to have survived and just concentrating on crossing the uneven ground? It's impossible to know for sure, but one thing is certain: They received a very different reception from the one they got fifty years before.

Across the field, at the stone wall of the Bloody Angle, the 170 Union troops had it relatively easy. All they had to do was wait for the old Confederate soldiers to show up. However, the crowd at the Bloody Angle was thick, and spectators eager for a better view pushed the old soldiers

A group of Confederates marching across the field during Pickett's Last Charge. Reproduced from the *Fiftieth Anniversary Report.*

back and shoved them out of the way. When the Confederates arrived, no one was ready to greet them.

There is a strong desire to sanitize this event and say it went off without a hitch. But the truth of the matter is that it was poorly organized, and *The Philadelphia Inquirer* didn't hold back in its criticism of the rude spectators for making it difficult for the aging veterans to take their places. To add to the chaos, a modern-day wire fence had been erected a few yards in front of the stone wall, and that obstacle had to be overcome before the Confederates could reach their position.

When the Confederate color bearer stopped at the wire fence, he looked ahead at the sea of spectators and said, "Well, where are the Yanks?"[24] The veterans laughed, breaking the tension. But things kept going sideways.

It was unclear what was to happen next, but Major Thomas Holland wanted to get out of the sun, so he took matters into his own hands. "Column right, forward march." The old soldiers marched along the wire fence and headed for a cluster of trees. Once under the shade, the order was given to "rest," and the tired old men slumped to the ground.

Meanwhile, the veterans from the Philadelphia Brigade formed up and, as a unit, pushed their way through the civilian spectators. Soon they stood in position on their side of the stone wall, determined not to let any more civilians through.

No sooner had the Confederates sat down under the shade than some low-ranking but well-meaning organizer ordered them back on their feet. Begrudgingly, the Confederates stood up and followed the organizer on a fool's errand. They marched back along the wire fence to a gate near the Bloody Angle. There, they passed through the opening and climbed over the stone wall. They soon found themselves on the wrong side of the field, *behind* their former enemies. They were now deep within the federal lines, farther than they had reached fifty years before. Things were quickly getting out of hand. In order of position, there was the stone wall, then the Philadelphia Brigade, followed by ten thousand spectators, and then the Confederates, who were pressed close to the parked cars on Hancock Avenue.

Colonel James Schoonmaker, who had planned the event, realized he had lost control. He rushed over to correct the situation, but the organizers were all yelling different instructions, and no one was listening. Schoonmaker threw his hands into the air in frustration. "Very well," he said. "I shall wash my hands of the entire matter."

If any heated words were exchanged during the day, it was by the organizers trying to rein in the chaos.

Finally, Major Thomas Holland had had enough. He ignored the bickering and took command of the situation. He ordered his Confederates to form up once more. They forced their way through the crowds, back across the stone wall, and into the space between the old stone wall and the new wire fence. Under Holland's instruction, the Confederates soon faced off against their Union counterparts with nothing between them except the stone wall, just as it should be.

However, it didn't last. The reporter for *The Philadelphia Inquirer* wrote:

> *The crowd had swept in on all sides of the gallant band of Union and Confederate survivors and showed absolutely no respect for the men who had waited patiently for fifty years to take part in the great event. With*

> *a total lack of courtesy, they jostled aside the aged rows of veterans and crowded into the front line.*
>
> *No attempt was made to keep them back except the trembling, weary lips of the men of a generation gone, who were forced to see the event for which they had been planning and preparing almost completely wrecked by the large crowd.*[25]

Just when it seemed the chaos had peaked, a politician seized the moment to make things even worse. Representative Joseph Hampton Moore of Philadelphia clambered onto the stone wall and launched into a tedious, self-important speech that dragged on for a grueling thirty minutes. He rambled about the "glory and valor" of battle, seemingly oblivious to the exhausted veterans standing under the scorching sun. They weren't inspired—they were irritated. They had come for a solemn reenactment, not to hear a politician's grandstanding.

This photograph captures the chaos of Pickett's Last Charge on the afternoon of July 3, 1913. Civilians jostle the veterans to get a better view. The tree at left is the same one featured in the posed handshake photo at the stone wall. Courtesy of the Library of Congress.

As Moore droned on about the men who had fallen fifty years before, one of the old Confederates said, "I feel like I'm going to fall over now."[26] Even the press had little patience for the spectacle. One reporter later summed up Moore's long-winded remarks in three words: "It was long."

Only after Moore finally silenced himself was Pickett's Last Charge allowed to proceed, thankfully free of further political interference.

The Confederate color bearer stepped forward, proudly waving the tattered Rebel flag, while the Union color bearer met him at the stone wall. The two crossed their flags in a symbolic gesture. Then a third man approached, carrying a leather roll. From it, he pulled out a brand-new silk American flag. The crowd cheered as the Stars and Stripes were raised high above the two battle flags. This flag was a gift from the Philadelphia Brigade, meant for the survivors of Pickett's Charge.

Captain R. W. Douthett of the Eleventh Virginia stepped forward to accept the American flag on behalf of the Southern veterans. Though weary and parched from the sun, the old Confederates ripped off their hats, let out the piercing Rebel Yell, and surged toward the stone wall once more.

The Union color bearer cried out, "Boys, there's Pickett's men, God bless them, they are charging again!" The Union men then cheered them on: "Hurrah! Hurrah!"

Some of the old Confederates stumbled and fell into the tall hay. Others, too tired to take another step, slid to the ground, but the rest pushed onto the stone wall. Meanwhile, the Union men could not hold back any longer—some jumped across the wall and rushed into the arms of the Southern men. Others waited for the Confederates to get closer, extended their hands, and helped the old men cross the stone wall.

Men who had stabbed each other fifty years earlier were now locked in an embrace, tears streaming down their faces without shame. The two armies intermingled and broke into smaller groups to relive the battle together.

William H. Turpin of the Fifty-Third Virginia[27] proudly wore the same uniform he had on when he first charged behind Pickett. Time had taken its toll—the fabric was worn and dingy, the buttons long gone, held together only by patches and string. Instead of shoes, he wrapped his feet in rags, just as he had during the charge of 1863. With pride, he marched up and down the line, showing off his tattered uniform to the old Union veterans.

As he did, he came face to face with Isaac E. Tibben from Frankford, Pennsylvania, who, by coincidence, was also wearing the same uniform from that fateful battle. Tibben even carried the rifle he had used to fire on the Confederates of Pickett's Charge. The two former enemies came together, laughing and joking as they examined each other's uniforms—a moment of camaraderie born from the shared history of war.

William H. Turpin was quoted in *The New York Times*: "I'm jest about as hot as I was the last time we-all charged, but I ain't so scairt. And the Yankees ain't a-goin' to get my tobaccy this time the way they did then, either."[28]

Turpin may have changed his mind on that last sentiment. Captain Pack from Mississippi was also in the crowd watching the reenactment of Pickett's Charge. He reported:

> *With yells they rushed to the old stone fence when each side halted, and the blue and the gray ranks grasped hands across the stone barrier once drenched in blood. It was then an old reb, in tattered gray uniform and*

William H. Turpin (Confederate) and Isaac E. Tibben (Union) shake hands during Pickett's Last Charge, both wearing the uniforms they wore fifty years earlier. Turpin holds his "peace pipe" in his left hand. Reproduced from the *Fiftieth Anniversary Report*.

> *feet tied up in rags as many of our boys went in that battle, loaded an old clay pipe and reed stem with tobacco, took a couple of puffs, and then passed the pipe of peace to an old union veteran in a tattered blue uniform. As the yank seized the pipe and gave it a puff, a mighty shout went up from both ranks, and a hearty shaking of hands and love feast ensued. When you met a Yank, he generally had his arms locked with a Johnnie Reb, and they were apt to be swapping badges and tobacco.*[29]

Soon after, a photographer captured the now-famous image of the veterans shaking hands over the stone wall. It's often criticized because "no one looks very happy," but let's be real—after everything they had just been through, who would be?

First, this wasn't some spontaneous, emotional snapshot frozen in time. The veterans had just trudged a mile through a hayfield in the sweltering July heat, reliving a moment they had never expected to survive the first time. Instead of being able to embrace old comrades and swap stories, they were forced to stand in the sun and listen to some self-important politician deliver an unimportant speech. By the time they finally reached the wall, emotions ran high—there were tears, confusion, and more than a few exhausted men trying not to keel over from heat and memories alike. Then, just as they were settling into long-awaited conversations, an overeager photographer swooped in, wrangled a few of them into place, and insisted they "look friendly."

In addition to their physical and emotional exhaustion, there was one more thing: People didn't smile for photos in the early twentieth century. Portraits were seen as serious affairs, and after decades of being told to hold still and look dignified, grinning for the camera wasn't part of the routine.

So when you look at that photo and wonder why no one seems happy, imagine yourself in their shoes: physically drained, emotionally overwhelmed, roasting under the summer sun, and suddenly told to pose like it was a pleasant social gathering. If you had just marched through all that, you wouldn't be smiling either!

But they did it anyway. Despite the exhaustion, the heat, and the forced formality of the moment, they stood together, shook hands, and allowed history to be captured in a single frame. And whether they looked happy or not, that photo has endured as one of the most iconic images of

(*Top*) Posed photograph of Union and Confederate veterans shaking hands over the stone wall at the Bloody Angle in 1913. Courtesy of the Library of Congress. (*Bottom*) The Bloody Angle, Gettysburg, photographed by the author in 2025.

the Grand Reunion—a powerful testament to reconciliation, resilience, and the weight of memory that no posed picture could ever fully capture.

With the picture out of the way, many of the Confederates wanted to visit the site where General Armistead had fallen. Drewry B. Easley of the Fourteenth Virginia reflected on what he had seen fifty years before:

*I was on the end of my regiment's line. And somehow, another regiment overlapped our line at the Bloody Angle and separated me from my comrades. Now, I wasn't doin' anything smart, and I don't want you to think I was; it just happened that way, I ran in front of them and got over that stone fence, and I found myself among a whole passel of Federals. I dropped my gun and they just let me pass behind them. Then I saw Armistead come along and put his hand on that cannon and fall.*

Easley became emotional as his mind drifted back to that distant day. Clutching his empty corncob pipe, he raised it to his lips, pretending to take a slow draw. His hands trembled, and his eyes filled with tears. For a long moment, he was silent. Then, at last, he looked up and found his voice:

*He fell. And he was an old man, past sixty. Think of that. I didn't believe it at first, he was dead. I thought it must be sunstroke, or something. But when I saw he was dead, I grabbed up a gun, though I had surrendered, and reached for some ammunition, but just then I saw three bayonets pointed at my breast, and I put it down.*[30]

General Lewis Armistead did not die on the battlefield. He was shot three times during the charge and fell wounded at the Bloody Angle, where he was cared for by the Union soldiers. He was eventually brought to a field hospital but died two days later. The Confederates who survived the charge reported back that Armistead had been killed outright, and it wasn't until much later that they learned otherwise. Even some of the Union troops were misinformed about Armistead's death.

Charles E. Scouten was the color bearer for the Fifty-Ninth New York Infantry. During the reunion, he was asked whether he had seen any other Confederates with Armistead when he fell.

*I didn't see but one man. He laid hold of a Union gun and was instantly killed. That, of course, was Armistead. I saw no one else. Still, you must remember that it wasn't possible to keep tabs on everything that was going on just then. My ramrod was too hot to work, and I bent it double and threw it into the Johnnies, and then grabbed up some rocks and threw them in their faces as they came up to the fence. Then I was lying down, and somebody stepped on my head. That's all I remember.*[31]

In his book *Hand Grips* (1913), Walter Blake records a similar account of two veterans—one from the North and the other from the South—as they stood on the battlefield.

Edward G. Freeley, an old Confederate, pointed to the ground and said, "There it is, right there, sir. No one got any further than that, and there three of them beat me down with the butt ends of their muskets." He looked out across the field, the weight of the memory heavy on his shoulders.

Ross Graydon, a Union veteran, stood silently for a moment, eyes narrowing as he thought back to that day. Finally, he spoke, his voice calm but intense: "Comrade," he said, "I wouldn't be a bit surprised if I was one of those fellows who hit you over the head. I remember slamming a Johnny who had gotten ahead of his men and made it all the way up to the guns of the battery we were supporting. Maybe you're the one I hit—now I wonder."

Freeley's eyes met his, a wry smile playing at the edges of his lips. "Maybe I am,"[32] he said. They stood together, their eyes fixed on the battlefield, two veterans from opposite sides of the conflict, silently sharing the weight of the past.

According to the American Battlefield Trust,[33] approximately two hundred Confederate soldiers pierced the Union defenses at the stone wall. One of them was Calvin Deering from the Twenty-Eighth Virginia Infantry, who was captured during Pickett's Charge and spent the rest of the war in prison at Fort Delaware.

Deering wrote about his wartime experience:

*I was in the three days' battle at Gettysburg, was in Pickett's charge, and was with the command at the rock fence where General Garnet was killed. Just as I started to get over the fence, a piece of shell or a large ball struck my gun, shattered it, and left me without a gun. I noticed a Mississippi rifle lying by the side of a dead boy and picked it up. Everybody who ever saw one knows how hard it is to cock. I naturally thought the gun was empty, so I rammed a load into it and fired. I supposed the gun must have been half full of lead, as the recoil sent me back some ten feet in a double somersault, the gun going backward over my head and sticking in the ground, stock up. I was dazed for a moment and thought I had been struck by a cannonball.*[34]

Deering was quickly captured by the Union soldiers and removed from the direct line of fire. From his position, he witnessed Pickett's Charge's grinding halt and his flag's capture. This is the story that was only alluded to in the last chapter.

According to the Regimental History of the Twenty-Eighth Virginia Infantry,

*Private John J. Eakin of Company C carried the 28th Virginia's colors into the breastworks. There, he received three severe wounds. He consequently relinquished the flag to Pvt. Graybill, who was shot down seconds later. Colonel Allen picked up the beloved flag and handed it to Lt. John A. I. Lee, who leaped onto the wall and defiantly waved it in the face of withering musket fire. A shell knocked it out of his hands as he fell wounded across the wall. Despite the wound, Lee continued to wave the colors until a "burly German" from the 7th Michigan took him prisoner.*[35]

Calvin Deering explained what happened after he surrendered: "Col. Allen was my Colonel, and he came from the same county I did. They laid him and me together, and he took his hat off a little, and he said, 'Deering, whar is the colors?' Then he put his hat back on his head and died right then."[36]

Deering was surrounded by a small group of Union troops at the reunion, eager to hear his tale.

"The Yankees were sho'ly very nice to us," he said. "They didn't shoot at us after we got into their lines, but just told us to surrender, and we did. . . . But the Yankees were very nice to us. I don't reckon they had a drink of water for a day, and they had marched for a day and a half, but they were good to us.

"Nobody could ever say anything against the Yanks when I was around. When they had us beaten, they did not try to kill us. They gave us what food they had and half of their water."[37]

"I don't reckon the folks at home will believe me when I tell them how fine I've been treated here. You can't get at any hotel such fine food as we've had from the army rations here. No, they won't believe me."[38]

Walter Blake witnessed another story and added it to his book:

> *Another startling meeting of former foes occurred at the "Bloody Angle." . . . There, where fifty years before the best blood of America had soaked the sod, A. C. Smith, a Confederate veteran, clasped hands with Albert N. Hamilton, of the Union forces. The Johnnie and the Yank had trudged over with friends to view again the scene of that awful struggle.*
>
> *"Here it was!" cried Smith, pointing to the wall, "here's where we leaped across! I got a yard beyond that wall, I reckon, when I got hit and down I went." He stopped momentarily and passed his hand across his forehead as he recalled that moment. "I remember a chap in Blue coming on a run to me and giving me a drink of water, and then he picked me up and carried me off. Next thing I knew, I was in a Yank hospital, and the boy who carried me away had gone."*
>
> *Again, there was a pause in the narrative. "I never saw him again," Smith finished sadly. "He's gone to his reward by this time, I reckon."*
>
> *Meanwhile, Hamilton had approached but had not heard a single word of what the Confederate had said. As he approached the Bloody Angle, he took up his story: "They (the Rebs) got about to here," he explained, "and then we beat 'em back." He studied his position carefully for a brief moment, and then resumed: "And it was right here that a Johnny fell into my arms. I lifted him up and gave him a swig of water, and then got him on my shoulders and carried him off, but—"*
>
> *Smith had caught the last few words of the speaker, and he sprang forward, listening intently now. Then he gazed searchingly into the other man's face. A mighty yell went up from his lips. "Praise the Lord!" he shouted. "Praise the Lord, it's YOU, brother!" and at those words, the*

> *two old foes fell into each other's arms, embracing. "Yes, sir—fifty years ago," cried Hamilton, as the crowd gathered around and cheered them—"Fifty years, and he's here NOW! Praise the Lord, comrade, praise Him! I'm Hamilton, of the Seventy-third Pennsylvania!"*
>
> *"And I'm Smith, of the Fifty-sixth Virginia," volunteered the other. It was a dramatic meeting, surely.*[39]

After witnessing Pickett's Last Charge, Colonel Schoonmaker said:

> *My regret is that every man, woman and child of our beloved country, North and South, was not with us at Gettysburg to have heard the addresses of the Northern and Southern soldiers, who vied with each other in expressions of friendship and loyalty and to have witnessed the handshakes over the stone wall at the Bloody Angle which forever ended whatever sectional feelings might have prevailed previous to that time.*

Colonel Schoonmaker then presented Pickett's men with a medal to remember the occasion. On one side, it said, "The Philadelphia Brigade, July 3rd, 1863–July 3rd, 1913. Pickett's Division." On the reverse side, it said, "Presented by John Wanamaker through the Philadelphia Brigade as a token of peace." John Wanamaker was a United States postmaster general, but he is more well known for his chain of department stores across the Northeast. The Wanamaker's building still stands today and is a National Historic Landmark across the street from Philadelphia's City Hall.

"Pin that on tight," said an old vet in gray as he received Wanamaker's medal. "I wouldn't lose that for half my farm."[40]

Eighteen-year-old Philip Myers, the photographer's assistant, was on hand to watch the reenactment of Pickett's Charge. He watched the Southerners emerge from the woods just as they had done fifty years earlier, except it was not quite the same. "We could see not rifles and bayonets, but canes and crutches," Myers said. "We soon could distinguish the more agile ones aiding those less able to maintain their places in the ranks." Nearer they came toward the stone wall where the Union guns had waited and where so many of their comrades had fallen.

"As the Rebel Yell broke out after a half century of silence, a moan, a gigantic sigh, a gasp of unbelief rose from the onlookers. It was then that the Yankees, unable to restrain themselves longer, burst from behind the stone wall and flung themselves upon their former enemies," Myers said. "Not in mortal combat, but reunited in brotherly love and affection."

Philip Myers concluded his writings by saying, "Soldiers forgive; it is only civilians who cherish hatred through the years."[41]

Talifero G. Hubbard was one of the Confederates who participated in Pickett's Charge in 1863 and in Pickett's Last Charge in 1913. He joined the Twenty-Eighth Virginia Infantry at the age of thirteen and fought throughout the four years of war.[42] He later married and relocated to Liberal, Kansas. His goal at the Grand Reunion was to renew old friendships from his time in the war and form new ones. While still on the field, he wrote a letter to his hometown newspaper:

> *I am now on the ground that was the scene of Pickett's famous charge 50 years ago. We, the surviving members of Pickett's division, re-enacted the famous charge over the same ground, and again, after 50 years of reconstruction and cementing of differences, met face to face the surviving Union soldiers who opposed us on that historic occasion; not with bayonets, shells, and balls, however, but with the right hand of fellowship and brotherly love. It certainly was a touching scene, Yankees and Rebels shaking hands with such hearty goodwill.*
>
> *The reunion is the crown of a reunited country, and to be here is indeed a great pleasure to me. —T. G. Hubbard*[43]

In August 1913, the veterans from Maine held a meeting at which they discussed the reunion in great detail. Thirty-seven veterans were present, and many shared their experiences at Gettysburg. This was followed by the remarks by Lizzie R. Eames from Prospect, Maine. Eames did not attend the Grand Reunion but gave her perspective on the event:

> *I read in the daily papers with much interest of each day's program at your recent anniversary in Gettysburg; but what impressed me most forcibly and thrilled me through and through, was that charge up the hill by the Blue and the Gray, re-enacting the battle of fifty year ago, only*

> *to meet at the summit and clasp hands in brotherly love over that stone wall. To me, this is one of the grandest deeds of Christian love, which history will ever record; and we can but feel respect and admiration for the boys in Gray, for we realize how hard it is for the vanquished to accept defeat in the spirit of love and forgiveness.*[44]

Before the reunion, the Pennsylvania Commission faced significant criticism for allowing the Confederate flag to be displayed at the event. Nevertheless, according to *The Philadelphia Inquirer*, the veterans from the North openly praised the Commission for permitting the Confederate flag to fly. In fact, the men of the Philadelphia Brigade insisted on it: "And the sight of the old battle flags of the Confederacy is as welcome to the Union veterans as it is to the men who fought under them." Additionally, it states that "The Philadelphia Brigade are most unanimous in praising the commission for its stand. Every living member of the four old regiments recruited in the City of Brotherly Love is enthusiastic over the reproduction of the great charge. And they unite in declaring that only with the battle flags ahead could the scene be accurately pictured after a lapse of fifty years."[45]

If the Union veterans, the guys who fought against the Confederacy, could accept seeing the Confederate flag as a way to honor shared history and healing, then maybe we should try to see it in a similar way today.

The veterans of both sides saw the flag not as a symbol of division but as a part of their collective experience. They recognized that, while they had fought under different banners, they had ultimately reunited as Americans. If the men who suffered the most from that war could embrace this perspective, then the Confederate flag, in certain contexts, can be acknowledged as a historical artifact rather than an emblem of hatred.

Of course, the flag has been used in ways since then that have changed how people see it, which makes things more complicated. However, looking back at 1913, one could argue that the flag can still serve as a poignant reminder of history, reconciliation, and how the deepest wounds can heal over time with mutual respect.

As the old soldiers from both sides gathered and talked, a new idea took shape—a monument dedicated to peace and reconciliation at the very spot where they had once fought to the death: the Bloody Angle.[46] These men had seen war up close, had lost friends, and endured unimaginable hardships. Yet, fifty years later, they weren't there to relive the fight but to honor the fact that they had moved past it. They wanted future generations to see that, despite the bloodshed of 1863, by 1913, the country had truly come back together.

This push for a peace monument speaks volumes about how these veterans saw their own history. They weren't trying to erase the past or pretend the war hadn't happened—they were acknowledging it while choosing to focus on unity rather than division. That's a critical perspective when thinking about the Confederate flag today. If the men who fought under those banners could stand side by side, shake hands, and even propose a monument to peace, then maybe we should take a step back and consider how we approach these symbols.

Examining what those veterans sought to convey in 1913, it's clear that their primary focus was on healing, not hostility. Perhaps there's something to learn from this viewpoint.

Plans were made to erect a $250,000 monument at the Bloody Angle, but it never materialized. World War I broke out the following year, and at its conclusion, a new generation of veterans returned home, and the Civil War vets slipped further into obscurity.

Twenty-five years later, a peace monument would be dedicated at Gettysburg, just in time for the seventy-fifth anniversary of the battle. The monument stands on a large granite pedestal with a forty-five-foot-tall vertical shaft. It was built using granite from Maine and limestone from Alabama, symbolizing the unity of North and South. At the top of the shaft burns a continuous flame, representing eternal peace. An inscription reads, "An enduring light to guide us in unity and fellowship." It was named the Eternal Peace Light Memorial and was dedicated on July 3, 1938, by President Franklin D. Roosevelt. The monument commemorates the healing that took place during the 1913 Grand Reunion. However, few Civil War veterans were still alive to attend the dedication.

The Eternal Peace Light Memorial is one of the most prominent monuments at Gettysburg, symbolizing the reconciliation between North and South. However, it sits roughly three miles from the Bloody Angle, closer to where the fighting began on the first day of battle. As a result, its significance in relation to Pickett's Charge and the Grand Reunion feels disconnected due to its location.

However, placing such a large, imposing monument at the Bloody Angle would have been an absolute eyesore. At fifty feet tall, with its towering eternal flame, it would have drastically altered the battlefield's sightlines and felt out of place among the more understated markers in that area. In that sense, its current location makes sense.

Still, it's hard not to wish that some monument existed at the Bloody Angle specifically to honor the Grand Reunion of 1913, something more directly tied to the veterans who returned to make peace. Perhaps even a simple inscription: "They waged war here, and 50 years later, those same men came back to make peace."

Such a tribute would serve as a powerful reminder that while Gettysburg was once a place of bloodshed, it has also become a symbol of healing.

Not all of the stories from Pickett's Last Charge had a happy ending. Joseph Husted from New York suffered from severe illness but was determined to be a part of the Grand Reunion. He was wounded during Pickett's Charge and wanted more than anything to be a part of the reenactment fifty years later. Unfortunately, Husted fell sick on July 3 and spent the time during Pickett's Last Charge lying ill in the cot of his tent. Three friends chose not to participate in the reenactment so they could be by Husted's side. Later that night, he was sent home, and his condition worsened. Joseph Husted died on July 7.[47]

Husted wasn't the only casualty of the day. On July 3, Captain George Wall of Lewisburg, Pennsylvania, died in one of the field hospitals in the Great Camp from uremia. He was sixty-nine years old.

Each day, another veteran was taken to the morgue. It seemed cruel that some had survived the battle only to pass away at the reunion. It was a heartbreaking reality, but at least the official death toll remained low. Almost too low.

Whispers began circulating that the numbers were being fudged, that the reunion organizers were discreetly hiding how many old soldiers were dropping like flies, perhaps to avoid causing panic among families back home. After all, nothing kills the spirit of a grand celebration like the realization that some guests might not return home.

The Trenton *Times* claimed:

> *Only two deaths were reported in or near the great camp yesterday, but it was learned from reliable sources that news of deaths was being held back by the authorities until the last day, in order not to needlessly scare the veterans away from the camp. It was stated in other quarters that nineteen persons had died in town and camp and that the terrible heat had killed at least 15 of them.*
>
> *In spite of the efforts of the authorities, wild rumors of deaths have been floating around the camp all day.*
>
> *Two men died in the New Jersey camp yesterday, and other veterans saw them pass away. The veterans were astonished when they saw no mention of it in the papers, and came to the correspondents' camp to ask why no notice had been printed. They did not know the names of the men who had died.*[48]

Colonel William Beitler was a member of the Pennsylvania Commission and was responsible for organizing the 1913 Gettysburg Reunion. He heard the rumors and was quick to shut them down, insisting that while the reunion was memorable, it wasn't that deadly:

> *The absolute correct list of dead up until noon today was seven. That will be corroborated at the morgue. We would have absolutely no reason at all to suppress the deaths. I am more than sorry that such a rumor became current. It's only result would be to worry the relatives of the many of the veterans here camped.*
>
> *Of the seven deaths, three already have been sent home, and the remainder will be dispatched just as soon as our officials can get in touch with the relatives.*[49]

Meanwhile, back at the Bloody Angle, thousands of spectators watched as the old soldiers shook hands and swapped tales. Among them were two notable individuals who did not have the opportunity to witness it the first time. The first was Helen Longstreet, who was only three months old when the original charge took place, and the second was that crazy bastard, General Sickles, who was already back in Washington, DC, minus one leg.

Sickles was driven to the Bloody Angle in a convertible automobile and shared the ride with Helen Longstreet. After Pickett's Last Charge, many veterans from both sides of the battle gathered around the car to shake Sickles's hand and tip their hats to Mrs. Longstreet. Sickles listened with rapt interest as many of the eyewitnesses spoke about what it was like to survive Pickett's Charge.[50]

Most old soldiers hung around the Bloody Angle swapping war stories until the supper bell rang. As much as they loved reliving the past, there was nothing quite like the promise of a full belly. Meanwhile, the civilian spectators quickly grew bored—after all, there's only so much charm in watching a bunch of old men chat. The sun was blazing, so they wandered off to find some shade.

With the crowd thinning out, Sickles signaled to his driver to drop Helen Longstreet off and ordered the car to head straight for the Great Tent. The official program was still going on, and Sickles wanted to hear the rest of the speeches.

Now, in case you haven't been paying attention, Sickles was a dramatic man, and he took this opportunity to make a grand entrance. Governor James McCreary of Kentucky was speaking to a crowd of several thousand, but all that came to a screeching halt when the tent flaps were flung open and four men strutted in, carrying the wheelchair-bound general like he was royalty.

"It's Dan Sickles!"

A cheer erupted from the crowd as Sickles was deposited on the stage, derailing whatever McCreary said. Let's be real: McCreary's speech? Forgotten. Sickles was now the star of the show.

And what did Sickles do next? He pulled out an unlit cigar and chomped on it like he was the coolest guy in the room. Meanwhile, an attendant got to work fanning the general with a straw hat. Once he was settled, Sickles waved a weary hand at McCreary, indicating that the governor should continue.

You can bet McCreary was furious, but he kept his cool like a true professional. He swallowed his pride, picked up his dignity, and carried on. Meanwhile, Sickles showed his support for the governor by closing his eyes and falling asleep. His snores only helped to punctuate McCreary's speech. McCreary remained calm and finished his speech without so much as a twitch or a raised eyebrow. A true professional, indeed. Then he turned the podium over to Governor William Sulzer from New York.

The crowd applauded; Sickles sprang awake and clapped wildly to let everyone know he was still the most important person in the room.

What a bastard.

After that, the official program settled into its rhythm. The governor of Virginia, William Mann, said, "If we had known each other as well in 1861 as we do now, the war would have been impossible."[51] He went on to say, "They say it took Moses 40 years to lead the children of Israel to the promised land. My friends, Stonewall Jackson would have trotted them through in a week."[52] That got quite a laugh from the crowd.

Mann then concluded on a serious note:

> *We will never have another civil war in this country. We got enough of it 50 years ago, all of us. And we won't let anybody else get the better of us. . . . And let me tell you this, the young men of the South will fight as bravely for the Union as the daddies fought against it.*[53]

Governor William T. Haines from Maine said:

> *As I rode over the field today, it occurred to me that 50 years ago was the saddest and most sorrowful day in American history. And as I went down through its tented fields and met and saw the blue and gray shaking hands with expressions of fraternity and love upon their faces, I said, "today is the greatest day of sunshine and happiness that has ever shown upon American soil."*[54]

After all the governors had given their speeches, the program concluded with a performance of "America."

That night, supper included pork and beans, cucumbers, pickles, rice fritters, fresh bread, hard bread, butter, and, of course, coffee.[55] After the meal, many veterans found a good spot to see what was coming next. The Pennsylvania Commission planned a two-hour fireworks display that would launch from Little Round Top, where Joshua Lawrence Chamberlain and his men from Maine had repelled the Confederates on July 2, 1863. The fireworks display cost $10,000, which would be about $250,000 in today's money, and according to reports, it must have been an impressive show of pyrotechnics.

Newspapers nationwide advertised the fireworks display, and the state police had to manage an astonishing amount of automobile traffic that evening. Most people arrived by train, but it is estimated that more than twelve thousand cars entered the town, nearly all coming for the day and leaving that evening. These vehicles jostled down the avenues heading toward Little Round Top with their headlights flickering along like fireflies. One newspaper reported that sixty thousand veterans were in camp, and an additional 150,000 civilian spectators came out solely to see the fireworks.[56]

The plan called for a 200-foot-wide by 120-foot-high American flag made of fireworks. Within the flag would be two giant figures, one representing a Union veteran and the other a Confederate veteran shaking hands, with a dove of peace outlined above their heads. The display required ten train cars to transport to Gettysburg—one carload contained rockets and two tons of red, white, and blue fireworks. This included one hundred thousand square feet of lance and framework used for set pieces, as well as four thousand shells ranging from three to thirty inches in diameter. Gettysburg hadn't seen that much ordnance since 1863.

At 8:45 p.m., a lone cannon rang out, letting the spectators know the show was about to begin. Many vets brought soapboxes for camp chairs so they could relax and watch the spectacle. "We were not toting camp chairs 50 years ago tonight," said a veteran from Virginia. "Son, let me tell you what we were doing. You see the ridge over there?" he pointed toward Seminary Ridge. "Well, sir, we were hiking south from that ridge so fast that you could've played seven-up on our coattails without losing a jack."

"We saw you going," replied a veteran from Pennsylvania. "But we were none too keen to chase you. I guess we had enough of gunpowder for one spell."

"Yes, enough to last 50 years," said the vet from Virginia.[57]

And then, BANG, the most amazing rockets in the world exploded over the treetops, leaving no time for swapping stories except for the exchange of "oohs" and "aahs."

"Lie down, boys, lie down!" an old soldier called out between bursts, just like they had heard so many times fifty years before. This was accompanied by much laughter; these were harmless fireworks, not the lethal shells of artillery.

Another old soldier called out during a lull in the fireworks, "Look out for the charge!" This caused more laughter from the vets.

When the fireworks went off again, someone shouted, "Now they're getting the range!" The old soldiers were truly enjoying themselves.

*The Pittsburgh Press* described the fireworks display:

> *With the coming of dark, the shooting commenced. There was a booming noise, and then a rocket curved its way heavenward, its fiery course reminiscent of the terrible battle: reaching its zenith, it burst in a glow of brilliant colors as though indicating the glory of the present reunion, and as the old vets watched admiringly turned suddenly to falling streaks that appeared as tears falling from the heavens, because of the sad affair of a half century ago. Scores of bombs shot upward and burst, causing no carnage, and one beautiful set-piece after another glowed forth from the darkness that was thick in spite of the few million stars.*[58]

The North and South corps badges blazed into the night sky throughout the two-hour show. One of the more unique displays called for a "special balloon shell" that fired into the sky and floated an American flag through the air.

Most of the veterans enjoyed the fireworks, but not everyone was pleased. Some gathered on the observation deck of the Pennsylvania Monument. It's the tallest monument on the battlefield and offers a 360-degree panoramic view. One old soldier up there was less than impressed with the pyrotechnics. "I thought they were very poor. They did not compare with those on Pennsylvania night at the Philadelphia Centennial, which cost $35,000."

The newspaper reporting this story offered a counterpoint to the old soldier's criticism:

> *This old fellow had gone back to 1876, the year of the great centennial exposition at Philadelphia, when his state had spent $35,000 in one evening's fireworks display for a comparison. It did not seem to occur to him that $35,000 would more than feed the army of veterans gathered*

*at Gettysburg for one day, and it would be somewhat extravagant to say the least, to spend that amount in fireworks when the object was to make the veterans as comfortable as possible during their reunion.*[59]

The *Adams County News* also gave a middling review of the fireworks: "The display could be seen for several miles and, while beautiful and greatly enjoyed, was not so elaborate as anticipated in view of advanced announcements. The concluding feature, as a huge flag of fire, came far from meeting its promised grandeur, due, it is said, to the smoke."[60]

It was a still night, and as the fireworks burst overhead, thick clouds of smoke billowed into the air, lingering longer than usual. Soon, Little Round Top was shrouded in haze, the view entirely obscured. The pyrotechnicians stopped for a moment to let the smoke clear. The crowd, unable to see anything through the smog, began to murmur in confusion. Some even feared that something had gone wrong, such as a malfunction or an accident.

Then a gentle breeze cleansed the air. As the haze dissipated, the fireworks resumed, lighting up the sky once again. The crowd breathed a sigh of relief, and the celebration continued without further interruption, the brief moment of worry quickly fading into the night.

As the fireworks ended, the veterans returned to camp to settle in but found it nearly impossible to rest. Thousands of vehicles crawled down the Emmitsburg Pike, which ran parallel to the camp. Engines rumbled, car horns blared, and policemen blew whistles to grab the drivers' attention. In town, the state police managed every intersection to keep the traffic moving. With all this commotion, it took nearly two hours to clear all the vehicles from the battlefield.

Although it had been a hot day and the old soldiers were tired, the fireworks had reenergized many veterans. They sensed the reunion was winding down, and no one wanted to go to bed just yet. Union vets from Pennsylvania, Massachusetts, and other Northern states marched toward Seminary Ridge yelling, "We've got the Johnnies this time!"

"All right, boys, come on! We're all ready for you!" replied the Confederates.[61]

In ranks, the veterans marched forward, some with only one leg, others missing an arm, and many hobbling along on crutches. The Confederates received them with open arms, and soon the entire Confederate camp was intermingled with the Blue and the Gray. The fife, drum, and bugle came out, and the military music of the 1860s drowned out the rumbling of the car engines. As the evening wore on, many former enemies sat together to swap stories around campfires.

At nearly every Confederate campfire were a half dozen Union men, while a fair number of Southerners invaded the Union campfires. A good deal of laughing came from all corners of the Great Camp. This camaraderie lasted through the night and into the small hours of the morning. Around 4:00 a.m., over at the headquarters of the Stonewall Brigade, four men from Jackson's fife and drum corps took up their instruments and struck up the tunes. The band marched through the Virginia camp, and the music was infectious. With shouts of joy, the Virginians rallied behind the music, pulling the visiting Union troops into line with them.

The song changed, and the old voices took up "Marching Through Georgia," a song that no true-born Southerner would have sung fifty years earlier.[62] The lyrics reference William Tecumseh Sherman's "March to the Sea" and the capture of Savannah, Georgia, in 1864. And here it was in 1913, being performed by the Confederate band. The impromptu parade enthusiastically sang the song as they marched toward the Union camp, picking up stragglers as they went.

> Bring the good old bugle, boys, we'll sing another song
> Sing it with a spirit that will start the world along
> Sing it as we used to sing it, fifty thousand strong
> While we were marching through Georgia.
> (Chorus)
>
> Hurrah! Hurrah! we bring the jubilee!
> Hurrah! Hurrah! the flag that makes you free!
> So we sang the chorus from Atlanta to the sea
> While we were marching through Georgia.
>
> How the darkeys shouted when they heard the joyful sound
> How the turkeys gobbled which our commissary found
> How the sweet potatoes even started from the ground
> While we were marching through Georgia.
> (Chorus)

Yes and there were Union men who wept with joyful tears,
When they saw the honored flag they had not seen for years;
Hardly could they be restrained from breaking forth in cheers,
While we were marching through Georgia.
(Chorus)

"Sherman's dashing Yankee boys will never reach the coast!"
So the saucy rebels said and 'twas a handsome boast
Had they not forgot, alas! to reckon with the Host
While we were marching through Georgia.
(Chorus)

So we made a thoroughfare for freedom and her train,
Sixty miles in latitude, three hundred to the main;
Treason fled before us, for resistance was in vain
While we were marching through Georgia.
(Chorus)

The parade was met in the Union camp with cheers, and at the conclusion of the song a federal band formed and struck up "Dixie." The parade was made up of old men who had rediscovered their youth on the fields of Gettysburg. The old men acted just like the boys they were when they first marched out behind Grant, Lee, Jackson, and Sherman. They marched with their hands on each other's shoulders or their arms around each other's necks. Regardless of which side they fought for, the veterans had the time of their lives.

"This is the grandest thing I ever heard of," declared an old Confederate. "I never expected to strike hands on this field with the men I crossed bayonets with 50 years ago. But boys, this is the right thing. We're one people under God, as Abraham Lincoln said."[63]

They went round and round the camp until, finally, the merrymaking was enough to wake General Liggett from his sleep. The general appeared wearing his pajamas and found himself cheering and laughing at the sight of almost five thousand veterans marching past his tent.[64]

Meanwhile, many army officers didn't find it quite so amusing. They feared the veterans were overdoing it and tried to get the old men to calm down and go to bed, but they would have none of it. They were not going to waste one minute of what was left of the Grand Reunion.

"Reckon we can get all the sleep we want when we go home," an old Confederate said when it was suggested that it was time for bed. "Reckon we will all go to have a little more visiting around the ranks."[65]

Moments like this demonstrated that the bitterness of war had passed away, far more than any speech could. If this was the culmination of joy and camaraderie that came out of the Grand Reunion, then every dollar the government used to bring them together was money well spent.

# 8

# July 4—Friday

On the morning of July 4, 1863, two battered and bruised armies stared across the field at each other. General Lee anticipated a counterattack from General Meade, but after a tense day of waiting, the attack never came. That evening, Lee realized there was nothing more he could accomplish at Gettysburg, so the Confederate army began its retreat back to Virginia.

Whenever I visit the Gettysburg Battlefield, no matter what the calendar says, it always feels like July 4. The battles of July 1 to 3 are over, and the old soldiers are long gone, but if you look closely at the placards, markers, and monuments, you'll see the ghost armies lined up in battle formation. Both sides are positioned and ready for an attack that will never come. The equestrian statues of General George Meade and General Robert E. Lee, separated by a mile, face off against each other, just as they did on July 4, 1863. Neither move, but both are forever watching and ready to resume the battle.

But in July 1913, the equestrian statue of Robert E. Lee did not yet exist. Neither did the seven bronze soldiers who would one day adorn the base. The Virginia Monument was only half-finished, consisting of nothing more than a granite pedestal. It was a mere placeholder for what was still to come. The Virginia Monument was the first Confederate state monument permitted on the battlefield, and it was placed near the location where General Lee had watched Pickett's Charge unfold. They held a brief dedication ceremony during the Grand Reunion, but the official dedication would not take place until 1917, when the monument was completed.

When the sun rose on July 4, 1913, many veterans were still awake and swapping tales around the campfire embers. Breakfast that morning consisted of puffed rice, fried eggs, fried bacon, cream potatoes, fresh bread, hard bread, butter, and coffee.[1]

After breakfast, ninety-six men from the Union and Confederate signal corps divided into their respective sides and advanced across the battlefield. These men hailed from eighteen different states and were provided with seven tents in the Great Camp for their use. The Union signalmen ascended Little Round Top and took positions close to the statue of General Warren.

Sergeant Charles Marcy peered through his field glasses at his Confederate counterparts, who were setting up over two miles away at the base of the unfinished Virginia Monument. "He is ready,"[2] Marcy announced to the group of veterans perched on the rocks of Little Round Top. Marcy then handed his field glasses to a comrade and took up the signal flag.

During the Civil War, the signal corps on both sides used the wig-wag system to communicate over vast distances. Various-sized flags were waved, with the most common size being a two-foot by two-foot square. A white, red, or black flag was used to help the flag stand out against the scenery. For instance, a black flag would be used during the winter months when snow was present, but the most common color was a white flag with a small red square at its center. The flag was held vertically and then swiftly waved down to the left or the right. Each letter in the alphabet was assigned up to three motions, and the recipient could decipher the message with a pencil and paper.

Using this method, Sergeant Marcy waved out a message to the Confederates: "Peace on Earth, Good Will to Men."

At the Virginia Monument, Lieutenant George Carr Round and the other Confederate signalmen watched the motion through their field glasses and made notations in their ledger. With the message received, George Round picked up his signal flag and replied, "Glory to God in the Highest."

Back and forth, the two sides exchanged messages. The Union Signal Corps responded with the famous quote from General Grant: "Let Us

(*Top*) A group of Civil War musicians at the base of the Virginia Monument during the 1913 Grand Reunion before the bronze statues were erected. Courtesy of The Horse Soldier, a Civil War–focused antiques dealer in Gettysburg. (*Bottom*) The same location in 2025, photographed by the author.

Have Peace." To which the Confederates replied with a quote from Robert E. Lee: "Duty is the sublimest word in our language."

From Little Round Top came another message: "America. All hail to thee. Thanks be to God who made us free." The Confederates replied, "North, south, east, west, hand clasped in hand, united, we thy children stand."[3]

After exchanging messages for over an hour, the flags were once more furled, and the signal corps from both armies converged on the Great Tent for a joint reunion.

Earlier in the book, we briefly discussed William Durst, one of the few navy veterans to attend the Grand Reunion. "These fellows insist on talking about charges and camps and all that sort o' thing," said Durst. "Not one of them know a thing about sailing. I guess I'll have to go back home. An inland battlefield is no place for an old sailor man."[4]

He was persuaded to stay at the reunion despite his intention to leave. He wandered around the battlefield in his old sailor's uniform, and it attracted a lot of attention. His attire made him a novelty in camp, and everyone wanted to hear his story. And what a story he had.

William Durst was born in 1839 in Austria and soon immigrated to the United States with his family. He enlisted in the navy as a coalheaver and transferred to the USS *Monitor* on February 25, 1862.

Durst, who was Jewish, encountered prejudice on board the *Monitor* and was often referred to as the "Dusty Jew" by his shipmates. The nickname came from a combo of his heritage and the fact that he was frequently covered in soot after feeding coal to the engines. One of his shipmates said this about Durst: "He was the only Jew on board either *Monitor* and the only Jew I ever saw on any United States vessel."

The USS *Monitor* was an ironclad warship built by the Union during the Civil War. It was the first of its kind and sat low in the water, which presented a very small footprint for opposing ships to attack. Most of the vessel was submerged with a revolving turret just above the waterline. Because of this design, it was often called "The Yankee Cheesebox on a Raft."

The Union wasn't the only one to have an ironclad. The Confederates had the *Merrimac*, which also sat low in the water and looked like "a floating barn roof." On March 8, 1862, the *Merrimac* sailed into Hampton

Roads and sank two Union ships. It returned the following day to wreak more havoc on the Federal Navy, but the USS *Monitor* intercepted it.

William Durst described the battle in his own words:

*March 9, 1862, was the date . . . I remember it all as well as if it had happened yesterday. We were ordered into action early in the morning to protect the Minnesota, a wooden ship from the Merrimac. The Merrimac had already done a lot of damage.*

*The fog was thick over the water, and we sighted the Merrimac so sudden-like that everybody on both boats was surprised.*

*While we were creeping through the fog we had been wondering how our little "cheesebox" would compare with the pride of the Confederate navy. She seemed to be about three times as big as our Monitor. Several men were running along the deck. One of them yelled something at us. I couldn't hear what it was.*

*The two ships were pretty close together. The Merrimac opened fire—two shots—bang, bang; both fell short and splashed up the water. . . . We had closed in by that time. We let fly a broadside as we passed. Then we came back. Both ships began banging away at each other. We were at close range. The boats stayed that way during most of the battle, until Merrimac was disabled. The shells bounced off our armor like water off a duck's back.*

*I was in the pilot house with Lieutenant Worden. . . . He was the commander. A shell exploded, and pieces of iron hit him in the head. He fell back into my arms, and I carried him out of danger.*

*We maneuvered around the Merrimac several times and licked her in great shape. History books that say we ran into shallow water where the Merrimac couldn't follow us are wrong. We drove her away and saved the Minnesota. The fight began at 6 am and lasted half the day.*[5]

The history books that Durst said were wrong claim that the battle between the two ironclads was a draw. I'll leave it up to the reader to discern the truth of the matter.

In October 1862, the USS *Monitor* entered dry dock for repairs, and the crew was granted a furlough. William Durst went to New York City and never returned to the *Monitor*. He claimed:

*I was sick from some trouble to my heart and stomach, contracted from the bad air on the Monitor, and when my liberty expired, I was still sick and unfit to return, and after the expiration of my furlough, I was afraid to return on account of fear of punishment, and enlisted under the name of Walter David, aboard the US* [sic] *Catskill and served 1 year and 3 months.*

Indeed, William Durst was marked as a deserter and given a dishonorable discharge by the US Navy. It was later determined that his illness was from typhoid fever. While Durst was recovering, the USS *Monitor* finished her repairs and set sail. Tragedy struck only a few weeks later. While sailing through a ferocious storm, the *Monitor* capsized and sank, sending sixteen sailors to a watery grave.

In retrospect, the typhoid fever may have saved William Durst's life.

After the war, Durst cleaned up his record, and the navy awarded him an honorable discharge.

In 1913, Durst attended the Grand Reunion in hopes of meeting other sailors. He was considering leaving for his home in Philadelphia when he heard a survivor from the Confederate navy might be at Gettysburg.

"Wouldn't I like to meet him, though?" declared the Philadelphian. "I didn't know whether there were any more of those fellows alive anymore. He's a man I'm going to look up, surely."

Durst had his opportunity on the afternoon of July 4 when he encountered Samuel Golder, one of the sailors from the *Merrimac*. How did these two ancient enemies greet each other?

With a hug.

With the introductions out of the way, Durst said, "Honest, Samuel . . . you had us scared. We thought we were goners. But we licked you finally, but not before you sent some of our good ships to the bottom."

"You did more than lick me," responded the Southern sailor. "A piece of a shell struck my left shoulder, and here's the mark." Golder bared his shoulder, revealing a large scar. "Three months in the hospital, too," added Golder. "No hard feelings now, my hearty, are there?"[6]

Unfortunately, the reporter didn't record the rest of the conversation, but I can speculate on what happened next. Durst had waited all week to meet another Civil War sailor, and I bet the two of them sat down and had a nice, long conversation.

July 4, 1913, was Independence Day and the final day with an official program for the Grand Reunion. Initially, the Pennsylvania Commission wanted to use July 4 as a day when the president of the United States dedicated a monument between the Blue and the Gray in honor of the reunion. The original concept called for a large-scale "peace monument" established at the Bloody Angle, near the high-water mark of Pickett's Charge. However, with all the planning involved with the reunion and everything else that needed to be done, there was no way such a monument would be finished in time, so it was proposed that the president dedicate just the cornerstone on July 4.[7] However, these plans were quickly abandoned in early 1912 for budgetary reasons. When that fell through, there was still hope that the president would address the old veterans on the last day of the reunion.

Throughout the planning stages of the Pennsylvania Commission, William Howard Taft was the president of the United States. President Taft visited Gettysburg in 1909 to dedicate the monument to the United States Regulars. However, he lost his reelection campaign to Woodrow Wilson, who took office on March 4, 1913, just a few months before the reunion. Wilson was invited to speak during the final day's program but declined. The Commission then asked former president Taft to speak, and he accepted the invitation. At the end of June, a strange reversal occurred. Taft changed his mind and decided not to attend the reunion after all; soon after, Wilson also reversed his decision and chose to speak at the reunion.

President Wilson arrived by train at 11:00 a.m., where Governor Tener and a crowd of cheering onlookers greeted him. Meanwhile, a twenty-one-gun salute was fired off from Gettysburg College. Wilson was escorted to a car and whisked over to the Great Camp. Once there, his car passed through two rows of Boy Scouts standing at attention on its way to the Great Tent. As Wilson entered the tent, the band struck up "Hail to the Chief."

With a brief introduction from Governor Tener, President Wilson took the stand and launched into his speech:

> *Friends and fellow citizens, I need not tell you what the Battle of Gettysburg meant. . . . These gallant men in blue and gray sit all about us here. Many of them met upon this ground in grim and deadly struggle. . . . But 50 years have gone by since then and I crave the privilege of speaking to you for a few minutes of what those 50 years have meant. . . . They have meant peace and union and vigor and maturity and might of a great nation. How wholesome and healing that peace has been. We have found one another again as brothers and comrades, in arms, enemies no longer; generous friends rather, our battles long past, the quarrels forgotten—except that we should not forget the splendid valor, the manly devotion of the men then arrayed against one another, now grasping hands and smiling into each other's eyes.*[8]

The president spoke slowly and carefully, but the breeze rippling through the canvas tent and the clomping feet of those who arrived late made it difficult for the old men in the rear seats to hear the speech. The estimated crowd was only around ten thousand people inside the Great Tent, and Wilson was interrupted only twice by cheering. Woodrow Wilson was born in Virginia and was the first Southern president elected since the start of the Civil War. Before serving as president, Wilson was the governor of New Jersey. Because of his Southern heritage, many old Confederates came to hear his speech and outnumbered the men in blue.

President Wilson's speech lasted just ten minutes. After some polite applause, the band played "The Star-Spangled Banner."[9] Wilson shook a few hands and exited the tent, where he got into his car and headed back to the train station. Altogether, President Woodrow Wilson spent forty-six minutes in Gettysburg.

President Wilson's visit to the Grand Reunion felt more like a symbolic gesture than a personal investment. He was like a celebrity making a brief cameo appearance in a Hollywood movie; it was nice to see him, but he didn't really contribute to the storyline. He delivered a carefully crafted keynote about unity and healing, but it was a little too safe and sanitized. Ultimately, his speech was simply that—just another speech that seemed to fulfill one of his presidential obligations.

And maybe that's okay. The reunion was never really about speeches or official ceremonies. It was about the veterans returning to the very fields where they had fought and bled, no longer as enemies but as old men seeking to make peace. What truly mattered weren't the words from a podium but the shared moments between old soldiers who had every reason to hate each other and yet chose not to.

The president had barely left town when the regular army paid tribute to the fallen soldiers of the Civil War. The Grand Reunion was for the survivors, those who had made it through the war and lived to see a day of peace. But those who didn't make it were never far from their thoughts. According to the American Battlefield Trust, approximately 620,000 lost their lives in the line of duty. To put it in more sobering terms, one in four soldiers never returned home:

> *The 26th North Carolina, hailing from seven counties in the western part of the state, suffered 714 casualties out of 800 men during the Battle of Gettysburg. The 24th Michigan squared off against the 26th North Carolina at Gettysburg and lost 362 out of 496 men. Nearly the entire student body of Ole Miss—135 out of 139—enlisted in Company A of the 11th Mississippi. Company A, also known as the "University Greys," suffered 100% casualties in Pickett's Charge.*[10]

These numbers reveal the true cost of war. Everyone at the reunion was deeply affected by the loss of a brother, a neighbor, a tentmate, or a commander they began the war with but who didn't survive to see the end. Fifty years had passed, but the memories remained vivid. How could they return to Gettysburg and not visit the place where they lost a friend? Although the veterans enjoyed their time together and also with their former enemies, every open field, hill, stone wall, swale, and woods served as a painful reminder of someone they knew who had suffered and died. The Great Camp had plenty of laughter and camaraderie, but an equal number of tears were shed in the quiet moments.

At noon, the church bells in town rang out, followed by a lone bugler playing Taps. The giant American flag at the camp headquarters was slowly lowered to half-mast; the other US flags installed around the Great Camp were also lowered. General Liggett faced the flag, clicked his heels together, and stood at attention.[11] The guns of the Third Battery bellowed at intervals for a total of forty-eight times, one for each state in the Union. As the roars echoed across the battlefield, a solemn silence fell over the camp.[12] Every officer and enlisted man from the past and the present stopped what they were doing and faced the flag. People who did not understand what was happening were compelled to silence. Even the clatter of pots and pans in the mess tents was hushed, and the calls of the cooks dropped to a whisper. For five full minutes, the camp was quiet as each individual turned their thoughts to those who gave the last full measure of devotion.

*The Philadelphia Inquirer* described the effect that the five minutes of silence had on the veterans: "The old men wept as they stooped. Into each heart had come memories almost unbearable."[13] All of them had lost someone during the war, and standing together but alone in their hearts, they mourned each one of them. Major Thomas Holland, who led the Confederates during Pickett's Last Charge, may have been thinking about General Lewis Armistead and how they had crossed the stone wall together just before Armistead was cut down. That crazy bastard, Dan Sickles, might have been gazing into the field where he lost his leg. The first Confederates in town, Brawner and Page, might have been reminiscing about their Third Musketeer, whose body ended up in a burial trench on Culp's Hill. William Durst didn't fight at Gettysburg, but during the five minutes of silence, his thoughts might have turned to his shipmates onboard the USS *Monitor*, who perished while he was recovering from typhoid fever. Henry S. Huidekoper, who conceived the initial idea for the Grand Reunion, might have been reflecting on the spot where he lost his arm and all of his comrades who died during the first day of battle. Helen Longstreet may have been thinking of her husband, who would have loved to see this moment of peace and reconciliation.

A reporter from Iowa summed it up like this: "There was an eloquence in the silent tribute of the regular army to the soldiers who have fought their last battle that by comparison made all the Gettysburg speech making seem rather cheap and tawdry."

Silence lingered in the air for several seconds after the forty-eighth and final artillery shell echoed across the valley. Then a lone bugle played a joyous tune, the American flag rose to its peak, and forty thousand voices erupted in cheers for the reunited red, white, and blue. The band played

Confederate and Union veterans clasp hands across a cannon barrel. Courtesy of the West Virginia and Regional History Center, A&M 1809 Collection 038318.

the national anthem, and as it concluded, so did the Grand Reunion of the Fiftieth Anniversary of the Battle of Gettysburg.

A new sound filled the air at the end of the five minutes of silence. The Pennsylvania Commission planned for the Fourth of July to be a real feast day. And so commenced the Great Chicken Massacre of 1913. Twenty thousand live chickens[14] were brought into the camp to feed the hungry veterans.

Confederate colonel D. A. Dickert wrote about the feast, "Did we have plenty to eat? Yes, and spare . . . Munroe Harris took a fright at a spread of dressed chickens, that I don't think he will forget during life. He led me to it. It was a table about five feet wide, more than two hundred feet long and piled as high as you could reach with the fattest chickens I ever saw. I was leaving for home, but 'Mun' said he would stay to eat of those chickens 'if it took all summer.'"[15]

The full lunch menu consisted of fricasseed chicken, peas, corn, ice cream, cake, cigars, fresh bread, hard bread, butter, coffee, and iced tea. It was a fine holiday dinner, and some veterans wished they could stay a few days longer, while others had seen enough and were ready to go home.

With lunch over, thousands of veterans packed their bags and headed for the train depot at the center of the Great Camp. Even though the official program had concluded, the Great Camp would continue to operate until after breakfast on Sunday, July 6. Those who wanted to avoid the crowds settled in for a few more days. Later that night, the strains of "Auld Lang Syne" could be heard coming from a campfire.

One of the Southerners spoke up and said, "We have not long to live. In a few years, we shall all be in our graves. What could the country do for us more fitting than to bring us here that we might in the face of the world take the hands of our brothers, once our foes, on this sacred ground and show the world that we are ready to pass on, content with what God has done for us and with peace in our hearts for our fellow Americans of the North."[16]

Another voice said, "Glory to God, brothers, glory to God!"

As the reunion wound down, many veterans set off for home, and by the evening of July 4, the Great Peace Camp had thinned down to twenty-five thousand veterans. Five hundred men marched down to the train depot and marched right back when they saw the congestion. Many were content to wait for the crowds to die down and stay in camp until it closed on Sunday morning.

The Grand Reunion transformed many foes into friends. A. T. Dice, the vice president of the Reading Railroad, witnessed a poignant scene:

> *Two old soldiers met for the first time at Gettysburg and quickly became close friends, one from the North and one from the South. They spent the entire week together, taking in the sights, touring the battlefield, and visiting the monuments. When it was time to part, they arrived at the train depot in tears. The soldier in blue lived in Oregon, while the soldier in gray resided in New Orleans. They lingered at the depot, watching train after train depart, delaying the inevitable farewell. The man from Oregon couldn't figure out how to return home from New Orleans, and his friend in gray was eager to visit the West but lacked the money for a*

*train ticket. Throughout the reunion, they had become fast friends, but they knew they would never meet again due to the distance. As their train stood waiting, the two old soldiers made a decision. They slowly removed their uniforms and exchanged them in front of a crowd of witnesses. The man who wore blue proudly returned home equally proud to wear gray, and vice versa.*[17]

Nearly every newspaper in America printed this story.

The Great Camp was clearing out, and it was time to start disassembling the tents. The Lost and Found Bureau was located underneath the bleachers at the back of the Great Tent. Throughout the week, they had acquired a considerable collection of oddities, and most had yet to be claimed. At least one hundred crutches were in the collection, and the veterans who came looking for them rarely left with their original ones.

Several sets of false teeth were found. An old veteran from Vermont had removed his teeth to give his jaw a rest. He slipped them into his pocket, but they fell out and were lost. When he saw how many sets were in the Lost and Found, he couldn't determine which was his. He inspected each set and came up with a brilliant idea. "Suppose I try 'em in," he suggested, glancing up at the attendant.

The curator wasn't having it. "You've got to take 'em by faith, Yank."[18]

The most unusual items in the collection were two female corsets and a wooden prosthetic leg.[19] The Boy Scouts found the wooden leg under a tree and presumed that a one-legged man unbuckled it from his stump while enjoying some shade beneath the tree but was overcome by the heat and carried to one of the field hospitals, leaving the wooden leg behind. Unfortunately, its owner was never found.

Regarding the corsets, who can say for sure? The old soldiers were the only ones invited to stay in the Great Camp, but once the crowds thinned out, many others found their way to unoccupied tents. Most likely, one of the veteran's wives found an empty cot and left her corsets behind.

By November, there were still seventeen sets of false teeth, several crutches, and one unclaimed woman's corset. This situation caused Colonel Lewis Beitler to issue a note in the newspapers: "If any of your veterans are 'shy' any of these useful commodities, let me know, and we will try to fit him out."[20]

While some veterans had lost their possessions, others were going home with new ones. Many of the old soldiers took home walking canes whittled from trees that had grown up over the very ground where they once fought. A few chipped away souvenirs from the rocky slopes of Devil's Den, eager to carry a tangible piece of Gettysburg back home.

These next two tales ought to be taken with a very large grain of salt. I can't vouch for their accuracy, but they're too good not to share.

The first account comes from W. P. Whitaker, an old soldier from Georgia, who was walking across the battlefield with a fellow veteran. When they reached the spot where his comrade's regiment had stood during the fight, the man stopped and said, "Here's where my command was, and right here the spear was shot off the top of our flagstaff. I'm going to look in the weeds and see if I can find it."

Whitaker watched as his friend poked about in the leaves and dirt, his hands black with soil, his face creased with excitement. Then, with a sudden shout, he bent down and snatched something from the ground, a slender, rusted bit of metal that he clutched to his chest. Against all odds, he had found the very spear from his flagstaff, lying there undisturbed for fifty years.[21]

The next story is just as unlikely, maybe even more so. Alfred Tennet, a Union veteran who fought on Culp's Hill, once found himself separated from his regiment and far too close to Confederate lines for comfort. Knowing he'd have to make a run for it, he decided his ten-pound rifle would slow him down. Spotting a hollow in a nearby beech tree, he stashed the gun inside, hoping to come back for it later. Of course, the battle raged on, and he never got the chance.

But for fifty years, that hidden rifle stayed in his memory. When Tennet returned to Gettysburg for the Grand Reunion, he set out on a personal mission to find it. He wandered across Culp's Hill until, at last, he found the same old beech tree—now gnarled and thick with age. Digging into its hollow, he pulled out the remnants of his long-lost musket. "The stock was worm-eaten and fragile," he reported, "the lock and barrel rusted, but in a fair state of preservation."[22]

Tennet was overjoyed and carried the relic back to camp like a trophy, showing it to anyone who would listen. Not only did he take home a unique souvenir, but he also had quite the tale to go with it.

Did either of these stories really happen? Who knows? But the newspapers printed them, and that's good enough for me to pass them along.

However, the following stories are far more credible.

Jefferson Sefton came from Iowa to attend the reunion and revisited where he had fought on July 2. On his last day at Gettysburg, he returned to the spot again and filled two suitcases full of soil to take back home. He said, "This is more precious to me than anything else. I fought on the spot where I gathered the soil, and I want to take some of it back home. I shall make a garden box of it."[23]

Sefton wasn't the only one with that idea.

Henry Hodges from Union Hill, North Carolina, was an old Confederate who enjoyed a week at Gettysburg. He had participated in Pickett's Charge in 1863 and Pickett's Last Charge at the reunion, but on July 5 it was time to head home. He left his tent shortly after dawn and made one final trip back to the Bloody Angle. Like Jefferson Sefton, he filled a suitcase with soil from the spot he had reached fifty years earlier. With one last look at the battlefield, Henry Hodges walked to the train station. The newspapers claim that he went to the Gettysburg station, not the train depot inside the Great Camp. The distance from the Bloody Angle to the Gettysburg station is almost two miles—a long way to carry a suitcase full of dirt.

When he arrived, he struck up a conversation with others waiting for the train. He told them about the suitcase full of soil and how much it meant to him. As he spoke, some of the listeners in the crowd noticed Hodges was starting to grow weak. They suggested he head into the waiting room to sit down, but Hodges rejected the idea.

"I am feeling sickly, for that suitcase is heavy," Hodges said. "I had to tote it from the Bloody Angle here. There weren't any buses around. I would willingly carry it all the way to my old home, for that ground will be placed in my front yard, and I will plant flowers there, so I can always remember when we of the South met the men of the North the second time at Gettysburg."[24]

No sooner had he said this than he placed his hand on his heart and fell over, dead.

Henry Hodges was the ninth fatality that took place at the reunion and also the only Confederate death. He was seventy years old.

Union and Confederate veterans using the train station as they depart from the Grand Reunion, 1913. Courtesy of Laura Hedgecock.

The railroad officials sent the suitcase of soil back with the body so that it could be placed in his grave.

During the reunion, the men from Vermont who bristled at the thought of the Confederate flag softened their stance the more time they spent with the Southerners. Toward the end of the week, a lone Confederate wandered into the Vermont camp, looking sad and out of sorts.

Colonel Henry Clark called out to him and invited him into his tent to rest for a while. "What's the matter now, Johnny?"

"Well, I'll tell you," said the Confederate, "last night, I lost all of the money I had."

"How much did you lose?" Henry asked.

"Five dollars."

"Haven't you any money to get home with?"

"No."

So Henry reached into his pocket, took out a five-dollar bill, and handed it to the Confederate. After this, the hat was passed around, and a collection of eighteen to twenty dollars was given to the old Confederate. "When you were here 50 years ago, any of these fellas would have shot you if they could; now they are giving you money. What do you say to that?" Henry asked.

"I wish to thank you all. May God bless you!"[25] The old Confederate walked away with tears in his eyes.

State Health Commissioner Samuel Dixon said in an interview:

> *That the fact that only nine deaths have occurred during excessive heat despite the presence of 50,000 to 60,000 veterans and civilians, the majority of them were of advanced age, probably was due to several causes. In the first place, the old soldiers represent the survival of the fittest. Secondly, the sanitary arrangements were considered with the utmost care and have been of the most advanced character. Another factor that is difficult to calculate and yet undoubtedly responsible to some degree is the stimulation naturally accompanying the meeting of old comrades and the revisitation of old scenes. All of these have combined to keep the mortality down to such a low point. It is a matter of congratulations for the officials who have been in charge and a happy refutation of the calamity howlers' predictions that the celebration would be marred by an excessively high death rate.*[26]

Of the nine who died, eight were Union veterans and one was a Confederate veteran. Thankfully, the reunion wasn't as deadly to the veterans as their first trip to Gettysburg.

There were 1,009 cases of veterans receiving medical attention at the reunion in some form or another; the vast majority were minor inconveniences.[27] The number one ailment was heat exhaustion. Some of the medical cases were quite serious, such as a hernia, tuberculosis, a fractured hip, and cystitis. But others were to be expected, considering the environment of the Great Camp, and these were cases of overexertion, aggravated sunburn, poison ivy, and insect bites. There were also quite a few throat afflictions and cases of laryngitis, probably from giving the Rebel Yell so loud and so often. The medical report mentioned eight cases of assault, which were probably from the knife fight in the Gettysburg Hotel. There was also an injury reported as a result of a runaway horse.

A more common ailment was tired faces from too much smiling and aching hands from too many handshakes. Alonzo Loucks of Roscoe, New York, said:

> *There were 280 acres of tents. I never before in all of my life saw such a great thing. It was a famous but sad sight to view the cemetery on the battlefield, where so many unidentified men who fought in the war are buried. You can say there were more than 10,000 "Johnnies" there too. I was almost weary from shaking hands with men whom I fought against 50 years ago.*

Confederate John B. Nicholson, who fought with the Thirty-Seventh North Carolina, expressed a similar sentiment. He survived the Battle of Gettysburg but lost a brother during the fighting. Despite that painful memory, he enjoyed his time at the Grand Reunion. While returning home to Huntersville, North Carolina, he said he never received such a reception as he had at Gettysburg. "Soldiers from New York, Pennsylvania, and other Northern States came to my tent in crowds and my hands are actually sore from shaking hands,"[28] he said.

It's possible that Alonzo Loucks and John B. Nicholson exchanged handshakes with their tired hands.

With the tents nearly empty, it was time to dismantle the Great Camp. Brigadier General Hunter Liggett was organizing the teardown when an unnamed veteran from New York approached him. Liggett had just finished breakfast in his tent at the camp headquarters and noticed the old man seemed troubled and hesitant to ask for assistance. Through some simple questions, Liggett discovered that the veteran had somehow lost his return train ticket to New York State and was anxious about getting home.

"I guess we can fix you up all right," Liggett said. Many veterans had lost their tickets during the week, so this was not an unusual request. He took a scrap of paper, wrote a quick note, and signed it. His signature was enough to cut through any red tape the old soldier might encounter.

"Take this to the depot," said General Liggett. "And if they don't honor it, come right back and let me know."

The veteran was overcome with relief. What had seemed an insurmountable obstacle was brushed aside with the stroke of a pen. He thanked the general and said he was anxious to get home because he wasn't feeling very well.

"If you are sick," said General Liggett, "why don't you go to the hospital and stay there two or three days until you get rested up? We will be very glad to take care of you, and I think it would do you good. You might drop out on the way home."

With tears in his eyes, the old soldier thanked the general but declined the offer. He knew the best care he could receive was waiting for him back home, where his wife and daughters could look after him.

Liggett nodded in understanding, but he wanted to make sure that the vet was properly fitted out for his journey. "Have you had breakfast?"

"Yes, sir."

Liggett nodded again and carefully scrutinized the old soldier in front of him, who seemed worn out. "Comrade, maybe a little stimulant will help you on your way to the depot. But you must be careful not to take too much."

Liggett opened a desk drawer and pulled out a bottle of whiskey (reserved for such occasions as this). He found a glass, poured a finger's width over some ice, and mixed it with water. With a smile, Liggett handed it over to the vet, who drank it with relish. The old veteran thanked him yet again. Suitably fortified, he was now ready to make the journey home. General Liggett was happy to help. Throughout the Grand Reunion, there had been hundreds of little incidents like this, and Liggett considered it an honor to serve the old soldiers, regardless of their uniform color.[29]

North Carolina was a state that was unable to provide transportation for its veterans to the reunion, but Henry C. Albea from Lexington, North Carolina, didn't let that stop him. The round-trip train ticket cost $10.50, and he knew that once he reached Gettysburg, the food and lodging would be provided free of charge to the veterans. So he reached out to other local vets to see who had the money and the interest in going with him. Eight friends and seventeen others from Lexington made the journey. They boarded a train on Sunday, June 29, at 3:45 p.m. and finally arrived in Gettysburg at 4:00 a.m. on Tuesday, July 1. Once they were settled in, it was time to go exploring. Henry Albea and his friends trampled up and down the fields, retracing their steps from fifty years ago. "On the field, I met some Union soldiers I fought there. They took my hand and told me how they ran to get away from us. They said that 'Rebel Yell' they could not stand. They were proud to meet me and walked with me some distance."[30]

On the evening of July 3, Albea explored the battlefield one last time. He wasn't interested in the fireworks and figured he could see them almost anywhere on the battlefield. Instead, he wanted to be alone with his thoughts and soak in the memories, so he left his friends behind. He didn't return until late in the evening, and when he did, he found that his tentmates had left for home without him, and only one of his friends remained. They held down the tent together that night and figured they could avoid some of the crowds by leaving before President Wilson arrived at camp. They had seen enough of the multitudes and knew they could always read the president's speech in the newspaper. While traveling home on the train, they had a "jolly time" with two veterans from Massachusetts. Throughout their ride, they exchanged addresses and promised to write to each other.

"You will hear from us when we get home," Albea said. One of the vets from Massachusetts gave Albea his photograph and a souvenir gun; they were very friendly traveling companions and prominent businessmen from Boston. The small group parted ways in Hagerstown, Maryland. "If you ever come to Massachusetts, let us know. We will meet you and give you a good time while there."[31]

Friendly exchanges like this happened all the time at the reunion, proving once again that the anger and hostilities from fifty years earlier were long gone.

As the veterans were departing the camp and making their way to the train depot, Confederate soldiers from the South and their Northern counterparts were given ovations from the townsfolk. Confederate flags and the Stars and Stripes were carried, with Johnny Rebs and Billy Yanks marching side by side. The newspapers said that "strong men wept" and "women waved handkerchiefs and threw kisses to the departing old soldier."

"Goodbye, Johnny; we wish you a safe journey home."

"Goodbye, Yank; hope you get home alright."[32]

One of the first stops the trains made was in Harrisburg, Pennsylvania, the state capital and, more important, home to something Gettysburg sorely lacked: showers. Sure, the Great Camp provided food, shelter, and sanitation, but when it came to bathing, the best the veterans could hope for was a quick splash from a spigot in the company streets. Now, picture yourself camping in July, in a tent, for a whole week, without a proper wash. Now, imagine thousands of old soldiers doing the same. The stench alone would have sent Lee and Grant running for the hills.

So, when the weary veterans rolled into Harrisburg, they made a beeline for the local YMCA like it was the Promised Land.[33] In the early twentieth century, the Young Men's Christian Association was a hub of social services, fitness, and wholesome living. And while "young men" might have been a bit of a stretch for these grizzled old warriors, they knew one thing for sure: The YMCA had showers. Visiting the YMCA in Harrisburg became one of the unofficial stops of the Grand Reunion for a long-overdue scrub-down.

After a week of baking in the July heat, covered in dust, sweat, and the lingering scent of battlefield nostalgia, a cold, refreshing shower must have felt like heaven. And, let's be honest, it was probably a public service, too. Rejuvenated and slightly less fragrant, the old soldiers climbed aboard their trains, ready to complete their journey home—cleaner, calmer, and significantly easier on the nose.

Throughout this book, I've tried to recover and highlight the stories of Black veterans, men who are often left out of the popular telling of Gettysburg's fiftieth anniversary. Some have claimed they were intentionally excluded, but I've found ample evidence to suggest otherwise. They were there—present, seen, and welcomed alongside their White counterparts. Their stories deserve to be remembered and celebrated, not lost to silence. And that's why it's so important to challenge what I've called the "Myth of the Uninvited Black Soldier."

The final story I have of a Black veteran attending the reunion is, unfortunately, the most mysterious. The details are scarce, and I haven't been able to find his name in any Civil War database or obituary. But that doesn't mean he didn't exist or was a figment of the imagination.

According to *The Roanoke Times*, Henry Merchant, who was described as an "aged colored man," left Clifton Forge with members of the Alleghany Camp of Confederate Veterans to attend the Grand Reunion at Gettysburg. Shortly after arriving, he vanished into the enormous crowd. For days, no one could find him. When he finally returned home, exhausted and disoriented, he couldn't explain where he'd been or how he'd made it back. His once-new clothes were now worn and tattered.[34] Interestingly, he returned home a week after the others.

Where was he during that time?

Was he a victim of foul play?

He was unable to say. Once home, he went to bed in a nervous condition and remained there for the rest of the day. Sadly, there was never a follow-up article on what happened to him afterward.

Although the newspaper never explicitly called him a veteran, the fact that he traveled and camped with Confederate veterans suggests he had some sort of association with them. I can't help but wonder if Henry Merchant had once been enslaved and was brought to Gettysburg in 1863 as a teamster, cook, or servant. That might explain why his name doesn't appear in any official records. Perhaps, fifty years later, he returned on his own terms—walking on the ground where he had once been forced to go. That's speculation, of course, but I hope that one day someone uncovers more information about Henry Merchant, the man who got lost at Gettysburg and somehow found his way back home.

Regardless of his official status, Henry Merchant's name deserves to be recognized among those who attended the reunion. Only around three hundred members of the United States Colored Troops were recorded as present, but they were there and denying that is to erase a part of our collective history. My hope in sharing these stories is to bring their names, however few we know, back into the light and to remind us that they, too, returned to Gettysburg, fifty years later, to stand once more on that sacred ground.

But something strange happened on the evening of July 4. As the crowds thinned and the Great Camp grew quieter, the cooks and kitchen helpers found themselves with nothing to do. Among them, a group of young Black cooks devised what they likely thought was an entertaining game. They threw themselves into it wholeheartedly, laughing until they could hardly breathe. Their excitement attracted a crowd.

One of the cooks, a large Black man, was placed on top of a stump. Another stepped forward, taking on the role of an auctioneer. With a theatrical flourish, he called out to the gathering of cooks and old soldiers, urging them to step closer and place their bids in a mock slave auction.

"He's a strong man, standing 5 feet 10 inches tall, in great shape, weighing 175 pounds. Who in the crowd wants to take him home for $100? Come on, place your bids!"[35]

Laughter echoed. The Black men roared at their performance, and even the old veterans who had endured the war that ended such spectacles found themselves chuckling along. However, it was nervous laughter. Beneath the surface of their mirth lay something else—something colder.

The laughter didn't quite reach their eyes. The veterans, who had seen the horrors of war firsthand, couldn't escape the ghosts this little performance had stirred. The scene before them was a shadow of something real, something they had once fought to destroy. And now, decades later, here it was again—brought back to life in a place where the echoes of the past had never truly faded.

The Grand Reunion was a product of its time, striking a delicate balance between celebration and remembrance. However, not everything was sunshine and rainbows. It was intended as a time for healing and for old enemies to shake hands and set aside the bitterness of war. On the surface, all seemed cordial and dignified, and many were on their best behavior. Yet beneath that veneer of civility, wounds had never fully closed, and memories had never truly faded.

Perhaps that night's strange spectacle was a way of letting off steam, of releasing tensions that could not be spoken aloud. Maybe the cooks, in their laughter, were mocking a past that had shaped their lives in ways they could never escape. And perhaps the veterans, chuckling along, were doing their best to convince themselves that time had softened the jagged edges of history.

This is an uncomfortable story, but history is rarely neat or easy. It would be convenient to let moments like this one fade into obscurity and smooth over the rough edges of the past. But doing so would mean losing an honest glimpse into the complexities of memory, reconciliation, and the lingering shadows of history. Some stories must be remembered, no matter how uneasy they make us feel.

That night, the camp felt different. The revelry of past evenings had faded, leaving behind an eerie stillness. The fife and drum had gone quiet, and the few remaining fires burned low, their embers pulsing like the last heartbeats of the reunion. Most of the tents stood empty, their flaps stirring ever so slightly in the night breeze, like ghosts shifting in their sleep.

The remaining veterans gathered around the dying fires, their faces bathed in the warm, flickering glow. Their voices were low, in quiet reverence of the moment. They spoke not just of war but also of the reunion itself—the old friends they had embraced, the unexpected encounters with the enemy, and the bittersweet memories stirred by the landscape.

As the night deepened, their conversation turned to those absent, the comrades who had not lived to see this day. Their names were spoken with sorrow and pride, their stories retold with the care of those who knew how precious remembrance could be. It was not just grief that hung in the air but also gratitude—for the friendships forged in hardship, for the years they had been granted, for the chance to come together one last time.

The Grand Reunion had come to an end. Soon, these men would part ways, returning to their homes and their lives. But as the last embers smoldered in the pit and the stars stretched high over the quiet battlefield, they knew that some things would always remain: the bonds they had formed, the sacrifices they had made, and the memories of those who had gone before them. These were not things that could simply fade away; they would be carried forward in the hearts of those who lived them.

9

# July 5 and Beyond

THROUGHOUT THIS BOOK, MY GOAL HAS BEEN TO RAISE THE DEAD, TO turn back the sands of time, and to breathe life back into the lungs of these old soldiers. It has been my privilege to share their stories, but now it's time to return them to their rest.

Corporal Charles H. Mettee was promoted to captain during the reunion. He had a splendid time at the event, but now it was time to pack up and head home. Mettee took down his flag after breakfast on July 5. He was the first to raise the Confederate flag in the Great Camp and the last to take it down. He was initially wary about raising the flag; he had come to Gettysburg in peace and didn't want to stir up any controversy, but his Union neighbors had insisted on seeing it, and he felt compelled to oblige. He was glad he did; the flag attracted a lot of attention, and, thankfully, it was all positive. Nothing was left to do after the flag was folded and tucked away for the trip home. He was packed and ready to go; the only thing left was to say goodbye. Mettee then crossed the company street to the Union side of the Maryland camp and said, "Well, boys, the war is over; I'm going home."

Captain J. Leonard Hoffman of the Union camp said to him, "I'm sorry to see you leave us. We've had a good time together."

"You bet we have," Mettee said, "but if there had been more of us here, we would have captured you Yanks."

There were more handshakes and pleasant farewells. Although they had fought as enemies the first time they met at Gettysburg, they were leaving this time as friends. General David L. Stanton was the ranking officer at the Union Maryland camp. "This is not the first great reunion of the blue and gray as I look at it," Stanton said. "The first reunion took place at Appomattox. Immediately after General Lee surrendered, the Johnnies came into our camp, and we had a good time together. They were good fellows."[1]

Charles Mettee headed for the train depot after bidding a fond farewell to the old soldiers on both sides of the Maryland camp.

Charles H. Mettee returned to his home in Northeast Baltimore, where he resided with his wife of forty-three years. He had joined the Confederate army in 1861 at the age of sixteen and served in the Baltimore Light Artillery under various commanders, including Stonewall Jackson. He died peacefully in his home on June 20, 1915.[2]

The Great Camp continued to empty, with many veterans waiting in line for hours for an open seat on the train. As the day wore on, clouds rolled in, and a gentle breeze cooled the air. By dinnertime, the crowds had thinned from tens of thousands to mere hundreds, and by nightfall, there were more empty tents on the Gettysburg Battlefield than there were people.

However, not everyone was in a rush to leave. According to *The Baltimore Sun*, on July 5, four gray sentinels stood guard over the evacuated tents along the Confederate line. William F. Brawner and William Page, the first Confederates to arrive, were determined to be the last to depart. They shared this sentiment with their companions, John L. Obernderfer and John R. Wade. A thunderstorm rolled in that night, and the old soldiers felt content tending a small campfire as the rain tapped a rhythm on the empty canvas sea. The flashes of lightning and rumbles of thunder brought to mind an artillery battle, making it a fitting way to spend their last night on the field.

Someone walked by and called out, "Still holding the fort, I see," to which Brawner replied, "Just as we used to try and do."

Brawner and Page were both seventy-eight years old and had fought through the war together. As old men, they became roommates in the Confederate Home in Pikesville, Maryland. Brawner still carried a treasured artifact with him. It was his parole pass that he received at Appomattox Courthouse in April 1865 when General Lee surrendered his army to General Grant. It was a rectangular sheet of paper that claimed the bearer was a paroled prisoner of the Army of Northern Virginia. This paper allowed the Confederates to return to their homes without risk of further persecution from the United States of America, so long as they did not take up arms against their country again. Thirty thousand were printed at Appomattox, and Brawner still had his almost forty-eight years later.

"I had my discharge, too," William Page said. "But I lost it. We both served from the beginning of the war to the end of it, and we have been here from the beginning and shall stay until they tell us to go home."[3]

On Sunday morning, July 6, the camp cooks made the final meal of the reunion. It consisted of puffed rice and milk, hard-boiled eggs, bacon, fresh bread, butter, coffee, and iced tea. After breakfast, Brawner, Page, Obernderfer, and Wade decided to call it quits and head home. They spoke with the highest regard about their treatment at the camp; they'd had more food than they could eat, and it was well cooked, too. Overall, they didn't have any complaints, although they wished they could have stayed in camp for a week longer.

They were tired but enthusiastic when they got off the train station near their home in Pikesville, Maryland. Brawner pulled out a red handkerchief as the train pulled away and waved to the departing veterans. William Page joined in, and the two old soldiers called after the lumbering train until it was out of sight. "Goodbye, Yanks," they cried out.

"Goodbye, Johnnies," came the reply.[4]

I don't know what happened to William Page after the reunion. He spent the rest of his days in the Pikesville Old Soldiers' Home, but I could not find an obituary or a grave marker.

William Brawner had enlisted in the Confederate army in October 1862 and surrendered at Appomattox in April 1865. I don't know why he fought for the South, but Brawner said on his first day at the reunion that he thought secession from the Union was the correct action at the time. However, after the war, he grew out of his old opinions and wasn't too proud to admit it.[5] How often have we done something in our youth only to regret it afterward? Lincoln and General Grant let the Confederates off easy at Appomattox, and from that point on, Brawner lived a life worthy of such mercy and grace. He spent his career as a carpenter and entered the

Old Soldiers' Home in Pikesville, Maryland, in May 1910. He lived there until his death on June 15, 1917.

One final point about Brawner and Page: The newspapers report that they were the same age. On June 28, 1913, *The Baltimore Sun* stated they were both seventy-three years old. Oddly enough, only a few days later, on July 6, 1913, that same paper reported they were now seventy-eight. Perhaps it was just a simple typo; after all, a "3" and an "8" look similar on paper. However, it goes deeper than that. William Brawner's death certificate claims he was seventy-five at the time of his passing in 1917, and yet his granite grave marker in Loudon Park Cemetery in Baltimore clearly states he was only sixty-eight. Which is correct? Who knows?

I mention this point to explain that while researching this book, I've done everything possible to verify facts and figures. I've encountered conflicting information countless times, so I've learned to hold the facts loosely and roll with it. I don't claim to be a historian, but if I were, it would probably drive me crazy trying to determine whether Brawner was truly seventy-three or seventy-eight in 1913 and how to reconcile that with his age at death in 1917, at either sixty-eight or seventy-five. However, as a storyteller, I find it doesn't really matter. I don't doubt that the man existed, but at times I've had to accept the details on faith with a large grain of salt. And that's good enough for me.

Leopold Wolf was the homeless veteran who walked to Gettysburg and lost his coat and discharge papers. He wandered through the Great Camp all night long until he was rescued by Lieutenant Lawrence and brought to one of the field hospitals. He summed up his experience at the Grand Reunion like this: "But now I'm happy. I've met lots of the old soldiers I once knew, and I wish this camp would last forever. Then, I would not have any fears for the future. Isn't it grand to see these men, who were once our enemies, now ready to shake us by the hand and call us friends? I'm glad I'm an American."[6]

When the reunion ended, the doctors felt Leopold Wolf needed additional medical attention. He was transferred, along with twenty other veterans, to the Harrisburg Hospital. The newspapers referred to them as "enemies on the battlefield but friends forever because of the Great Gettysburg Reunion."[7] On their first night in the hospital, one of the Southerners started to sing with a squeaky old voice: "I wish I were in

Dixie, hurrah, hurrah!" At first, the others only listened in, but the sounds of "Dixie" were infectious, and soon they all joined in, with the song echoing down the hospital hallways.[8] Afterward, they moved on to other wartime favorites and sang the night away. A man with a powerful bass voice led the tunes, and when others didn't know the lyrics, they hummed along and joined in the chorus.

As the old soldiers grew tired, one final song ended the night. The words seem so fitting for men nearing the end of their days. The title is "Oh, That Will Be Glory," by Charles H. Gabriel:

> When all my labors and trials are o'er,
> And I am safe on that beautiful shore,
> Just to be near the dear Lord I adore,
> Will through the ages be glory for me.
> (Refrain)
>
> Oh, that will be glory for me,
> Glory for me, glory for me,
> When by His grace I shall look on His face,
> That will be glory, be glory for me.
>
> When, by the gift of His infinite grace,
> I am accorded in heaven a place,
> Just to be there and to look on His face,
> Will through the ages be glory for me.
>
> Friends will be there I have loved long ago;
> Joy like a river around me will flow;
> Yet just a smile from my Savior, I know,
> Will through the ages be glory for me.

The final chorus echoed down the hallways, followed by a profound silence. The old soldiers went to sleep with peace in their hearts. Leopold Wolf's story seems to end on a positive note. He applied for and was accepted into one of the county homes for old soldiers.

I pause as I write this. I so want to give Leopold Wolf a happy ending. He had been through so much in his life and faced quite the ordeal at the reunion, but I wanted to know what happened to him once he left the hospital. Despite his trials, he left with a smile on his face and a song in his heart, but it wouldn't last.

Years later, in 1920, newspapers reported a story about a homeless man named Leopold Wolf. He was gentle and disturbed no one, but that didn't prevent a group of young boys from tormenting him. They harassed the old man until he finally fought back. Leopold Wolf pulled out a knife and slashed an eight-year-old boy across the neck. Fortunately, it was a superficial wound, but the police were called, and Leopold Wolf was arrested and taken to jail. Eventually, the charges were dropped, but the police didn't believe Wolf could live independently and placed him in a mental institution.

I don't know what happened to Leopold Wolf after that, and I could not find an obituary. He mentioned that he had no living relatives, so when he died, he was likely buried in an unmarked grave in a potter's field.

As the reunion concluded, Helen Longstreet was in awe of the event. She had come to Gettysburg with a job as a special correspondent for more than fifty newspapers across the country. However, she felt so overwhelmed by the magnitude of the event that her attempts to write about it fell flat; she remarked that the reunion was too big for description. Another veteran, J. A. Watrous, managed to capture what many—including Helen—were struggling to say: "This greatest and most valuable of all reunions ever held is drawing to a close. . . . Goodbye, Gettysburg; let me look down upon you on the hundredth anniversary of the battle."[9]

Helen didn't live to see the one hundredth anniversary, but she was there in 1938 for the seventy-fifth anniversary. The highlight of that reunion was the dedication of the Eternal Light Peace Memorial by President Franklin D. Roosevelt. It has undergone some changes over the years, but the eternal flame still burns bright and commemorates the lasting peace established at the Grand Reunion of 1913. However, by 1938, the ravages of time had claimed most of the Civil War veterans; less than two thousand of the old soldiers attended, and of that number, only twenty-five had fought in the Battle of Gettysburg. It was a novel event, but a mere shadow of what happened in 1913.

While the men were off fighting in World War II, the government encouraged women to join the workforce and to do the jobs historically done by men. Helen Longstreet answered the call and, at eighty years old, became one of the famous "Rosie the Riveters." She worked at the Bell plant in Marietta, Georgia, helping to produce the B-29 Superfortress bombers. She showed up every morning at 7:00 a.m., ready to work, and never missed a day. Helen was quite proud of her contributions during the war effort. She eventually retired and, a few years later, was asked about her time on the assembly line. She said, "Do I still know how to work a rivet gun? I'll have you know, I'm no lowly riveter. I'm an assembler, although I sometimes filled in as a riveter in emergencies."[10] Her foreman claimed that her work was ranked among the best done in the plant.[11]

Helen Longstreet died on May 3, 1962, just one year short of the hundredth anniversary of the Battle of Gettysburg.

Before leaving Gettysburg, Micajah Weiss, the oldest veteran at the reunion, stopped in one of the field hospitals for free health care. The 112-year-old soldier asked the doctors to pull one of his remaining teeth. "The durn thing is bothering me considerably," he said. The doctors warned that at his age, it would be dangerous to try to pull it.

"All right, I'll pull it myself," he replied. With his knotted hand, he reached in and came out with the bothersome tooth. "You folks is too squeamish these days,"[12] Weiss told the doctors as he picked up his cane and hobbled away.

After the Grand Reunion, Micajah Weiss, his wife Christina, and their two adult children headed home in the family automobile. They decided to take the long way home and spent the night of July 4 in Allentown, Pennsylvania. The following day, they went "bee shopping." Weiss had an apiary on his farm in Sullivan County, New York; it was his pride and joy. With bees in tow, they drove to New York City and spent some time with that crazy bastard, Dan Sickles, before finally returning home.

For the next year or so, Weiss enjoyed the best of health and often went on joyrides in his car. He never wore glasses and didn't find much need for them, as he could neither read nor write. Although he was plagued by rheumatism, he still enjoyed life and laughed often. Despite his age, his memory was quite sharp. Weiss did not use any form of tobacco but enjoyed a nice glass of whiskey whenever he felt like it. He died on September 22, 1914, at the ripe old age of 113. He was the oldest Civil War veteran to receive a pension.[13]

With the reunion over, it was time to leave Gettysburg for the final time. General Dan Sickles reflected on the event:

> *My hand is tired tonight, my arm aches from the shaking it has received all day long from Confederates and Union men alike. . . . I am glad to be here and I am glad that so many of them have been able to get here. A little while longer and we shall all have passed away.*
>
> *One of my old boys shook my hands today. "General," he said. "I shall never see you again. God bless you. We are meeting on the old field for the last time."*
>
> *And I said to him, "Pray that we shall gather together some time at the foot of the Almighty."*[14]

Sickles left the town of Gettysburg very differently from how he arrived. On Monday, he had a full military escort of mounted cavalry leading the way, but there was no fanfare to signify his departure. He was taken to the train station in town without ceremony. Once there, a handful of old soldiers—some in blue and some in gray—fussed over the one-legged general and helped him aboard the waiting train bound for New York City.

His (*cough-cough*) housekeeper, Eleanor Wilmerding, watched the general closely as the veterans carried him to his seat. "General Sickles has been busy enough with receptions to kill a horse," she said. "They did not give him time to take a nap in the afternoon. But he feels none the worse for having made the trip and gone through the trying ordeals of the campaign which has just closed. As a matter of fact, I think he feels better than when he came to Gettysburg."[15]

Sickles looked across the battlefield one last time as the train pulled away from the station. He was almost ninety-three years old and knew he would never return. Despite that realization, his heart was at peace. Sickles said, "Today, I feel 50 years younger."

Sickles returned to New York City, but his days were growing short. On February 11, 1914, his (*cough-cough*) housekeeper, Eleanor Wilmerding, died.[16] She had been his constant companion for fifteen years and the cause of a long-standing rift between Sickles and his second wife, Carmina. With Wilmerding finally out of the picture, Carmina and Sickles reconciled, though it was short lived. Sickles suffered a stroke only three weeks after Wilmerding's death.

A reporter called up the Sickles residence to see what his prognosis was. A voice answered, "Yes, this is Sickles. Am I ill? Nonsense! Never better in my life. Nothing to the story. It's all a damn lie. Goodbye."[17]

Despite the bravado, Sickles suffered a second stroke a few weeks later. He was confined to his bed and grew weaker and weaker each day. He died on Sunday evening, May 3, 1914, surrounded by his wife and son.[18]

General Daniel Edgar Sickles's funeral was held on May 8, 1914, at Saint Patrick's Cathedral in New York City. He was given full military honors and interred in Arlington Cemetery just outside of Washington, DC.

Many people loved Sickles, and thousands attended his funeral. But he had made a lot of enemies, too. The South Carolina *Columbia Record* concisely announced his demise: "Dan Sickles is dead. The least said the better."[19]

Losing his leg at Gettysburg might have ended Dan Sickles's days on the battlefield, but it sure as hell didn't end him. The man was a force of nature—equal parts audacity, arrogance, and an uncanny ability to land on his feet, even when missing one. General George Meade wanted nothing more to do with him and removed Sickles from command. This decision only fueled a bitter rivalry between them that lasted for the rest of their lives. Yet, in a plot twist worthy of a dime-store novel, Sickles and Confederate general James Longstreet—his onetime enemy—became good friends. Both had been vilified for their decisions at Gettysburg, and neither had patience for the "armchair generals" who critiqued them from the comfort of their parlor chairs. Somehow, they understood each other in a way no one else ever could.

After the war, Sickles didn't fade into the shadows—he owned history. He secured his legacy as a champion of Gettysburg's preservation through sheer determination (and no small amount of political maneuvering). As chairman of the New York Monument Commission, he oversaw the erection of eighty-eight monuments dedicated to New York regiments. And just in case future generations ever forgot who was behind all this, he made sure his name was carved into a fair number of them. Subtlety was never his strong suit.

But Sickles wasn't just about monuments—he was about monumental influence. His most outstanding achievement came when he helped establish the Gettysburg National Military Park, shaping its layout in ways that still exist today. He may have nearly lost the battle, but he made sure he owned the battlefield forever.

During the 1913 Gettysburg Reunion, someone asked him, "Why isn't there a monument to General Sickles?"

Sickles, never one to downplay his importance, fired back, "Hell, the whole damn battlefield is a monument to General Sickles!"

And he wasn't wrong. Walk through Gettysburg today, and you'll find his fingerprints everywhere: a marker where his leg was blown off, a monument for his headquarters, brigade positions scattered across the field. His name lingers across the landscape like a turd that won't flush.

Among the many monuments dotting Gettysburg, one stands out, not for what's there but for what's missing. The grand Excelsior Brigade Monument was supposed to feature a stone bust of none other than General Dan Sickles himself. To make it happen, $23,000 was raised.[20] But in classic Sickles fashion, the money mysteriously *vanished.*

Did he embezzle it? Some people certainly thought so. Was it ever proven? Of course not. This is Dan Sickles we're talking about—he had a lifetime habit of slipping out of trouble like a greased pig in a mud pit.

But even without the missing bust, Sickles made sure his name was everywhere. The massive half-circle of the New York Auxiliary Monument? His name is on it. The monument to Lincoln's Gettysburg Address inside the Soldiers' National Cemetery? His name is on that one, too. And if you take a drive to Little Round Top, chances are that you'll find yourself on Sickles Avenue—a long, winding road through the heart of the battlefield, just like the long, winding tale of the man himself.

Because if there was one thing Dan Sickles never lacked, it was the determination to make damn sure history never forgot him.

But the crown jewel of his legacy, the most jaw-dropping, utterly Sickles thing he ever did, was the witness fence. When Lafayette Park in Washington, DC, decided to replace its wrought iron fence, Sickles swooped in and shipped it to Gettysburg, where it was quietly installed in the cemetery. At first glance, this seems like just another battlefield addition—until you realize what fence this was.

A series of monuments referencing Dan Sickles. (*Left*) The Excelsior monument was meant to house a marble bust of Sickles, but the appropriated funds went missing. Photographed by the author (2025).

This was the very fence Philip Barton Key was leaning against when Sickles shot him dead.

Coincidence? Hardly. Some say Sickles placed it there as a not-so-subtle nod to his infamous past, a final testament to the fact that he had quite literally gotten away with murder.

And that, my friends, is why General Dan Sickles is one crazy bastard.

# Epilogue

By all accounts, the Grand Reunion of 1913 was a remarkable success. Fifty years after the battle that had once torn them apart, former enemies stood together as friends. The veterans returned to Gettysburg for many reasons—some to reunite with old comrades, others to walk the hallowed ground where they had once fought, tracing their steps through history. Some may have even come for the speeches.

The summer heat proved too much for many, sending them home early, while others endured, determined to soak in every moment. Few arrived with reconciliation as their goal, but that is exactly what happened. Those still burdened by bitterness had chosen to stay away.

Of course, not everyone in attendance was able to forgive and forget. Confederate colonel D. A. Dickert offered a candid perspective on the Grand Reunion:

> *Speaking on general principles of the good cheer and love feast of the recent reunion, I went to that meeting with fifty years of bitterness and hatred pent up in my soul, more than the majority of the Southern veterans, for in my line of duty I had opportunities to see more of the wrongs done our women and country than most men, but I came away with ill feeling for none. Not that I have forgiven the North for everything they did to us, for fifty years is too short a time to forget and forgive all the South endured.*
>
> *But since talking with any number of intelligent men from the North, and hearing their version of war, I have become greatly mollified, enough at least, to keep me from cutting any of their throats. As a man said to me, from the old "Iron Brigade" from Michigan, "You men entered the army for a principle, we of the North, to get bread for our families; our mines, workshops and factories were all closed and we had to either enlist for the bounty offered, or starve. All that talk you hear about the Northern men entering the army and fighting to save the Union is all*

*stuff, gotten up by the newspapers, while as a fact, we didn't care a damn whether you were in or out of the Union, so long as we had bread for ourselves and families." Well, I believe there is a lot of truth in this, but these sentiments were no reason why they should burn our houses.*[1]

Dickert's words reveal mixed but evolving feelings about the Union veterans he met. Initially, he harbored deep resentment, but after hearing their perspective, he softened. Many Northern soldiers, he realized, had enlisted out of economic necessity rather than ideological commitment to preserving the Union. Still, his final remark about the burning of houses suggests that, while he gained some understanding, full reconciliation remained out of reach. Yet even that slight shift—from hostility to reluctant acceptance—was a step in the right direction.

A Chicago paper said this: "The enmities of '61 are not forgotten. They are remembered, but only as memories by the brave survivors of those stirring days. Nothing of the rancor remains."[2]

The *Charleston News and Courier* also stated exactly what the Grand Reunion was celebrating:

*We are holding a celebration, but we are not celebrating the battle. We are celebrating the valor of the men who faced without flinching a thing that was infernal. If we fail to make this distinction, the celebration at Gettysburg may do more harm than good. If it thrills us with the glory of war's heroes, but does not sadden us with the sorrow and the agony of war's victims, we lose a vitally important part of the lesson which it should teach.*[3]

For some, the Grand Reunion was more than a gathering—it was a testament to time's healing power. This sentiment was reflected in an article in the *National Tribune*:

*The great Peace Jubilee is now over, and we can, in the quiet thoughtfulness of our homes, review it calmly and critically. There can be no question that it was one of the most important events in the country's history, that it will be productive of immense good, and that everyone who was present will recall it as one of the happiest and most noteworthy events of his life.*[4]

Amid the formal ceremonies, there were also moments of personal reconciliation. On his last night in camp, a Confederate corporal offered a toast to his new Union friends. They passed around a bottle of applejack brandy to fill their tin cups. With his hand over his heart, the Confederate declared, "There is no malice in my heart. The man who can hold malice in his heart for fifty years should have died forty years ago."[5]

For many veterans, attending the reunion was an act of duty, a final service to their country. Before leaving for Gettysburg, one of the veterans knew that the trip would strain his old body. He told his anxious wife:

> *This is most likely the last chance I'll have to do anything for the Union, and I'd like to do it fifty years from the time the Union was saved. It's going to mean something to all the younger generation to have us old fellows get together and show there isn't any hard feelings. It will take away the last excuse for young people to cherish any sectional hatred. It's a duty we owe the country, about the last we can fill, most of us and I figure out I ought to do it.*[6]

Despite the powerful symbolism of the reunion, some questioned whether younger generations would grasp its full significance. A *Washington Post* reporter reflected: "It is hard for the man who has never 'smelled powder' to realize the peculiar and the full significance of this reunion. Can we who have had no share in the terrific battle understand the complex feelings of the grizzled veterans who clasp the hand of the very man who raised his saber to deal him a deathblow?"[7] Perhaps not. But the more people learn about the Grand Reunion, the more they can understand its message of grace, mercy, and forgiveness—a story that never grows old.

The reporter for *The New York Times* wrote a statement that we should be mindful of today: "The men who did the fighting in the war between the states were the first to accept its termination as final, and it was the noncombatants and later generations in both North and South that did most to prolong its animosities."[8] This statement is a powerful reminder today, especially when modern voices still debate the legacy of the Confederacy. I think of this quote when I hear people say the Confederates were all traitors and should have been hanged.

The *Harrisburg Daily Independent* said, "There was no doubt in the minds of those who saw that so far as these men who have gathered here are concerned, the war has ceased to be a source of hatred and rancor."[9]

One of the veterans from North Carolina said, "We got one flag, and we love it. These old boys in blue are Americans, just as we are. Our differences are settled and for all time. I am ready to pass on to the last camping ground, happy to see this day."[10]

In its final reflection on the event, *The Washington Post* captured the reunion's true significance:

> *Nothing could possibly be more impressive or more inspiring to the younger generation than this gathering. They feel the thrill of bygone days, without a knowledge of its bitterness, which, thank God, has passed us all. But even more touching must be the emotions of these time-worn veterans, as they assemble on an occasion that in itself constitutes a greater victory than that of half a century ago, and one too, in which every section of a reunited country has common part.*[11]

Governor James Cox of Ohio offered a fitting farewell:

> *The two armies are now near the Great Divide, facing the sunset, waiting for the sun to go down. Silhouetted on the evening skies we see couriers arm in arm, the Blue and the Gray entering the shadows. Let us give them a message to Grant and Lee, Sheridan and Jackson—to their comrades beyond the skies—a message that both armies have won the greatest victory, and that one flag shelters a reunited republic.*[12]

This brings us back to Abraham Lincoln's immortal words from the Gettysburg Address: "The world will little note, nor long remember what we say here, but it can never forget what they did here."

Gettysburg unfolds like a three-act drama: the first act was the battle; the second, the Gettysburg Address; and the final act was the Grand Reunion of 1913. Though its memory has faded, the story endures. The war began in conflict, but it ended in reconciliation, and what once divided these men had been transformed into something like peace.

"This is the old soldier's show—they paid the price of admission fifty years ago."[13] —*The New York Times*, June 29, 1913

*The end*

# Acknowledgments

I began working on this project in the fall of 2019, and now, six years later, in the fall of 2025, I'm finally completing it. There are many people to thank along the way, and my sincerest apologies if I have left anyone out.

First off, I need to thank my father-in-law, Mike Bell, who initially told me the story of the old veterans and triggered a decades-long obsession with the subject. As a filmmaker, it sparked an idea for a documentary about the Grand Reunion, and one that I still hope to make. Mike introduced me to his good friend Andy DeCusati, who worked at the Horse Soldier in Gettysburg. Both Mike and Andy have a depth of knowledge about the Civil War that far exceeds my own. Andy read an early draft of my script and painstakingly went through it, correcting many of my historical deficiencies. Andy said, "I think that if you do bring this production to a successful conclusion, the feeling of acceptance and reconciliation exhibited by the veterans to each other in the stories you have included may go a long way in explaining to young people of today why we should still honor the Confederate soldier even though his cause was a mistaken one." Unfortunately, Andy has since passed, but I am so thankful for his support.

During lunch one day, Donna Basilicato listened as I lamented my struggles to get the documentary off the ground. She was the one who said, "Why not turn it into a book?" Without her prompting, this story might never have been written.

Of course, I cannot write an acknowledgment without also thanking my wife, Rikki. She listened to my crazy idea for this story, declared it needed to be told, and said I was the right man for the job. For years, she has listened to every little nugget and discovery I made while researching the Grand Reunion and joyfully tagged along on almost every research trip to Gettysburg. I hope I have done her and the veterans proud.

Rick Garland is one of the best storytellers I have ever personally met. I have to thank him for telling me some stories of that crazy bastard, Dan Sickles, in the most humorous way possible. He said if he could have a beer with any historical figure, he would pick Sickles hands down, and I have to agree with him. Another great yarn spinner I know is Dave Jackson, who read one of the versions of this book and encouraged me to lean into the storytelling aspect of the Grand Reunion and make it sound more like a conversation than a lofty history book. Esther Wilson also read an early draft and nudged me to better define some of the Civil War terms that might stump a modern reader. (Just how many men were in a regiment, anyway?)

Others I need to thank include John Hesier, an excellent historian from the Gettysburg National Military Park. I've heard several of his talks on the Grand Reunion and was also lucky enough to sit down for a chat and go over the details. He was able to point me in the right direction for my research efforts. John also introduced me to Greg Goodell, the park's curator, who graciously opened the archives and helped me sift through old correspondence and photographs of the reunion. Chris Brenneman from the Gettysburg Foundation unlocked the wonders of the Gettysburg Cyclorama for me—a stunning piece of art that the old soldiers once marveled at and that we're fortunate to still have preserved today. And finally, Jennifer Haase, also from the Gettysburg Foundation, helped me untangle the historical linguistics surrounding the Gettysburg Lincoln Railroad Station—both during the battle and at the reunion.

I also want to thank Michael Wicklein, a documentary filmmaker whose encouragement came at exactly the right moment. Mike was extraordinarily generous with his time, his connections, and his belief that this story could reach readers well beyond seasoned Civil War enthusiasts, which meant more to me than he probably knows.

I also must thank Dave Reisch, my publisher at Stackpole Books, who read my manuscript and saw its potential. I truly appreciate his patience and willingness to answer all of my endless questions. Thank you for making this easy for me!

I've been to Gettysburg many times, but my first visit wasn't until I was around thirty. While talking to my dad about it, I was surprised to hear he had never been, but it was a place he very much wanted to visit. I had hoped to take him there one day, to walk those fields together, but, sadly, we never got the chance. This book is dedicated to him.

And finally, I thank you, my dear readers: I hope this isn't just another "history slog." My wish is that it brings to life the old soldiers who fought and returned to Gettysburg to make peace with one another and with the past. History is only as alive as the people who care to tell it and the readers who care to listen. Thank you for letting me share this story with you and for keeping the memory of these men alive a little bit longer.

# Notes

## Chapter 1

1. "The Listener," *Boston Evening Transcript* (Boston, MA), July 2, 1913, 17.

2. Stone Sentinels, "Strengths and Losses of States at the Battle of Gettysburg Ranked," in *The States at Gettysburg, Battle of Gettysburg Facts*, StoneSentinels.com, 2025, https://gettysburg.stonesentinels.com/battle-of-gettysburg-facts/the-states-at-gettysburg/.

## Chapter 2

1. *The War of the Rebellion: A Compilation of the Official Records of the Union and Confederate Armies*, Series 1, vol. 27, pt. 1, Reports (Washington, DC: Government Printing Office, 1889), 347.

2. Congressional Medal of Honor Society, "Henry Shippen Huidekoper," *Stories of Sacrifice*, accessed September 29, 2025, https://www.cmohs.org/recipients/henry-s-huidekoper.

3. "Tener Arbitrates Uniform Quibble," *The Philadelphia Inquirer* (Philadelphia, PA), January 25, 1913, 16.

4. "Dr. Eastman Resolution Is Heralded," *Star-Gazette* (Elmira, NY), February 26, 1913, 3.

5. "The Boys in Gray at Gettysburg," *Natchez Democrat* (Natchez, MS), April 23, 1913, 9.

6. "Letters to the Editor," *The Baltimore Sun* (Baltimore, MD), June 28, 1913, 8.

7. "Gray of South Again Appears in Gettysburg," *The Philadelphia Inquirer* (Philadelphia, PA), June 27, 1913, 1.

8. Pennsylvania, *Fiftieth Anniversary of the Battle of Gettysburg: Report of the Pennsylvania Commission*, ed. and comp. Lewis Eugene Beitler (Harrisburg, PA: Wm. Stanley Ray, State Printer, 1913), 15.

9. Pennsylvania, *Fiftieth Anniversary of the Battle of Gettysburg: Report of the Pennsylvania Commission*, ed. and comp. Lewis Eugene Beitler (Harrisburg, PA: Wm. Stanley Ray, State Printer, 1913), 16.

10. Pennsylvania, *Fiftieth Anniversary of the Battle of Gettysburg: Report of the Pennsylvania Commission*, ed. and comp. Lewis Eugene Beitler (Harrisburg, PA: Wm. Stanley Ray, State Printer, 1913), 144.

11. Pennsylvania, *Fiftieth Anniversary of the Battle of Gettysburg: Report of the Pennsylvania Commission*, ed. and comp. Lewis Eugene Beitler (Harrisburg, PA: Wm. Stanley Ray, State Printer, 1913), 48.

12. Edward S. Ellis, *Library of American History* (Chicago: Jones Brothers Publishing, 1918), 206.

13. "New York Grand Army in Gettysburg Charge," *New York Tribune* (New York, NY), July 1, 1913, 3.

14. Congressional Medal of Honor Society, "Joshua Lawrence Chamberlain," *Stories of Sacrifice*, accessed September 29, 2025, https://www.cmohs.org/recipients/joshua-l-chamberlain.

15. "Veterans of Battle of Gettysburg Start from Union Station," *Portland Sunday Telegram* (Portland, OR), June 29, 1913, 1.

16. Pennsylvania, *Fiftieth Anniversary of the Battle of Gettysburg: Report of the Pennsylvania Commission*, ed. and comp. Lewis Eugene Beitler (Harrisburg, PA: Wm. Stanley Ray, State Printer, 1913), 24.

17. Pennsylvania, *Fiftieth Anniversary of the Battle of Gettysburg: Report of the Pennsylvania Commission*, ed. and comp. Lewis Eugene Beitler (Harrisburg, PA: Wm. Stanley Ray, State Printer, 1913), 37–38.

18. "Gettysburg," *The Washington Herald* (Washington, DC), July 2, 1913, 6.

19. Pennsylvania, *Fiftieth Anniversary of the Battle of Gettysburg: Report of the Pennsylvania Commission*, ed. and comp. Lewis Eugene Beitler (Harrisburg, PA: Wm. Stanley Ray, State Printer, 1913), 38–39.

20. Pennsylvania, *Fiftieth Anniversary of the Battle of Gettysburg: Report of the Pennsylvania Commission*, ed. and comp. Lewis Eugene Beitler (Harrisburg, PA: Wm. Stanley Ray, State Printer, 1913), 50.

21. Pennsylvania, *Fiftieth Anniversary of the Battle of Gettysburg: Report of the Pennsylvania Commission*, ed. and comp. Lewis Eugene Beitler (Harrisburg, PA: Wm. Stanley Ray, State Printer, 1913), 87.

22. "Big Army Pouring into Camp," *The Pittsburg Press* (Pittsburgh, PA), June 29, 1913, 4.

23. "Big Army Pouring into Camp," *The Pittsburg Press* (Pittsburgh, PA), June 29, 1913, 4.

24. "Philadelphia, PA," *The New York Age* (New York, NY), June 19, 1913, 3.

25. "First Boys in Gray Are Here," *Adams County News* (Adams County, PA), June 28, 1913, 1.

26. "Greatest Tented Field in Nation's Annals Where Veterans Meet," *The Baltimore Sun* (Baltimore, MD), June 28, 1913, 18.

27. Congressional Medal of Honor Society, "James M. Schoonmaker," *Stories of Sacrifice*, accessed June 22, 2025, https://www.cmohs.org/recipients/james-m-schoonmaker.

28. "James Martinus Schoonmaker (1842–1927)," National Park Service, last updated October 5, 2022, https://www.nps.gov/jofl/learn/historyculture/james-martinus-schoonmaker.htm.

## Chapter 3

1. "Civil War Veteran Plans Long Walk," *Altoona Times* (Altoona, PA), May 15, 1913, 6.
2. "Veteran Ends His Long Hike," *Adams County News* (Adams County, PA), June 14, 1913, 5.
3. "Walter's Theatre," *The Gettysburg Times* (Gettysburg, PA), June 17, 1913, 1.
4. "Two Old Confederates Capture Gettysburg," *The Baltimore Sun* (Baltimore, MD), June 28, 1913, 8.
5. "Two Old Confederates Capture Gettysburg," *The Baltimore Sun* (Baltimore, MD), June 28, 1913, 8.
6. "Maryland Is First with Stars and Bars," *The Baltimore Sun* (Baltimore, MD), June 30, 1913, 1.
7. Pennsylvania, *Fiftieth Anniversary of the Battle of Gettysburg: Report of the Pennsylvania Commission*, ed. and comp. Lewis Eugene Beitler (Harrisburg, PA: Wm. Stanley Ray, State Printer, 1913), 89.
8. "50th Anniversary Is Here," *The Gettysburg Compiler* (Gettysburg, PA), July 2, 1913, 1.
9. Walter Herbert Blake, *Hand Grips: The Story of the Great Gettysburg Reunion, July 1913*, comp. Frank Ernest Channon (Vineland, NJ: G. E. Smith, 1913), 73.
10. Walter Herbert Blake, *Hand Grips: The Story of the Great Gettysburg Reunion, July 1913*, comp. Frank Ernest Channon (Vineland, NJ: G. E. Smith, 1913), 151.
11. Walter Herbert Blake, *Hand Grips: The Story of the Great Gettysburg Reunion, July 1913*, comp. Frank Ernest Channon (Vineland, NJ: G. E. Smith, 1913), 15.
12. "Over 40,000 Now in Camp," *The Gettysburg Times* (Gettysburg, PA), July 1, 1913, 1.
13. "Veterans Here but Few Others," *The Gettysburg Times* (Gettysburg, PA), July 1, 1913, 1.
14. "Parade of Automobiles Through Town of Dillsburg," *Harrisburg Daily Independent* (Harrisburg, PA), July 2, 1913, 2.
15. "Over 40,000 Now in Camp," *The Gettysburg Times* (Gettysburg, PA), July 1, 1913, 1.
16. "Gettysburg Camp Housed 65,000 Men in 2 Mile Square Says Commander," *The Bridgeport Evening Farmer* (Bridgeport, CT), July 5, 1913, 1.
17. "Maryland Is First with Stars and Bars," *The Baltimore Sun* (Baltimore, MD), June 30, 1913, 2.
18. "50th Anniversary Is Here," *The Gettysburg Compiler* (Gettysburg, PA), July 2, 1913, 1.
19. "Over 40,000 Now in Camp," *The Gettysburg Times* (Gettysburg, PA), July 1, 1913, 1.
20. "3 Dead 100 Stricken by Heat at Gettysburg," *The Baltimore Sun* (Baltimore, MD), July 2, 1913, 2.
21. "3 Dead 100 Stricken by Heat at Gettysburg," *The Baltimore Sun* (Baltimore, MD), July 2, 1913, 2.

22. "Thieves Busy in Camp," *The Baltimore Sun* (Baltimore, MD), July 2, 1913, 2.
23. "John Francis Key Arrives at Camp," *The Evening Sun* (Baltimore, MD), June 30, 1913, 1.
24. "Maryland 500 Strong," *The Baltimore Sun* (Baltimore, MD), July 1, 1913, 2.
25. "Correct Records of Old Soldiers," *Harrisburg Daily Independent* (Harrisburg, PA), July 7, 1913, 7.
26. Timothy B. Smith, "Timothy B. Smith," *Essential Civil War Curriculum*, Virginia Center for Civil War Studies, Virginia Tech, accessed June 22, 2025, https://www.essentialcivilwarcurriculum.com/timothy-b.-smith.html.
27. "Local News," *The Evening Star* (Washington, DC), February 28, 1859, 3.

## Chapter 4

1. "Old Guns Roar Again," *The Baltimore Sun* (Baltimore, MD), July 1, 1913, 2.
2. "Vets Not Pleased with Reunion," *The Tribune*, July 3, 1913, 5.
3. "Capt. French Back from Gettysburg," *The Bridgeport Evening Farmer* (Bridgeport, CT), July 5, 1913, 1.
4. "Many Veterans Leave Gettysburg," *The Pittsburg Press* (Pittsburgh, PA), July 2, 1913, 2.
5. "Gettysburg Camp Housed 65,000 Men in 2 Mile Square Says Commander," *The Bridgeport Evening Farmer* (Bridgeport, CT), July 5, 1913, 1.
6. "Oldest in Gettysburg," *The Boston Globe* (Boston, MA), June 30, 1913, 5.
7. "Key Is a Boy of 82," *The Evening Sun* (Baltimore, MD), June 28, 1913, 1.
8. "Maryland 500 Strong," *The Daily Banner* (Greencastle, IN), July 2, 1913, 1.
9. "Sidelights of Gettysburg Reunion," *The Capitol Hill Beacon* (Washington, DC), July 10, 1913, 8.
10. "Veterans Organize," *The Baltimore Sun* (Baltimore, MD), July 2, 1913, 2.
11. "Pathetic Story Brings Results," *The Philadelphia Inquirer* (Philadelphia, PA), July 4, 1913, 3.
12. The Editors of Encyclopaedia Britannica, "Draft Riot of 1863," *Encyclopaedia Britannica*, last modified July 4, 2023, https://www.britannica.com/event/Draft-Riot-of-1863.
13. "Pathetic Story Brings Results," *The Philadelphia Inquirer* (Philadelphia, PA), July 4, 1913, 3.
14. "Death Visits Gettysburg Camp," *The Daily Notes* (Canonsburg, PA), June 30, 1913, 1.
15. "Thousands Walk in Palpitating Heat," *The Boston Globe* (Boston, MA), July 1, 1913, 5.
16. Walter Herbert Blake, *Hand Grips: The Story of the Great Gettysburg Reunion, July 1913*, comp. Frank Ernest Channon (Vineland, NJ: G. E. Smith, 1913), 57–62.
17. "Camp Holds Its 40,000," *The Boston Globe* (Boston, MA), July 1, 1913, 5.
18. "Eluded His Family," *Adams County News* (Adams County, PA), February 21, 1914, 3.
19. "Out the Window," *The Gettysburg Times* (Gettysburg, PA), July 2, 1913, 1.

20. "Veteran Soldier Outwits Family," *Harrisburg Telegraph* (Harrisburg, PA), July 2, 1913, 2.
21. "Confederates Hold Reunions," *The Baltimore Sun* (Baltimore, MD), July 2, 1913, 2.
22. "Editorial Comments," *The Patterson Morning Call* (Patterson, NJ), July 1, 1913, 4.
23. "Maryland 500 Strong," *The Baltimore Sun* (Baltimore, MD), July 2, 1913.
24. "50th Anniversary Is Here," *The Gettysburg Compiler* (Gettysburg, PA), July 2, 1913, 1.
25. T. C. Cheney, F. Kenfield, and Vermont Gettysburg Commission, *Vermont at Gettysburg, July, and Fifty Years Later* (Rutland, VT: Tuttle Co., 1914), 29.
26. "Negro Vets at Gettysburg," *The Twin City Star* (Minneapolis, MN), July 11, 1913, 2.
27. "Comrade Middleton—At Rest," *The Twin City Star* (Minneapolis, MN), October 9, 1914, 3.
28. "Gettysburg Field Fills with Vets," *Evening Journal* (Wilmington, DE), June 26, 1913, 1.
29. "Comrade Middleton—At Rest," *The Twin City Star* (Minneapolis, MN), October 9, 1914, 2.
30. "Hundreds of Veterans from B'klyn Ready to Start for Gettysburg," *The Brooklyn Citizen* (Brooklyn, NY), June 29, 1913, 1.
31. "Trenton Veterans Having Big Time," *The Times* (Trenton NJ), July 3, 1913, 12.
32. "Five Surviving Members in Stevens Post No. 520," *Harrisburg Telegraph* (Harrisburg, PA), May 30, 1930, 7.
33. "Real Invasion of Gettysburg Began This Morning," *Harrisburg Daily Independent* (Harrisburg, PA), June 28, 1913, 3.
34. "Tent Resounding with Cheers and Yells," *Harrisburg Telegraph* (Harrisburg, PA), July 2, 1913, 7.
35. "Documents Prized by Auter," *Harrisburg Daily Independent*, June 19, 1914, 8.
36. "Five Surviving Members in Stevens Post No. 520," *Harrisburg Telegraph* (Harrisburg, PA), May 30, 1930, 7.
37. "Retired State Messenger Dies," *Harrisburg Telegraph* (Harrisburg, PA), February 17, 1932, 18.
38. "Citizens Republican Club History," *Goin' North*, accessed June 22, 2025, https://goinnorth.org/history_crc#.
39. "Five Surviving Members in Stevens Post No. 520," *Harrisburg Telegraph* (Harrisburg, PA), May 30, 1930, 7.
40. "Candy for Children," *Harrisburg Daily Independent* (Harrisburg, PA), December 26, 1913, 3.
41. "Auter Again to Play Santa at Mansion," *The Evening News* (Harrisburg, PA), December 11, 1931, 12.
42. "50th Anniversary of Memorable Battle," *Gazette News-Current*, July 16, 1913, 6.

43. "Here and There," *The Times Leader* (Wilkes-Barre, PA), July 30, 1913, 13.
44. "Negro Troops Sing," *The Evening Sun* (Baltimore, MD), July 4, 1913, 2.
45. *Plessy v. Ferguson*, 163 U.S. 537 (1896).
46. "Events of the Week in GAR Circles," *The Philadelphia Inquirer* (Philadelphia, PA), June 15, 1913, 20.
47. "50,000 Veterans Camped Together," *The Gazette*, July 16, 1913, 6.
48. Edward Sylvester Ellis, *Library of American History* (New York: Jones Brothers Publishing, 1918), 210.
49. Walter Herbert Blake, *Hand Grips: The Story of the Great Gettysburg Reunion, July 1913*, comp. Frank Ernest Channon (Vineland, NJ: G. E. Smith, 1913), 181–82.
50. "Gets a Place Again," *Chicago Tribune* (Chicago, IL), October 30, 1897, 6.
51. "Gets a Place Again," *Chicago Tribune* (Chicago, IL), October 30, 1897, 6.
52. "Why She Married Longstreet," *The Wilmington Messenger* (Wilmington, NC), September 19, 1897, 6.
53. "55,000 Veterans Defy the Great Heat," *New York Tribune* (New York, NY), July 2, 1913, 1.
54. Martin Blumenson, *The Patton Papers, 1885–1940* (Boston: Houghton Mifflin, 1972), 173.
55. "Boys in Blue," *Adams County News* (Adams County, PA), July 5, 1913, 7.
56. "Veteran of 110 Here on Way to Gettysburg," *The Allentown Morning Call* (Allentown, PA), June 30, 1913, 9.
57. "Personal and Pertinent," *The Times-Tribune* (Scranton, PA), October 23, 1912, 6.
58. "Weiss Is 112 but Attends Reunion," *The Scranton Truth* (Scranton, PA), July 3, 1913, 2.
59. "Personal and Pertinent," *The Times-Tribune* (Scranton, PA), October 23, 1912, 6.
60. "Drummer Boy Hero Is Marching Today," *The Washington Times* (Washington, DC), May 30, 1913, 5.
61. "Colonel John Clem, the 'Drummer Boy of Chickamauga,'" *The Ottawa Guardian* (Ottawa, ON), August 20, 1915, 1.
62. "Colonel J. L. Clem Civil War Veteran, in Active Service," *Springville Journal* (Springville, NY), May 29, 1913, 2.
63. "Colonel J. L. Clem Civil War Veteran, in Active Service," *Springville Journal* (Springville, NY), May 29, 1913, 2.
64. "Last Veteran of '61 to Leave the Army," *The New York Times* (New York, NY), August 8, 1915, 6.
65. "Here and There at Gettysburg," *The Evening Star* (Washington, DC), July 2, 1913, 2.
66. Walter Herbert Blake, *Hand Grips: The Story of the Great Gettysburg Reunion, July 1913*, comp. Frank Ernest Channon (Vineland, NJ: G. E. Smith, 1913), 53.
67. "That Flag Incident," *The Herald-Sun* (Durham, NC), July 8, 1913, 4.
68. "United US Veterans," *The New York Times* (New York, NY), July 2, 1913, 2.

69. "Flag Mystery Cleared Up," *Hartford Courant* (Hartford, CT), July 3, 1913, 16.
70. "Low Death Rate Among Veterans," *Adams County News* (Adams County, PA), July 5, 1913, 8.
71. "Deaths in Camp," *The Gettysburg Times* (Gettysburg, PA), July 1, 1913, 1.
72. Gregory A. Coco, *A Strange and Blighted Land: Gettysburg: The Aftermath of a Battle* (Gettysburg, PA: Thomas Publications, 1995), 86.
73. "From Washington," *The Indianapolis Star* (Indianapolis, IN), November 28, 1863, 2.
74. Letter from Edward Everett to Abraham Lincoln (letter book copy), November 20, 1863, retrieved from the Digital Public Library of America, https://www.masshist.org/database/1780, accessed June 22, 2025.
75. *Wilmington Journal* (Wilmington, DE), June 9, 1871.
76. Walter Herbert Blake, *Hand Grips: The Story of the Great Gettysburg Reunion, July 1913*, comp. Frank Ernest Channon (Vineland, NJ: G. E. Smith, 1913), 24.
77. "Obituary," *National Republican* (Washington, DC), July 2, 1863, 2.
78. *The Lancaster Examiner* (Lancaster, PA), July 8, 1863, 2.
79. *The Baltimore Sun* (Baltimore, MD), June 30, 1913, 2.
80. Walter Herbert Blake, *Hand Grips: The Story of the Great Gettysburg Reunion, July 1913*, comp. Frank Ernest Channon (Vineland, NJ: G. E. Smith, 1913), 119.
81. Walter Herbert Blake, *Hand Grips: The Story of the Great Gettysburg Reunion, July 1913*, comp. Frank Ernest Channon (Vineland, NJ: G. E. Smith, 1913), 151–52.

## CHAPTER 5

1. Walter Herbert Blake, *Hand Grips: The Story of the Great Gettysburg Reunion, July 1913*, comp. Frank Ernest Channon (Vineland, NJ: G. E. Smith, 1913).
2. "Hark Back to Days of '63," *The Washington Herald* (Washington, DC), July 1, 1913, 4.
3. Walter Herbert Blake, *Hand Grips: The Story of the Great Gettysburg Reunion, July 1913*, comp. Frank Ernest Channon (Vineland, NJ: G. E. Smith, 1913), 151.
4. "Pint of Coffee Not Enough," *The Boston Globe* (Boston, MA), July 2, 1913, 6.
5. "Incidents of the Big Reunion as Picked Up by the Reporters," *The Evening Sentinel* (Ansonia, CT), July 1, 1913, 4.
6. "Little Tales of Gettysburg," *The Washington Times* (Washington, DC), July 2, 1913, 2.
7. "Yank and Johnny Chums on Battlefield," *The Evening World* (New York, NY), July 1, 1913, 2.
8. "Only One Flag Now," *The Baltimore Sun* (Baltimore, MD), July 2, 1913, 2.
9. "55,000 Veterans Defy the Great Heat," *New York Tribune* (New York, NY), July 2, 1913, 2.
10. "Little Tales of Gettysburg," *The Washington Times* (Washington, DC), July 2, 1913, 2.
11. "Army Retreats from Big Camp," *Harrisburg Daily Independent* (Harrisburg, PA), July 2, 1913, 6.

12. "'Yanks' and 'Rebs' in Opening Exercises at Gettysburg," *The Wheeling Intelligencer* (Wheeling, WV), July 2, 1913, 1.
13. "'Yanks' and 'Rebs' in Opening Exercises at Gettysburg," *The Wheeling Intelligencer* (Wheeling, WV), July 2, 1913, 1.
14. Pennsylvania, *Fiftieth Anniversary of the Battle of Gettysburg: Report of the Pennsylvania Commission*, ed. and comp. Lewis Eugene Beitler (Harrisburg, PA: Wm. Stanley Ray, State Printer, 1913), 103.
15. "Rebel Yell Awarded Governor Tener at Veteran Exercises," *The Philadelphia Inquirer* (Philadelphia, PA), July 2, 1913, 2.
16. Pennsylvania, *Fiftieth Anniversary of the Battle of Gettysburg: Report of the Pennsylvania Commission*, ed. and comp. Lewis Eugene Beitler (Harrisburg, PA: Wm. Stanley Ray, State Printer, 1913), 101.
17. "Editorial Notes," *The New York Age* (New York, NY), July 10, 1913, 4.
18. "'Military Day' Is Fully Observed," *The Washington Times* (Washington, DC), July 2, 1913, 2.
19. "'Military Day' Is Fully Observed," *The Washington Times* (Washington, DC), July 2, 1913, 2.
20. "The Fine Arts," *Boston Evening Transcript* (Boston, MA), July 3, 1913, 11.
21. "Comrades at Gettysburg," *The Gettysburg Compiler* (Gettysburg, PA), July 16, 1913, 4.
22. T. C. Cheney, F. Kenfield, and Vermont Gettysburg Commission, *Vermont at Gettysburg, July, and Fifty Years Later* (Rutland, VT: Tuttle Co., 1914), 30.
23. "Confederates Hold Reunions," *The Baltimore Sun* (Baltimore, MD), July 2, 1913, 2.
24. "Old Vet Passes 88th Birthday," *The Times and Democrat* (Orangeburg, SC), April 22, 1930, 1.
25. "At Gospel Service," *The Baltimore Sun* (Baltimore, MD), July 2, 1913, 2.
26. "Last Rites for Veteran and Retired Minister," *The Columbia Record* (Columbia, SC), June 24, 1930, 2.
27. Edward Sylvester Ellis, *Library of American History* (New York: Jones Brothers Publishing, 1918), 209.
28. Edward Sylvester Ellis, *Library of American History* (New York: Jones Brothers Publishing, 1918), 210.
29. "Hard for 'Vets' at Gettysburg," *The Morning Call* (Allentown, PA), July 2, 1913, 1.
30. "This Veteran Was Satisfied," *The Morning Call* (Allentown, PA), July 3, 1913, 1.
31. "The Aftermath of Gettysburg," *The Morning Call* (Allentown, PA), July 7, 1913, 1.
32. Walter Herbert Blake, *Hand Grips: The Story of the Great Gettysburg Reunion, July 1913*, comp. Frank Ernest Channon (Vineland, NJ: G. E. Smith, 1913), 151.
33. "Low Death Rate Among Veterans," *Adams County News* (Adams County, PA), July 5, 1913, 8.

34. "Allan D. Albert," *Times Herald* (Burns, OR), July 3, 1913, 12.
35. "Wisconsin Veteran Dies," *Green Bay Semi-Weekly Gazette* (Green Bay, WI), July 5, 1913, 3.
36. "Veteran Killed," *Adams County News* (Adams County, PA), July 5, 1913, 8.
37. "Interesting Incidents," *The Wilmington Messenger* (Wilmington, NC), March 3, 1893, 4.
38. John B. Bachelder, *The Bachelder Papers: Gettysburg in Their Own Words*, ed. David L. Ladd and Audrey J. Ladd (Dayton, OH: Morningside House, 1994), 636.
39. Samuel P. Bates, *The Battle of Gettysburg* (Philadelphia, PA: T. H. Davis & Co., 1875), 144.
40. Harry W. Pfanz, *Gettysburg: Culp's Hill and Cemetery Hill* (Chapel Hill: University of North Carolina Press, 1993), 319–20.
41. "Veterans Organize," *The Baltimore Sun* (Baltimore, MD), July 2, 1913, 2.
42. "Gen Trippe Wounded on Culp's Hill," *The Baltimore Sun* (Baltimore, MD), July 3, 1913, 2.
43. "To 'Capture' Union Men," *The Baltimore Sun* (Baltimore, MD), July 1, 1913, 2.
44. "Both Badly Scared," *The Baltimore Sun* (Baltimore, MD), July 2, 1913, 2.
45. "Camp at Gettysburg Full of Oddities," *The Times-Dispatch* (Richmond, VA), July 4, 1913, 2.
46. "40,000 Veterans There," *The Baltimore Sun* (Baltimore, MD), July 1, 1913, 2.
47. "Slow Walk of Veteran of 85 Years," *The Boston Globe* (Boston, MA), July 3, 1913, 5.
48. "Harrisburgers Liven Up Camp," *Harrisburg Daily Independent* (Harrisburg, PA), July 2, 1913, 1.
49. Bruce Catton, "The Day the Civil War Ended," *American Heritage* 29, no. 4 (June/July 1978).
50. "Army Retreats from Big Camp," *Harrisburg Daily Independent* (Harrisburg, PA), July 2, 1913, 6.
51. "Little Tales of Gettysburg," *The Washington Times* (Washington, DC), July 2, 1913, 2.
52. T. C. Cheney, F. Kenfield, and Vermont Gettysburg Commission, *Vermont at Gettysburg, July, and Fifty Years Later* (Rutland, VT: Tuttle Co., 1914), 27.
53. Walter Herbert Blake, *Hand Grips: The Story of the Great Gettysburg Reunion, July 1913*, comp. Frank Ernest Channon (Vineland, NJ: G. E. Smith, 1913).
54. "Noted Custer Cannon for G.A.R. Encampment," *The Evening Star* (Washington, DC), July 29, 1915, 12.
55. "Here and There at Gettysburg," *The Evening Star* (Washington, DC), July 2, 1913, 2.
56. Martin Blumenson, *The Patton Papers, 1885–1940* (Boston: Houghton Mifflin, 1972), 255.
57. "District Men Fortunate," *The Washington Times* (Washington, DC), July 2, 1913, 2.

## CHAPTER 6

1. Pennsylvania, *Fiftieth Anniversary of the Battle of Gettysburg: Report of the Pennsylvania Commission*, ed. and comp. Lewis Eugene Beitler (Harrisburg, PA: Wm. Stanley Ray, State Printer, 1913), 121.
2. Pennsylvania, *Fiftieth Anniversary of the Battle of Gettysburg: Report of the Pennsylvania Commission*, ed. and comp. Lewis Eugene Beitler (Harrisburg, PA: Wm. Stanley Ray, State Printer, 1913), 125–26.
3. "Tented Gettysburg Swept by Storm," *The New York Times* (New York, NY), July 3, 1913, 3.
4. "Tented Gettysburg Swept by Storm," *The New York Times* (New York, NY), July 3, 1913, 1.
5. "Tented Gettysburg Swept by Storm," *The New York Times* (New York, NY), July 3, 1913, 3.
6. "Tented Gettysburg Swept by Storm," *The New York Times* (New York, NY), July 3, 1913, 3.
7. "Tented Gettysburg Swept by Storm," *The New York Times* (New York, NY), July 3, 1913, 3.
8. "Storm Brings Relief to Weary Veterans," *The Baltimore Sun* (Baltimore, MD), July 3, 1913, 2.
9. "Storm Brings Relief to Weary Veterans," *The Baltimore Sun* (Baltimore, MD), July 3, 1913, 2.
10. "Tented Gettysburg Swept by Storm," *The New York Times* (New York, NY), July 3, 1913, 3.
11. "Tented Gettysburg Swept by Storm," *The New York Times* (New York, NY), July 3, 1913, 3.
12. Pennsylvania, *Fiftieth Anniversary of the Battle of Gettysburg: Report of the Pennsylvania Commission*, ed. and comp. Lewis Eugene Beitler (Harrisburg, PA: Wm. Stanley Ray, State Printer, 1913), 128.
13. Pennsylvania, *Fiftieth Anniversary of the Battle of Gettysburg: Report of the Pennsylvania Commission*, ed. and comp. Lewis Eugene Beitler (Harrisburg, PA: Wm. Stanley Ray, State Printer, 1913), 133.
14. "Sickles Tells of Gettysburg Fight," *Adams County Independent* (Littlestown, PA), July 11, 1913, 7.
15. "Where Sickles Lost His Leg," *Adams County Independent* (Littlestown, PA), July 11, 1913, 7.
16. George Gordon Meade and George Meade, eds., *The Life and Letters of George Gordon Meade: Major-General United States Army* (New York: Charles Scribner's Sons, 1913), 354.
17. "Sickles Tells of Gettysburg Fight," *Adams County Independent* (Littlestown, PA), July 11, 1913, 7.
18. Mark Twain, *Mark Twain's Autobiography* (New York: Harper & Brothers, 1924), 337.

19. Mark Twain, *Mark Twain's Autobiography* (New York: Harper & Brothers, 1924), 339.

20. Congressional Medal of Honor Society, "Daniel Edgar Sickles," *Stories of Sacrifice*, accessed October 4, 2025, https://www.cmohs.org/recipients/daniel-e-sickles.

21. "Sickles Denied Report of Death," *Stockton Evening and Sunday Record* (Stockton, CA), July 5, 1913, 1.

22. "Sickles Tells of Gettysburg Fight," *Adams County Independent* (Littlestown, PA), July 11, 1913, 7.

23. "Sickles Tells of Gettysburg Fight," *Adams County Independent* (Littlestown, PA), July 11, 1913, 7.

24. "At Getteysbung [*sic*]," *The Jones County News* (Ellisville, MS), July 10, 1913, 4.

25. "55,000 Veterans Defy the Great Heat," *New York Tribune* (New York, NY), July 2, 1913, 1.

26. "At Getteysbung [*sic*]," *The Jones County News* (Ellisville, MS), July 10, 1913, 4.

27. "Hark Back to Days of '63," *The Washington Herald* (Washington, DC), July 1, 1913, 4.

28. "Gettysburg Receives, Dressed in Its Best," *The Baltimore Sun* (Baltimore, MD), June 29, 1913, 21.

29. "Ice Cream Sold Here Condemned," *Adams County News* (Adams County, PA), July 5, 1913, 4.

30. Pennsylvania, *Fiftieth Anniversary of the Battle of Gettysburg: Report of the Pennsylvania Commission*, ed. and comp. Lewis Eugene Beitler (Harrisburg, PA: Wm. Stanley Ray, State Printer, 1913), 59.

31. Pennsylvania, *Fiftieth Anniversary of the Battle of Gettysburg: Report of the Pennsylvania Commission*, ed. and comp. Lewis Eugene Beitler (Harrisburg, PA: Wm. Stanley Ray, State Printer, 1913), 56.

32. "Impressions of Gettysburg," *The Morning Call* (Allentown, PA), July 5, 1913, 1.

33. Pennsylvania, *Fiftieth Anniversary of the Battle of Gettysburg: Report of the Pennsylvania Commission*, ed. and comp. Lewis Eugene Beitler (Harrisburg, PA: Wm. Stanley Ray, State Printer, 1913), 56.

34. "Jackson His Reliance," *The Robesonian* (Lumberton, NC), July 7, 1913, 7.

35. "At Getteysbung [*sic*]," *The Jones County News* (Ellisville, MS), July 10, 1913, 4.

36. "Notable Pair of Brothers," *The Boston Globe* (Boston, MA), July 2, 1913, 9.

37. "Sidelights of Gettysburg Reunion," *Beaver County Republican* (Monaca, PA), July 18, 1913, 2.

38. "Sidelights of Gettysburg Reunion," *Beaver County Republican* (Monaca, PA), July 18, 1913, 2.

39. "Two Anthony's Meet After Fifty Years," *The Philadelphia Inquirer* (Philadelphia, PA), July 3, 1913, 2.

40. "Took Off His Arm," *Adams County News* (Adams County, PA), July 5, 1913, 6.

41. "Many Unique Scenes," *Evening Chronicle*, July 2, 1913, 1.

42. "'Rebel Yell' Rings Out Again at Gettysburg, but Now in a Friendly Fashion," *Harrisburg Telegraph* (Harrisburg, PA), July 1, 1913, 7.
43. "'Rebel Yell' Rings Out Again at Gettysburg, but Now in a Friendly Fashion," *Harrisburg Telegraph* (Harrisburg, PA), July 1, 1913, 7.
44. "Bury the Hatchet," *Lancaster News* (Lancaster, PA), July 4, 1913, 1.
45. "Miller at Gettysburg Celebration," *The Twin City Star* (Minneapolis, MN), August 8, 1913, 3.
46. Edward Sylvester Ellis, *Library of American History from the Discovery of America to the Present Time* (Philadelphia, PA: Jones Brothers Publishing Company, 1918), 212.
47. Edward Sylvester Ellis, *Library of American History from the Discovery of America to the Present Time* (Philadelphia, PA: Jones Brothers Publishing Company, 1918), 212.
48. "Colored Confederate Receives Pension," *Lexington Gazette* (Lexington, VA), March 6, 1912, 1.
49. "No Provision for Women," *The Baltimore Sun* (Baltimore, MD), July 2, 1913, 2.
50. "Seen by Mrs. Longstreet," *The New York Times* (New York, NC), July 3, 1913, 3.
51. "No Provision for Women," *The Baltimore Sun* (Baltimore, MD), July 2, 1913, 2.
52. "A Tribute to War Women," *The Baltimore Sun* (Baltimore, MD), July 2, 1913, 2.
53. "Greek Met Greek," *Creston Statesman*, July 25, 1913, 5.
54. "Stories That Show Spirit of the Reunion," *Boston Evening Transcript* (Boston, MA), July 2, 1913, 3.
55. "Is Doing Newspaper Work," *Pittsburgh Post-Gazette* (Pittsburgh, PA), July 3, 1913, 3.
56. "Work Under Difficulty," *Rosalie Rip-Saw* (Rosalie, NE), July 18, 1913, 5.
57. "His Meanest Trick," *Spencer Advocate* (Spencer, NE), July 24, 1913, 3.
58. "Thousands Going Home; Touching Scenes Staged," *Rosalie Rip-Saw* (Rosalie, NE), July 18, 1913, 5.
59. "Heat Too Great for the Old Vets," *Harrisburg Daily Independent* (Harrisburg, PA), July 2, 1913, 1.
60. "Heat Too Great for the Old Vets," *Harrisburg Daily Independent* (Harrisburg, PA), July 2, 1913, 1.
61. Untitled, *Carlisle Evening Herald* (Carlisle, PA), July 8, 1913, 4.
62. Untitled, *Carlisle Evening Herald* (Carlisle, PA), July 8, 1913, 4.
63. "Coffins Sent to Gettysburg Only Nine Were Used," *The Dispatch* (Lexington, NC), July 16, 1913, 2.
64. "Intense Heat Causes Vet to Return—Tells of Big Meet," *Daily Times* (Burlington, NC), July 3, 1913, 1.
65. "Heat Too Great for the Old Vets," *Harrisburg Daily Independent* (Harrisburg, PA), July 2, 1913, 1.
66. "That Coffin Story," *The Gettysburg Compiler* (Gettysburg, PA), July 16, 1913, 6.

67. "Undertaker Lost on Reunion Deal," *The Times-Dispatch* (Richmond, VA), July 12, 1913, 3.

68. "Low Death Rate Among Veterans," *Adams County News* (Adams County, PA), July 5, 1913, 8.

69. "Military Day Is Fully Observed," *Times Herald* (Burns, OR), July 2, 1913, 1.

70. Walter Herbert Blake, *Hand Grips: The Story of the Great Gettysburg Reunion, July 1913*, comp. Frank Ernest Channon (Vineland, NJ: G. E. Smith, 1913), 151–53.

71. "I Remember When Blue Met Gray Again at Gettysburg," *The Baltimore Sun* (Baltimore, MD), June 28, 1970, 184.

72. "Rex Theater Has Civil War Scene," *The Spokesman-Review* (Spokane, WA), July 13, 1913, 29.

73. "Make-Believe Vet. Hooted," *The Evening Star* (Washington, DC), July 5, 1913, 21.

74. "Struck by Runaway," *The Gettysburg Times* (Gettysburg, PA), June 30, 1913, 1.

75. "Fifty Washington Lad Honor Their Home City," *The Evening Star* (Washington, DC), July 2, 1913, 2.

76. "Fifty Washington Lad Honor Their Home City," *The Evening Star* (Washington, DC), July 2, 1913, 2.

77. *Harrisburg Daily Independent* (Harrisburg, PA), July 2, 1913, 1.

78. Edward Alexander, "Man's Best Comrade: Sallie and the 11th Pennsylvania," *Emerging Civil War*, February 6, 2015, https://emergingcivilwar.com/2015/02/06/mans-best-comrade/.

79. "Sallie Ann: Civil War Dog Hero," *Dogs in History* (blog), April 16, 2016, https://dogs-in-history.blogspot.com/2016/04/sallie-ann-civil-war-dog-hero.html.

80. "Man Who Resented Insults to Lincoln," *Altoona Tribune* (Altoona, PA), July 9, 1913, 1.

81. "Son of Major R. R. Henry," *The World-News* (Roanoke, VA), July 3, 1913, 2.

82. "Seven Stabbed in Fight at Reunion of the Veterans," *The Huntington Herald* (Huntington, WV), July 3, 1913, 1.

83. "Man Who Resented Insults to Lincoln," *Altoona Tribune* (Altoona, PA), July 9, 1913, 1.

84. "Six Civil Suits Against Henry," *Adams County News* (Adams County, PA), July 26, 1913, 1.

85. "Veteran Hobbles Home," *Pittsburgh Post-Gazette* (Pittsburgh, PA), July 9, 1913, 12.

86. "Six Civil Suits Against Henry," *Adams County News* (Adams County, PA), July 26, 1913, 1.

87. "Eight Stabbed at Local Hotel," *Adams County News* (Adams County, PA), July 5, 1913, 1.

88. "Wm. Byrd Henry Cases Closed," *The Gettysburg Times* (Gettysburg, PA), November 11, 1913, 1.

89. "I Remember When Blue Met Gray Again at Gettysburg," *The Sun Magazine*, June 28, 1970, 2.

90. "The Civil War Veteran," *The San Francisco Call* (San Francisco, CA), July 4, 1913, 1.

91. "Little Tales of Real Life at Gettysburg," *Harrisburg Telegraph* (Harrisburg, PA), July 3, 1913, 10.

92. "Stories That Show Spirit of the Reunion," *Boston Evening Transcript* (Boston, MA), July 2, 1913, 3.

93. "Little Tales of Gettysburg," *The Washington Times* (Washington, DC), July 2, 1913, 2.

94. "'Reb' Find Where His Battle Flag Went," *The Philadelphia Inquirer* (Philadelphia, PA), July 2, 1913, 2.

95. "A Distinguished Visitor," *The Morning Journal* (Lancaster, PA), July 5, 1913, 1.

96. *Richmond Times-Dispatch* (Richmond, VA), September 9, 1921, 1.

97. "Pathetic Story Brings Results," *The Philadelphia Inquirer* (Philadelphia, PA), July 4, 1913, 3.

98. Walter Herbert Blake, *Hand Grips: The Story of the Great Gettysburg Reunion, July 1913*, comp. Frank Ernest Channon (Vineland, NJ: G. E. Smith, 1913), 95.

## Chapter 7

1. Walter Herbert Blake, *Hand Grips: The Story of the Great Gettysburg Reunion, July 1913*, comp. Frank Ernest Channon (Vineland, NJ: G. E. Smith, 1913), 151–53.

2. "Friendships Are Cemented," *Harrisburg Daily Independent* (Harrisburg, PA), July 3, 1913, 1.

3. "But We Did Lick You," *Commercial*, July 3, 1913, 12.

4. "Pathetic Story Brings Results," *The Philadelphia Inquirer* (Philadelphia, PA), July 4, 1913, 3.

5. Walter Herbert Blake, *Hand Grips: The Story of the Great Gettysburg Reunion, July 1913*, comp. Frank Ernest Channon (Vineland, NJ: G. E. Smith, 1913), 66.

6. "22nd USCT," *The Second NJ Brigade*, accessed June 23, 2025, https://www.2dnjbrigade.org/22nd-usct.

7. Pennsylvania, *Fiftieth Anniversary of the Battle of Gettysburg: Report of the Pennsylvania Commission*, ed. and comp. Lewis Eugene Beitler (Harrisburg, PA: Wm. Stanley Ray, State Printer, 1913), 136.

8. Pennsylvania, *Fiftieth Anniversary of the Battle of Gettysburg: Report of the Pennsylvania Commission*, ed. and comp. Lewis Eugene Beitler (Harrisburg, PA: Wm. Stanley Ray, State Printer, 1913), 148.

9. Pennsylvania, *Fiftieth Anniversary of the Battle of Gettysburg: Report of the Pennsylvania Commission*, ed. and comp. Lewis Eugene Beitler (Harrisburg, PA: Wm. Stanley Ray, State Printer, 1913), 138.

10. "Governors Day at the Tent," *The Boston Globe* (Boston, MA), July 4, 1913, 5.

11. George E. Pickett, La Salle Corbell Pickett, and Woodrow Wilson Collection, *The Heart of a Soldier: As Revealed in the Intimate Letters of Genl. George E. Pickett* (New York: S. Moyle, 1913), 97–99.

12. George E. Pickett, La Salle Corbell Pickett, and Woodrow Wilson Collection, *The Heart of a Soldier: As Revealed in the Intimate Letters of Genl. George E. Pickett* (New York: S. Moyle, 1913), 106.

13. "Helped Defeat Pickett," *The Baltimore Sun* (Baltimore, MD), July 4, 1913, 2.

14. George E. Pickett, La Salle Corbell Pickett, and Woodrow Wilson Collection, *The Heart of a Soldier: As Revealed in the Intimate Letters of Genl. George E. Pickett* (New York: S. Moyle, 1913), 107.

15. George E. Pickett, La Salle Corbell Pickett, and Woodrow Wilson Collection, *The Heart of a Soldier: As Revealed in the Intimate Letters of Genl. George E. Pickett* (New York: S. Moyle, 1913), 214–15.

16. George E. Pickett, La Salle Corbell Pickett, and Woodrow Wilson Collection, *The Heart of a Soldier: As Revealed in the Intimate Letters of Genl. George E. Pickett* (New York: S. Moyle, 1913), 102.

17. Paul M. Angle, *Crossroads: 1913* (Chicago: Rand McNally, 1963), 142.

18. "Blunders Spoil the Rehearsal of Pickett's Charge," *The Philadelphia Inquirer* (Philadelphia, PA), July 4, 1913, 1–2.

19. "Another Pickett's 'Charge,'" *Transcript-Telegram* (Holyoke, MA), July 5, 1913, 7.

20. Walter Herbert Blake, *Hand Grips: The Story of the Great Gettysburg Reunion, July 1913*, comp. Frank Ernest Channon (Vineland, NJ: G. E. Smith, 1913), 178–79.

21. "Southerners Express No Regret," *The Boston Globe* (Boston, MA), July 1, 1913, 5.

22. "Another Pickett's 'Charge,'" *Transcript-Telegram* (Holyoke, MA), July 5, 1913, 7.

23. "Soldiers in Gray Make Onslaught on Blue Brothers," *The Times-Dispatch* (Richmond, VA), July 4, 1913, 1.

24. "Blunders Spoil the Rehearsal of Pickett's Charge," *The Philadelphia Inquirer* (Philadelphia, PA), July 4, 1913, 2.

25. "Blunders Spoil the Rehearsal of Pickett's Charge," *The Philadelphia Inquirer* (Philadelphia, PA), July 4, 1913, 2.

26. "Addresses for North and South," *The Boston Globe* (Boston, MA), July 4, 1913, 5.

27. "Many Picturesque Figures," *The Evening Star* (Washington, DC), July 4, 1913, 2.

28. "Pickett's Charge Fifty Years After," *The New York Times* (New York, NY), July 4, 1913, 3.

29. "At Gettysburg," *The Jones County News* (Ellisville, MS), July 10, 1913, 4.

30. "Pickett's Charge Fifty Years After," *The New York Times* (New York, NY), July 4, 1913, 3.

31. "Pickett's Charge Fifty Years After," *The New York Times* (New York, NY), July 4, 1913, 3.

32. Walter Herbert Blake, *Hand Grips: The Story of the Great Gettysburg Reunion, July 1913*, comp. Frank Ernest Channon (Vineland, NJ: G. E. Smith, 1913), 182–83.

33. American Battlefield Trust, "Gettysburg: Pickett's Charge, July 3, 1863," *Battlefields.org*, accessed June 23, 2025, https://www.battlefields.org/learn/maps/gettysburg-picketts-charge-july-3-1863.
34. *Confederate Veteran*, vol. 21 (1913): 592.
35. Frank E. Fields Jr., *The 28th Virginia Infantry Regiment* (1984), 52.
36. "Pickett's Charge Fifty Years After," *The New York Times* (New York, NY), July 4, 1913, 3.
37. "At Gettysburg," *The Waco Times-Herald* (Waco, TX), July 27, 1913, 17.
38. "Pickett's Charge Fifty Years After," *The New York Times* (New York, NY), July 4, 1913, 3.
39. Walter Herbert Blake, *Hand Grips: The Story of the Great Gettysburg Reunion, July 1913*, comp. Frank Ernest Channon (Vineland, NJ: G. E. Smith, 1913), 21–23.
40. "At Gettysburg," *The Waco Times-Herald* (Waco, TX), July 27, 1913, 17.
41. "I Remember When Blue Met Gray Again at Gettysburg," *The Baltimore Sun* (Baltimore, MD), June 28, 1970, 184.
42. "From Kansas," *The Bedford Bulletin*, July 3, 1913, 5.
43. "Liberal Vet at Gettysburg," *The Liberal News* (Liberal, MO), July 10, 1913, 1.
44. "Waldo County Veterans," *The Republican* (Oakland, MD), August 14, 1913, 1.
45. "Veterans Will Reproduce Pickett's Famous Charge," *The Philadelphia Inquirer* (Philadelphia, PA), July 3, 1913, 23.
46. "Great Charge Repeated at Gettysburg," *The Pittsburgh Press* (Pittsburgh, PA), July 3, 1913, 1.
47. "Dies After Return Home," *Harrisburg Daily Independent* (Harrisburg, PA), July 7, 1913, 7.
48. "Keep Death Secret," *The Times* (Trenton, NJ), July 3, 1913, 12.
49. "Two Deaths from Heat," *The Philadelphia Inquirer* (Philadelphia, PA), July 3, 1913, 2.
50. "At Gettysburg," *The Waco Times-Herald* (Waco, TX), July 27, 1913, 17.
51. Pennsylvania, *Fiftieth Anniversary of the Battle of Gettysburg: Report of the Pennsylvania Commission*, ed. and comp. Lewis Eugene Beitler (Harrisburg, PA: Wm. Stanley Ray, State Printer, 1913), 145.
52. "At Gettysburg," *The Waco Times-Herald* (Waco, TX), July 27, 1913, 17.
53. "At Gettysburg," *The Waco Times-Herald* (Waco, TX), July 27, 1913, 17.
54. Pennsylvania, *Fiftieth Anniversary of the Battle of Gettysburg: Report of the Pennsylvania Commission*, ed. and comp. Lewis Eugene Beitler (Harrisburg, PA: Wm. Stanley Ray, State Printer, 1913), 152.
55. Walter Herbert Blake, *Hand Grips: The Story of the Great Gettysburg Reunion, July 1913*, comp. Frank Ernest Channon (Vineland, NJ: G. E. Smith, 1913), 151–53.
56. "Fitting Climax to the Reunion," *Princeton Daily Clarion* (Princeton, IN), July 4, 1913, 1.
57. "Veterans March on the Field of Gettysburg," *The Buffalo News* (Buffalo, NY), July 5, 1913, 7.

58. "Old Warriors Make Merry in Observing 4th," *The Pittsburgh Press* (Pittsburgh, PA), July 5, 1913, 3.
59. "General Liggett Tells of Vexing Problems of Camp at Gettysburg," *The Buffalo Sunday Morning News* (Buffalo, NY), July 13, 1913, 33.
60. "Many See Fireworks," *Adams County News* (Littlestown, PA), July 5, 1913, 4.
61. "March on Rebs," *Adams County News* (Littlestown, PA), July 5, 1913, 1.
62. "Great Parade Chief Feature," *The Daily Republican* (Popular Bluff, MO), July 5, 1913, 3.
63. "Southerners Seethe with Sentiment," *The Boston Globe* (Boston, MA), July 2, 1913, 6.
64. "Great Parade Chief Feature," *The Daily Republican* (Popular Bluff, MO), July 5, 1913, 3.
65. "The One Big Fact," *The Sun*, July 5, 1913, 1.

## Chapter 8

1. Walter Herbert Blake, *Hand Grips: The Story of the Great Gettysburg Reunion, July 1913*, comp. Frank Ernest Channon (Vineland, NJ: G. E. Smith, 1913), 151–53.
2. "Signals of Peace Reunion's Climax," *The Evening Star* (Washington, DC), July 5, 1913, 21.
3. "Signal Corps to Meet Here in September," *Chattanooga Daily Times* (Chattanooga, TN), August 8, 1913, 9.
4. Walter Herbert Blake, *Hand Grips: The Story of the Great Gettysburg Reunion, July 1913*, comp. Frank Ernest Channon (Vineland, NJ: G. E. Smith, 1913), 181–82.
5. "William Durst, Hero of Monitor's Victory Over Merrimac Dead," *The Evening Public Ledger* (Philadelphia, PA), January 4, 1916, 3.
6. "Old Sea Foes Meet," *The Washington Times* (Washinton, DC), July 4, 1913, 3.
7. Pennsylvania, *Fiftieth Anniversary of the Battle of Gettysburg: Report of the Pennsylvania Commission*, ed. and comp. Lewis Eugene Beitler (Harrisburg, PA: Wm. Stanley Ray, State Printer, 1913), 174.
8. Pennsylvania, *Fiftieth Anniversary of the Battle of Gettysburg: Report of the Pennsylvania Commission*, ed. and comp. Lewis Eugene Beitler (Harrisburg, PA: Wm. Stanley Ray, State Printer, 1913), 174.
9. Pennsylvania, *Fiftieth Anniversary of the Battle of Gettysburg: Report of the Pennsylvania Commission*, ed. and comp. Lewis Eugene Beitler (Harrisburg, PA: Wm. Stanley Ray, State Printer, 1913), 175.
10. American Battlefield Trust, "Civil War Casualties," *American Battlefield Trust*, accessed June 24, 2025, https://www.battlefields.org/learn/articles/civil-war-casualties.
11. "Silence in Camp as Regulars Pay Tribute to Dead," *Richmond Times-Dispatch* (Richmond, VA), July 5, 1913, 1.
12. Pennsylvania, *Fiftieth Anniversary of the Battle of Gettysburg: Report of the Pennsylvania Commission*, ed. and comp. Lewis Eugene Beitler (Harrisburg, PA: Wm. Stanley Ray, State Printer, 1913), 177.

13. "Tribute to the Dead," *The Philadelphia Inquirer* (Philadelphia, PA), July 5, 1913, 1.
14. "20,000 Chickens Slain," *The Baltimore Sun* (Baltimore, MD), July 5, 1913, 2.
15. "High Water Mark of the Confederacy," *The Newberry Weekly Herald* (Newberry, SC), July 18, 1913, 2.
16. "We Have Not Long to Live," *The Boston Globe* (Boston, MA), July 2, 1913, 6.
17. "How Veterans Swapped Uniforms to See Each Other's Country," *Reading Times* (Reading, PA), July 5, 1913, 10.
18. Walter Herbert Blake, *Hand Grips: The Story of the Great Gettysburg Reunion, July 1913*, comp. Frank Ernest Channon (Vineland, NJ: G. E. Smith, 1913), 44.
19. "False Teeth Unidentified," *Pittsburgh Post-Gazette* (Pittsburgh, PA), July 4, 1913, 17.
20. "Of Interest to Veterans," *Fulton County Tribune* (Wauseon, OH), December 5, 1913, 2.
21. W. P. Whitaker, "A Georgia Veteran at Gettysburg," *Confederate Veteran* 21 (1913): 320.
22. "Finds Army Gun in Tree 50 Years After," *The Independent-Herald* (Hinton, WV), July 10, 1913, 1.
23. "Took Home Ground," *The Gettysburg Times* (Gettysburg, PA), July 3, 1913, 1.
24. "Pathetic Stories of Ninth Veteran's Death," *Public Opinion* (Chambersburg, PA), July 8, 1913, 3.
25. T. C. Cheney, F. Kenfield, and Vermont Gettysburg Commission, *Vermont at Gettysburg, July, and Fifty Years Later* (Rutland, VT: Tuttle Co., 1914), 30.
26. "The Great Peace Camp," *The Gettysburg Compiler* (Gettysburg, PA), July 9, 1913, 6.
27. Pennsylvania, *Fiftieth Anniversary of the Battle of Gettysburg: Report of the Pennsylvania Commission*, ed. and comp. Lewis Eugene Beitler (Harrisburg, PA: Wm. Stanley Ray, State Printer, 1913), 90.
28. "This 'Reb' Is Sore," *The Baltimore Sun* (Baltimore, MD), July 4, 1913, 12.
29. "Sorry to See Veterans Go," *The Baltimore Sun* (Baltimore, MD), July 7, 1913, 1.
30. "The Trip to Gettysburg," *The Dispatch* (Lexington, NC), July 16, 1913, 2.
31. "The Trip to Gettysburg," *The Dispatch* (Lexington, NC), July 16, 1913, 2.
32. "Touching Farewells Said," *The Baltimore Sun* (Baltimore, MD), July 6, 1913, 2.
33. "Vets Dash for Splash in Harrisburg Baths," *The Patriot-News*, July 5, 1913, 1.
34. "Lost at Gettysburg; Now Back at Home," *The Roanoke Times* (Roanoke, VA), July 13, 1913, 6.
35. "Depict Slave Selling," *The Pittsburgh Press* (Pittsburgh, PA), July 5, 1913, 2.

## Chapter 9

1. "Maryland Holds Fort," *The Baltimore Sun* (Baltimore, MD), July 6, 1913, 2.
2. "C. H. Mettee Dead," *The Evening Sun* (Baltimore, MD), June 21, 1915, 3.
3. "Maryland Holds Fort," *The Baltimore Sun* (Baltimore, MD), July 6, 1913, 2.
4. "Veterans Say Goodby!" *The Baltimore Sun* (Baltimore, MD), July 7, 1913, 2.

5. "Two Old Confederates Capture Gettysburg," *The Baltimore Sun* (Baltimore, MD), June 28, 1913, 8.
6. "Pathetic Story Brings Results," *The Philadelphia Inquirer* (Philadelphia, PA), July 4, 1913, 3.
7. "Veterans at Hospital Sing Old Time Songs," *The Courier* (Salsbury, MD), July 6, 1913, 1.
8. "Veterans at Hospital Sing Old Time Songs," *The Courier* (Salsbury, MD), July 6, 1913, 1.
9. "Veterans Cheer Patriotic Airs," *The Los Angeles Times* (Los Angeles, CA), July 5, 1913, 2.
10. "Another Longstreet Gets Ready for War," *The Baytown Sun* (Baytown, TX), December 23, 1950, 38.
11. "Helen Longstreet, 99, Widow of Confederate General, Dies," *The Daily Mail*, May 4, 1962, 1.
12. "Camp with Eclipses," *Richmond Times-Dispatch* (Richmond, VA), July 5, 1913, 2.
13. "The Oldest Pensioner in the United States," *Audubon County Journal* (Exira, IA), February 2, 1915, 4.
14. "Tired from Shaking Hands," *Adams County Independent* (Littlestown, PA), July 4, 1913, 1.
15. "Sickles Goes Home," *The Baltimore Sun* (Baltimore, MD), July 7, 1913, 1.
16. "Eleanor Wilmerding Dead," *Transcript-Telegram* (Holyoke, MA), February 11, 1914, 1.
17. "Chuck and Chickles," *Chattanooga Daily Times* (Chattanooga, TN), April 6, 1914, 4.
18. "Gen Dan E. Sickles Dead," *Mount Union Times* (Mount Union, PA), May 8, 1914, 2.
19. "Dan Sickles Is Dead," *The Columbia Record* (Columbia, SC), May 6, 1914, 4.
20. "Embezzled Monument Money," *Statesville Record and Landmark* (Statesville, NC), February 4, 1913, 2.

## Epilogue

1. "High Water Mark of the Confederacy," *The Newberry Weekly Herald* (Newberry, SC), July 18, 1913, 2.
2. "On the Field of Gettysburg," *The Inter Ocean* (Chicago, IL), July 2, 1913, 6.
3. Pennsylvania, *Fiftieth Anniversary of the Battle of Gettysburg: Report of the Pennsylvania Commission*, ed. and comp. Lewis Eugene Beitler (Harrisburg, PA: Wm. Stanley Ray, State Printer, 1913), 196.
4. Pennsylvania, *Fiftieth Anniversary of the Battle of Gettysburg: Report of the Pennsylvania Commission*, ed. and comp. Lewis Eugene Beitler (Harrisburg, PA: Wm. Stanley Ray, State Printer, 1913), 214.
5. "Veterans' Vigor Is Remarkable," *Harrisburg Daily Independent* (Harrisburg, PA), July 5, 1913, 1.

6. "Veterans Risk Their Lives, but Not Needlessly," *The Kansas City Star* (Kansas City, MO), July 5, 1913, 8.

7. "On to Gettysburg Fifty Years After the Battle," *The Washington Post* (Washington, DC), June 22, 1913, 1.

8. "Veterans Risk Their Lives, but Not Uselessly," *The New York Times* (New York, NC), July 1, 1913, 8.

9. "Handshakes; No Bullets," *Harrisburg Daily Independent* (Harrisburg, PA), July 3, 1913, 1.

10. "Nation United," *The Boston Globe* (Boston, MA), July 2, 1913, 6.

11. *The Washington Post* (Washington, DC), July 1, 1913, 21.

12. "Governor Cox, of Ohio, on Gettysburg Program Today," *Harrisburg Daily Independent* (Harrisburg, PA), July 3, 1913, 12.

13. "How Veterans and Others Will Be Cared for at Gettysburg," *The New York Times* (New York, NY), Junc 29, 1913, 38.

www.ingramcontent.com/pod-product-compliance
Ingram Content Group UK Ltd.
Pitfield, Milton Keynes, MK11 3LW, UK
UKHW040249150926
8627IPUK00002B/3